The Four Faces of
Affirmative Action

**Recent Titles in
Contributions in Legal Studies**

The Four Faces of Affirmative Action

Fundamental Answers and Actions

W. ROBERT GRAY

Contributions in Legal Studies, Number 99

GREENWOOD PRESS
Westport, Connecticut • London

Library of Congress Cataloging-in-Publication Data

Gray, W. Robert, 1947–
    The four faces of affirmative action : fundamental answers and actions / W. Robert Gray.
        p.   cm.—(Contributions in legal studies, ISSN 0147–1074 ; no. 99)
    Includes bibliographical references and index.
    ISBN 0–313–31559–0 (alk. paper)
    1. Affirmative action programs—Law and legislation—United States.   I. Title.   II. Series.
    KF4755.5.G73   2001
    342.73'087—dc21   00–042233

British Library Cataloguing in Publication Data is available.

Library of Congress Catalog Card Number: 00–042233
ISBN: 0–313–31559–0
ISSN: 0147–1074

First published in 2001

Greenwood Press, 88 Post Road West, Westport, CT 06881
An imprint of Greenwood Publishing Group, Inc.
www.greenwood.com

Printed in the United States of America

The paper used in this book complies with the
Permanent Paper Standard issued by the National
Information Standards Organization (Z39.48–1984).

10 9 8 7 6 5 4 3 2

To the Memory of
J. Gilbert McAllister
and
W. Alvin Pitcher

Contents

Acknowledgments

Several persons provided invaluable assistance and encouragement in the writing of this book. Without the encouragement, guidance, and the generous provision of intellectual capital given me by my friend Jonathan B. Eddison of Los Angeles, I could not have written the book. Denny O. Ingram and Ron McManus, colleagues at Texas Wesleyan University, read extensive portions of the manuscript and commented on it constructively. Racquetball colleague Fred Gunther gave me his exceedingly useful real-world reaction. My secretary Nicki Hargrave and my student assistant Kathryn Freed-Collier performed their respective duties with great aplomb. Jack Cella in Chicago provided his Chicago-style analysis and other help. I also want to thank Jim Clark, from my hometown of Carthage, Texas, for his constant friendly encouragement.

My editor at Greenwood, Heather Ruland Staines, has been kind, patient, understanding, and most helpful. Without her the book could not have been published. My thanks also go to John Donohue, who patiently worked with me on the preparation of the manuscript.

I also, of course, thank Texas Wesleyan University for giving me time for and assistance in the writing of this book.

Finally, my students have constantly challenged me to formulate new ideas and to refine old ones, and have never failed to provide inspiration. They have my utmost gratitude.

Despite all the assistance and encouragement that I have received, final responsibility for all errors that the book may contain belongs, of course, to me.

Introduction

Affirmative action is one of the most controversial, contradiction-riddled, and confusing public issues of our day. Its discussion and debate stir painful passions accumulated from over 350 years of tumultuous race relations in this country. "Indeed the phrase [affirmative action] has become an epithet for our time."[1] Simple introduction of the term into discourse can cause a logomachy (or "war of words") about whether affirmative action is a just remedy for the problem of racial injustice in this country or whether it produces a new racial injustice against a majority, an injustice that has no moral relation to the plight of minorities. Certainly both public opinion and judicial and other official action have begun to turn dramatically against affirmative action. In 1996 the people of California, a state known in recent years for its fair treatment of minorities in employment and public accommodations, approved an amendment to their state constitution, popularly called Proposition 209, which banned affirmative action in public employment, education, or contracting;[2] and the people of Washington have only recently approved a similar proposition against affirmative action.[3] The U.S. Court of Appeals for the Fifth Circuit within the past five years stunned the world of higher education, particularly professional education, by holding in the *Hopwood* case that the affirmative action plan devised by the University of Texas School of Law could not be constitutionally justified as a remedy for past educational discrimination either by the school or the State of Texas itself and that the justification of diversity was unavailable because it had become discredited, despite its origin in the Supreme Court.[4] And today there are two lawsuits pending against the University of Michigan attacking two of its affirmative action plans,[5] and a similar suit has been filed against the University of Washington Law School.[6]

With all the present opposition to affirmative action, it may be difficult to recall what has propelled it since the 1960s. Its purpose was categorically to address *en masse* the issues of racial injustice that have long lingered in this country, by means more widely effective than case-by-case litigation. The present grounds for opposition, which resist the racial classifications that affirmative action embodies, were well stated by Justice Antonin Scalia in these words, quoted by the Fifth Circuit in support of its *Hopwood* decision: " 'Racial preferences appear to "even the score" . . . only if our society is appropriately viewed as divided into races, making it right that an injustice rendered in the past to a black man should be compensated for by discriminating against a white.' "[7] The justice's plain implication is that our nation is not divided in such a manner and thus requires no measures to redress racial injustice at large. But two races or "two nations" are what scholars have constantly found to exist, with one race subordinated to the other like caste is subordinated to dominant society. Affirmative action is addressed to breaking this subordinating relationship.

Over fifty years ago the Swedish sociologist Gunnar Myrdal found that a person born black in the United States became a part of a "closed and rigid . . . caste system" akin to "caste" in the Hindu society of India.[8] Myrdal foresaw the decay of caste but with the retention of some of its features:

The Negro group is being permeated by the democratic and egalitarian values of the American culture. Since at the same time there has been increasing separation between the two groups [black and white], Negroes are beginning to form a self-conscious "nation within the nation," defining ever more clearly their fundamental grievances against white America.[9]

Fifty years later respected political scientist Andrew Hacker has found the same phenomena of separation and subordination: "White Americans of all classes have found it comforting to preserve blacks as a subordinate caste: a presence that despite all its pain and problems still provides whites with some solace in a stressful world."[10] And the problems of race relations are enduring—for in contrast to the complacent views of Justice Scalia, Professor Hacker finds that "[p]roblems associated with race continue to beset the nation, [exactly] as they have since its earliest origins."[11]

Affirmative action emerged as an attack on what at that time seemed to be a national, though not then an intractable, problem by redressing racial injustice through bringing more blacks and other minorities and women into the mainstream of American economic life, as well as into its highest levels of education. Now this optimistic and hope-filled view is on the wane. President Bill Clinton, from an obviously defensive position, has declared of affirmative action, "Mend It, Don't End It."[12] But the prospects for affirmative action continue to decline. One of the principal reasons seems to be that "few white Americans feel that they should be held personally responsible for racial discrimination."[13] The Supreme Court has even referred to the need to protect the jobs of "*innocent persons*," mostly white males.[14] There is apparently no sense of collective guilt, of guilt of the nation, and this fact runs contrary to our deepest historical experience. This historical experience extends from the first appearance of chattel slaves on our shores, though the institution of the Black Codes and then Jim Crow, to the de facto segregation and subordination of today.

When President Abraham Lincoln gave his Second Inaugural Address near the end of the great Civil War, he invoked the religious concept of expiation[15] to explain and make meaningful the suffering of that war as the means for release from collective guilt for slavery and to appeal for national unity.[16] "Fondly do we hope—fervently do we pray—that this mighty scourge of war may speedily pass away. Yet, if God wills that it continue until all the wealth piled by the bondsman's two hundred and fifty years of unrequited toil shall be sunk . . . , 'The judgments of the Lord [nonetheless] are true and righteous altogether.' "[17] Over 130 years later we have no such wisdom and prophecy to guide us, perhaps because there is no guilt—it is denied and repressed—and thus no need for the expiation that affirmative action, analogically if not directly, might provide. No one now speaks to the racial injustice to which affirmative action is related with the same singular and uncontradicted message as Lincoln did, as a brief tour through the legal and moral authorities on affirmative action will show.

The lawfulness of affirmative action relies primarily on two separate sources of law: the Equal Protection Clause of the Fourteenth Amendment[18] and Title VII of the Civil Rights Act of 1964.[19] A violation of the Fourteenth Amendment requires an *intention* to commit *invidious* racial discrimination,[20] and liability for such discrimination can attach equally for official discrimination against either whites or blacks.[21] By the same token, at the time of the civil rights movement of the 1960s, and especially during the congressional debate and enactment of the Civil Rights Act of 1964 and its Title VII—a statute of near-constitutional force—most officials and lawyers thought that the purpose of Title VII was solely to rectify, by a uniform standard, specific racial harms *intentionally* inflicted by employers (and later by government agencies) on victims of *either* race, not to promote racial preferences or "quotas."[22] This kind of color-blind, volitional standard was well summarized some twenty-five years later by the Ninth Circuit in registering its approval of California Proposition 209:

The standard of review under the Equal Protection Clause does not depend on the race or gender of those burdened or benefited. . . . Proposition 209 amends the California Constitution simply to prohibit state discrimination against or preferential treatment to any person on account of race or gender. . . . To be constitutional, a racial classification, regardless of its *purported* motivation [to benefit minority races], must be narrowly tailored to serve a compelling governmental interest, an extraordinary justification.[23]

Because, however, affirmative action depends on some form of preferential treatment of marginalized groups (or women) whose unjust treatment does not lend itself to redress through ordinary litigation based on conventional proof, these early views against proportional preferential treatment or quotas—through their persistence and reappearance—provide an unavoidable background against which the competing and conflicting justifications of affirmative action have emerged.

In contrast to these early color-blind and volitional rationales for antidiscrimination doctrine and their later acceptance to render affirmative action anathema in *Hopwood* and Proposition 209, affirmative action emerged in the late 1960s and early 1970s as a preferential (and sometimes preferred) method to attack racial segregation and discrimination in the operations of government contractors. These first plans sprang neither from the Equal Protection Clause nor from Title VII but from a series of presidential orders and decisions and administrative directives requiring overtly racial hiring by government contractors, generally without imposing a precondition of intent or design to discriminate against minorities on these contractors' parts. The plans were largely a pragmatic or commonsense response to the civil strife of the time, which fed on racial injustice.[24] These developments culminated in the creation of a contract compliance plan by President Richard Nixon, a traditional civil rights opponent, in the Philadelphia construction trades.[25] Remnants of this approach tying affirmative action to government contractors exist today, as the rejection of one such plan (congressionally mandated) in the *Adarand* case shows.[26]

It was not until 1978 that the Supreme Court rendered its first decision on affirmative action on the merits, in the *Bakke*[27] case. The justices, however, were severely split—some resting their opinions on statutory grounds and others, on constitutional grounds embodied in the Equal Protection Clause. The case, however, did leave open some ground for affirmative action under a First Amendment justification for racial and ethnic diversity in educational institutions.[28] But there was no clear resolution of the legal or constitutional status of affirmative action.

Earlier, at the beginning of the 1970s, the Supreme Court found in the *Griggs* case that statutory liability for discrimination under Title VII could be found not only under a theory of intent or disparate treatment but also under a theory of disparate impact, without proof of invidious intent by the employer—in effect, strict liability.[29] In 1979, implicitly building on *Griggs*, the Court in the *Weber* case held that a private employer could defend its voluntary affirmative action plan from Title VII attack by white workers or applicants, without having to adduce proof of its own invidious treatment of blacks, with a showing, instead, that the composition of its internal workforce showed a "manifest racial imbalance" with the relevant labor pool.[30] And in 1980 the Court in *Fullilove* approved under the Equal Protection Clause a congressionally enacted affirmative action plan where proof of antecedent intent to discriminate against the benefited minority businesses, as well as these minorities' correctly projected proportionate share of the government contracting market, was not subject to rigorous proof.

But all the while, controversy about affirmative action was building. *Weber*, like *Bakke*, was a very controversial decision, in large part because it involved a construction of Title VII that seemed to some lawyers and academics to contradict the plain meaning of the statute.[31] Then in the 1980s and into the 1990s, a group of justices on the Court, at first only a plurality but evolving into a majority, led first by Justice Powell and then by Justice O'Connor, perfected a constitutional theory and made it the dominant doctrine. In *Wygant,*[32] *J. A. Croson Co.,*[33] and *Adarand,*[34] the Court or a strong plurality propounded a causally taut theory of compensatory justice that would allow affirmative action only on proof of past injustices to a definite group, all under the gaze of strict scrutiny and according to a theory of color-blindness that rejects the concept of asymmetrical discrimination—that whites are harmed less by treatment according to race than are blacks. The less rigorous theories of Title VII have so far gone undisturbed in this period, but an attempt to transfer *Bakke* diversity to the Title VII employment context faltered when the *Piscataway* case was withdrawn from Supreme Court consideration by civil rights advocates who feared a calamitous ruling.[35] And in 1996 the *Hopwood*[36] court both stretched the prevailing Supreme Court doctrine so tautly that all but the most causally pristine of cases in higher education would be doomed, while it also, perhaps mortally, delivered a disparaging wound to diversity.

These, then, are the current perimeters of the problem: Affirmative action, as a projected resolution to prevailing racial injustice, is at a nadir of popular and official support, with an intellectual heritage that reveals confusion and conflict about its legitimacy and its effectiveness. Moreover, the problem of giving it a coherent rationale to resist its destruction as a potential remedy to address racial injustice is not going to disappear. To the end of clarifying these matters and placing them in order—as well as selecting among those arguments that have the most force—I use the approach of "philosophic semantics" formulated by the late Richard McKeon of the University of Chicago. This approach identifies the principles and methods of the writer of a text, including legal texts, and serves to preserve that identity in the clash with other writers and their principles and methods.[37] "[S]ince it is easy to refute other philosophers [or justices of the Supreme Court] within the framework of one's own philosophy [or legal doctrine],"[38] McKeon and his approach (frequently called a "metaphilosophy" because it abstracts to a level beyond that of the texts being studied) can clarify rationales for affirmative action and disentangle each of these from the distortions inflicted on them by combatants in the war of words over affirmative action.

This so far is interpretive analysis. But I shall also be engaged in a constructive inquiry aimed at resolving the problem of affirmative action itself. The former is descriptive in nature; the latter, prescriptive. The problem of affirmative action is treated here as an intellectual problem. As such it presents itself as whether affirmative action is capable of one or more lucid, persuasive, and just rationales in a society of pluralism of both thought and social conflict or whether it should be abandoned as unfit to address the larger race problem. I choose to proceed on the premise that fashioning one or more satisfactory rationales for affirmative action is a worthy project. In this light I define *affirmative action* as a remedial policy, sanctioned by law, of governmental or private collective entities that are otherwise subject to liability under the Constitution or by statute for discrimination against members of minority and certain other protected groups. Such a policy systematically favors, *under some rationale for social justice*, the conferral of benefits upon these constitutionally and statutorily protected groups *qua* groups—benefits to which they would not be entitled under the present operation of a hypothetically fair and unbiased market or selection procedure, in the absence of current actual discrimination. Put somewhat differently, under the remedy of affirmative action, employment, educational, and other fundamental types of social goods are preferentially allocated to blacks and other legally protected groups on a justification other than narrow compensatory justice, *i.e.*, without the contemporaneous remedial impetus of a distinct and palpable violation of the antidiscrimination laws resulting in harm to one or more members of a protected group. According to this entire viewpoint, the heart of any affirmative action plan is its underlying rationale for social justice.

The constructive use of McKeon's approach should enable me to reach a well-grounded conclusion of whether affirmative action can achieve, and *ought* to be used to achieve, justice between and among the races (and between the sexes). I proceed by illumining critical differences and by revealing significant similarities among the various constitutional and legal positions and the visions of social justice that they represent.

McKeon identifies four basic "modes of thought": dialectic, operational, problematic, and logistic; and their use is critical to my identifying and engaging in constructive analysis with the various justifications of affirmative action. Modes of thought themselves are broad groupings of philosophies with typical basic similarities, though each mode does not by any means have complete homogeneity within its own grouped philosophies.[39] A mode of thought is not a substantive philosophy but rather a heuristic device with the pragmatic aim to aid understanding—a concept of which a precise definition should not be expected. Its nature and usefulness emerge as my inquiry progresses.

Because the four modes of thought are arranged to be *mutually* exclusive and exhaustive, I will use them to account for every *type* of thought that might be found on this subject, without any overlap or lack of coverage among the modes of thought themselves. McKeon explains this mutual relation among the four types on the basis of *a priori* logic:

Even in non-technical considerations of thinking, four modes of thought may be distinguished: it is a process by which parts are put together, or englobing truths are approximated, or problems are solved, or arbitrary formulations are interpreted. The four are *formally* exhaustive of possibilities: [*the logistic mode*—] the assumption of least parts, but no whole except by composition; [*the dialectical mode*—] the assumption of an ontologically unifying principle, but no absolute least parts; [*the problematic mode*—]

the rejection of least parts and separated wholes, and the assumption of problems and natures encountered in the middle region; and [*the operational mode*—] the assumption that all distinctions are initially arbitrary. *The four modes of thought are mutually exclusive and exhaustive of all possibilities.*[40]

I shall use the four modes to identify four types of constitutional and statutory arguments found in the law to justify affirmative action.[41] Although I begin with abstract philosophical concepts to identify and "stake out" a mode of thought, I return to the law of affirmative action itself, now with new powers of explication gained from the foundation laid. Moreover, and by the same token, this is a reciprocal process, because the concrete examples from the law throw new light on the more abstract philosophical thought in the mode of thought.

This is why I am calling my book *The Four Faces of Affirmative Action: Fundamental Answers and Actions*—because I claim to present an in-depth and exhaustive treatment of all the *types* of supporting grounds of affirmative action in this book. The primary materials of this project (though last in order of presentation under each type of justification and its corresponding mode of thought) will be varying opinions of the justices of the Supreme Court, some lower court opinions, and some nonjudicial commentary on affirmative action. But first I examine works of a philosophical nature. Although (or because) these philosophical works are the most abstract, they reveal the basic presuppositions in a mode of thought and show most clearly—in relation to other philosophical work—how the four types of presuppositions underlying the problem of affirmative action are related. These I take up first in the order of my exposition because of their greater power to penetrate to the basic principles and methods supportive of the type of affirmative action under consideration. At the secondary or intermediate level (and second in the order of presentation), there will be texts of contemporary legal writers whose works I will show to have certain similarities to, or unities, with the primary legal materials. These intermediate texts will serve a transitional function between the more abstract philosophical writings and the traditional legal materials. Finally, I emerge from these more general discussions into the concrete law of affirmative action. These inquiries are designed to produce basic "answers" and to show that they are practical, *i.e.*, that they lead to "actions."

In Table 1, I show the various materials that I will use in their relation to one another and to the modes of thought from McKeon's work. This schema is not intended to be exhaustive of all *sources*, but it does include all possible points of view (or "modes of thought"), enabling me to attempt to expose clearly the divergent intellectual foundations of the affirmative action controversy. But as I indicated earlier, it may be possible to find that there is enough convergence among the positions to present a common basis for a definitive and widely accepted resolution. This was Richard McKeon's position when he worked on a committee to devise a philosophy for UNESCO (United Nations Educational, Scientific, and Cultural Organization)[42]—finding common ground among dif-

Table 1
The Modes of Thought and Affirmative Action

Mode of Thought	Philosopher	Intermediate Figure	Major Legal Justification(s)
Dialectic(al) (englobing whole but no least parts)	Jürgen Habermas, *Legitimation Crisis, Between Facts and Norms* (ultimately Plato in *Symposium*)	Bruce Ackerman, *Social Justice in the Liberal State, We the People*	*Diversity* (distributive justice*), by Powell, J., in *Bakke*, and by Brennan, J., in *Metro Broadcasting* (*not Powell, J.)
Operational (all distinctions initially arbitrary with meaning supplied by mind)	John Rawls, *A Theory of Justice, Political Liberalism* (ultimately Kant)	Ronald Dworkin, in "Reverse Discrimination" and other essays in *Taking Rights Seriously, A Matter of Principle, Law's Empire*	*Social Equality* (distributive justice), by Stevens, J., in, *e.g., Wygant* and *Adarand*
Problematic (neither least parts nor englobing wholes, but a series of problems or issues encountered in a middle region)	John Dewey, *The Public and Its Problems, Democracy and Education* (ultimately Aristotle)	Cass R. Sunstein, *The Partial Constitution* and other writings	*Social Causation* (distributive justice), by Brennan and Marshall, JJ., *e.g.,* Marshall in *J. A. Croson*, Brennan, J., in *Johnson v. Transp. Agency*
Logistic (least parts but no whole except by construction)	Robert Nozick, *Anarchy, State and Utopia* (ultimately Locke)	Richard Epstein, *Forbidden Grounds*; articles on strict liability	*Compensatory Causation* (corrective justice), by Powell, J., in *Bakke, Wygant*; O'Connor, J., in *J. A. Croson, Adarand* (the prevailing justification); Scalia, J., in *J. A. Croson, Adarand*

ferent ideologies. It may show, on the other hand, that the divergences are quite sharp. What I believe it *will* show is that a range of competing and even conflicting *ideas* (not passions, prejudices, or misconceived notions of race relations) is the ultimate cause of the controversy over the quality of support for affirmative action as a remedy for racial discrimination and that in these ideas lies a possible resolution of the place of affirmative action in promoting racial justice through restoring or creating racial equality.

Further, then, I conclude that of the four modes and their corresponding legal theories, dialectic and its doctrine of diversity, together with operational and its doctrine of social equality, are best suited to bringing affirmative action to a new ground of legitimacy and effectiveness. They are so suited, my inquiry will show, because of their universal, categorical approach to the rights of all individuals—*and* because of their alertness to the reality of group dynamics as well; their unfailing reliance on rational discourse to resolve key issues; their forward-looking perspective that concentrates on the structure of society in the future and not simply on causes from the past; and in a related vein, their lack of encumbrance to theories of compensatory justice that are ill suited to purging a continental nation of 280 million souls of racial injustice.

I begin with the most comprehensive and beckoning mode of thought of all— the dialectic—and with perhaps a surprising exponent, Jürgen Habermas, who is a post-Marxist social philosopher and the most important intellectual in Germany if not on the entire Continent today.

NOTES

The legal authorities relied upon and cited in this book are current through April 2000.

[1] ANDREW HACKER, TWO NATIONS: BLACK AND WHITE, SEPARATE, HOSTILE, UNEQUAL 123 (1995).

[2] Calif. Const. art. 1 § 31(a) (West 1999 Pocket Part) ("The state shall not discriminate against, or grant preferential treatment to, any individual or group on the basis of race, sex, color, ethnicity, or national origin in the operation of public employment, public education, or public contracting.").

[3] Sam Howe Verhovek, N. Y. TIMES, §B, p. 1, col. 1, "From Same-Sex Marriages to Gambling, Voters Speak," Nov. 5, 1998 ("In a vote expected to have national reverberations, Washington State residents dealt a stinging defeat to state-sponsored affirmative action.").

[4] Hopwood v. Texas, 78 F.3d 932 (5th Cir.), *reh'g denied*, 84 F.3d 720, *cert. denied*, 518 U.S. 1033 (1996), *on remand*, 999 F. Supp. 872 (W.D. Tex. Mar. 20, 1998), *appeal perfected*, Apr. 17, 1998. See Peter Applebome, N. Y. TIMES, §A, p. 19, col. 4–6, "Seeking New Approaches for Diversity—Universities Weigh Other Means of Keeping Racial Mix of Students," Apr. 23, 1997. See also Peter Applebome, N. Y. TIMES, §A, p. 10, col. 3–6, "Affirmative Action Bar Transforms Law School," Jul. 2, 1997.

[5] Grutter v. Bollinger, No. 97–75928 (E.D. Mich. Dec. 3, 1997) (against the Law School) (visited Apr. 20, 1998) <http://www.umich.edu/~newsinfo/Admission/grutter.html> and Gratz v. Bollinger, No. 97–75231 (E.D. Mich. Oct. 14, 1997) (against the under-

graduate College of Literature, Arts and Science) (visited Apr. 20, 1998) <http://www.umich.edu/~newsinfo/Admission/gratzham.html>; see also Grutter v. Bollinger, 16 F. Supp. 2d 797 (E.D. Mich. 1998) (two cases ruled not companion cases); Grutter v. Bollinger, 188 F.3d 394 (6th Cir. 1999) (minority applicants may intervene as of right).

[6] *Cf.* Smith v. Univ. of Washington Law School, 2 F. Supp. 2d 1324 (W.D. Wash. 1998), *aff'd sub nom.* Smith v. Marsh, 194 F.3d 1045 (9th Cir. 1999).

[7] *Hopwood*, 78 F.3d at 934–35 (quoting from City of Richmond v. J. A. Croson Co., 488 U.S. 469, 528 [1989] [Scalia, J., concurring]).

[8] GUNNAR MYRDAL, AN AMERICAN DILEMMA: THE NEGRO PROBLEM AND MODERN SOCIETY 668 (1944).

[9] Id. at 1003–04.

[10] HACKER, TWO NATIONS, supra Intro., note 1, at 244.

[11] Id. at 223.

[12] Title of a speech. Text reprinted in GEORGE E. CURRY (ED.), THE AFFIRMATIVE ACTION DEBATE 258–76 (1996) ("Affirmative action has not always been perfect, and affirmative action should not go on forever. It should be changed now to take care of things that are wrong, and it should be retired when its job is done. But the evidence suggests—indeed screams—that day has not yet come." Id. at 274.).

[13] HACKER, TWO NATIONS, supra Intro., note 1, at 136.

[14] Wygant v. Jackson Bd. of Educ., 476 U.S. 267, 280–84 (1986) (plurality opinion of Powell, J.) (emphasis supplied). See also Johnson v. Transp. Agency of Santa Clara County, Calif., 480 U.S. 616, 637–38 (1987) ("whether the Agency trammeled the rights of male employees.").

[15] See generally MAX WEBER, THE SOCIOLOGY OF RELIGION 141 (1922 Beacon ed. 1964) (voluntary suffering mollifies God for transgressions).

[16] See GARRY WILLS, LINCOLN AT GETTYSBURG: THE WORDS THAT REMADE AMERICA 185–89 (1992).

[17] PAUL M. ANGLE (ED.), THE LINCOLN READER 491, 492–93 (1947).

[18] U.S. Const. amend. XIV (1994).

[19] 42 U.S.C. §§ 2000e *et seq.*

[20] Washington v. Davis, 426 U.S. 229, 239–42 (1975) (citing, *inter alia*, Keys v. School Dist. No. 1, 413 U.S. 189 [1973]).

[21] See, *e.g.*, the opinions of Justice Powell in Regents of the University of California v. Bakke, 438 U.S. 265, 289–90 (1978), and Wygant v. Jackson Bd. of Educ., supra Intro., note 14, 476 U.S. at 273.

[22] McDonald v. Santa Fe Trail Transp. Co., 427 U.S. 273, 278–83 (1976); section 703(j) of Title VII, 42 U.S.C. § 2000e–2(j) (1994) (prohibiting any requirement that an employer grant preferential treatment to satisfy a racial quota); Bernard D. Meltzer, "The *Weber* Case: The Judicial Abrogation of the Antidiscrimination Standard in Employment," 47 U. Chi. L. Rev. 423, 425, 430–31 (1980).

[23] Coalition for Economic Equity v. Wilson, 122 F.3d 692, 702, 703 (9th Cir.), *cert. denied*, 118 S. Ct. 397 (1997) (emphasis supplied to show court's concern with motive or intent to discriminate against the majority).

[24] JOHN DAVID SKRENTNY, THE IRONIES OF AFFIRMATIVE ACTION: POLITICS, CULTURE, AND JUSTICE IN AMERICA 93, 101, 109, 110, 111, 114 passim (1996).

[25] Id. at 177–78, 181–82, 193–98. ("Nixon thus placed on the table something to help

African-Americans at the expense of unions, producing discontent and factional rivalry in two of the liberal establishment's major supporters." Id. at 182.)

[26] Adarand Constructors, Inc. v. Pena, 515 U.S. 200, 205–10 (1995) (provision of Small Business Act giving advantage in bidding to presumptively disadvantaged minority-owned firm declared unconstitutional).

[27] Regents of the University of California v. Bakke, Intro., note 21.

[28] Id. at 311–19 (opinion of Powell, J.).

[29] *Cf.* Griggs v. Duke Power Co., 401 U.S. 424 (1971).

[30] United Steelworkers of America v. Weber, 443 U.S. 193 (1979); see also Johnson v. Transp. Agency of Santa Clara County, Calif., supra Intro., note 14, 480 U.S. 616 (voluntary affirmative action plan approved despite no finding of illegal, intentional discrimination by local government agency).

[31] See, *e.g.*, Meltzer, "The *Weber* Case," supra Intro., note 22, 47 U. Chi. L. Rev. 423; George Schatzki, "*United Steelworkers of America v. Weber*: An Exercise in Understandable Indecision," 56 Wash. L. Rev. (1980).

[32] Intro., note 14, 476 U.S. 267.

[33] City of Richmond v. J. A. Croson Co., 488 U.S. 469 (1989).

[34] Intro., note 26, 515 U.S. 200.

[35] Taxman v. Bd. of Educ. of the Township of Piscataway, New Jersey, 91 F.3d 1547 (3d Cir. 1996) (en banc) (holding that diversity does not justify affirmative action discrimination against a white teacher in a suit based on Tit. VII), *cert. dism'd*, 522 U.S. 1010 (1997); see Linda Greenhouse, N. Y. TIMES, §A, p. 1, col. 5–6, cont'd at §A, p. 12 col. 1–6, "Settlement Ends High Court Case on Preferences—Tactical Retreat—New Jersey School Move Leaves Affirmative Action in Limbo"; "Rights, Groups Ducked a Fight, Opponents Say," Nov. 22, 1997. But note that in *Johnson*, 480 U.S. at 638, the Court adopted *Bakke* diversity to support an affirmative action plan that had been attacked under Title VII.

[36] Intro., note 4, 78 F.3d 932.

[37] See, *e.g.*, RICHARD MCKEON, FREEDOM AND HISTORY AND OTHER ESSAYS: AN INTRODUCTION TO THE THOUGHT OF RICHARD MCKEON [hereinafter FREEDOM AND HISTORY AND OTHER ESSAYS] (Z. MCKEON ED. 1990).

[38] RICHARD MCKEON, FREEDOM AND HISTORY: THE SEMANTICS OF PHILOSOPHICAL CONTROVERSIES AND IDEOLOGICAL CONFLICTS [hereinafter FREEDOM AND HISTORY] 23 (1952), reprinted in id. at 174.

[39] Thus thinkers as diverse as Hegel and Marx, on the one hand, and St. Augustine, Rousseau, and Kant, on the other, may share dialectical characteristics. McKeon, FREEDOM AND HISTORY, at 43–52, reprinted in FREEDOM AND HISTORY AND OTHER ESSAYS, at 192–203.

[40] Richard McKeon, "Philosophic Semantics and Philosophic Inquiry," 4 (unpublished contribution to the Illinois Philosophy Conference, held at Carbondale, Illinois, February 26, 1966, privately reproduced and distributed by the author; © 1987 by Zahava K. McKeon; copy in possession of the author of this book), reprinted in FREEDOM AND HISTORY AND OTHER ESSAYS, at 245 (all emphases supplied).

[41] I have deviated in one respect from McKeon's logical order of generation of the modes of thought by placing dialectic ahead of logistic. I prefer this ordering of the modes of thought in the text of my treatment because it allows me to deal first with diversity, a type of affirmative action that is holistic (it emphasizes the unity and national character of the nation), that does not involve the vagaries of causation, and that is primal

and fundamental in the development of affirmative action, having come early in *Bakke*. For those who would rather not begin with dialectic, either because it remains largely a stranger to American thought or because of my use of the highly abstract thought of Jürgen Habermas, it is entirely permissible to start with logistic or any other mode of thought with which the reader feels comfortable. After all, this is an operational system (as I explain), and its initial ordering is arbitrary. By the same token, it is only by comparing the different modes of thought with each other that one begins to understand any one of them.

[42] Richard McKeon, "A Philosophy for UNESCO," 8 Phil. & Phenomenology 573, 577 (1948).

1

Dialectic and Diversity

THE NATURE OF DIALECTIC

Justice Powell in the *Bakke* case determines that " 'the nation's future depends upon leaders [with] wide exposure' to . . . ideas and mores . . . as diverse as this Nation of many peoples. [O]f paramount importance [to this goal] is the 'robust exchange of ideas.' "[1] Dialectic is the mode of thought that best characterizes this desired intense dialogue filled with diverse and thus, not unexpectedly, with contrary, opposite, and seemingly incompatible opinions and ideas. Dialectic is the mode of thought, or worldview, that considers all distinctions and separateness in the phenomenal world as merely provisional, being ultimately subject to collapse and dissolution in a world behind the phenomenal world. In this latter world, being, rhetoric, human actions, or even material elements of existence variously become unified in a single ground that is the basis for all truth and justice.

Dialectic aspires to truth and justice by *transforming* the relations between opposites, contraries, or contradictories. It drives behind the contradictions of ordinary experience to reach an englobing whole in which diversity and its myriad distinctions, being but tentatively meaningful in the world of appearances, are dissolved and subsequently assimilated in the interest of approximating true reality found in comprehensive unity. Yet diversity and the identities of its elements—whether cultures, nations, or individual entities such as persons—are retained within the comprehensive unity. Among the requirements of this dialectical process is that concepts must be expressed in analogical (rather than in univocal) terms, and its truth, in system—without the precision and compartmentalization that are often demanded in the contemporary scientific world. Among the distinctions that disappear in this process are those between knowledge and action, and between truth and justice; for once a person experiences one of these qualities, he necessarily grasps its correlative, since the two ultimately share the same comprehensive ground of unity.

Dialectic, as originated by Plato and continued in the twentieth century by his followers Whitehead and Hartshorne (among others), is (or is based on) dialogue in which interlocutors are initially stymied because of the tension between the conflicts in their ideas—tensions reflected in such universal problems as being and becoming, the one and the many, or the universal and the particular. These tensions, however, are eventually dispelled when the dialogical juxtaposition of their conflicts reveals a ground for unity, as the interlocutors reach a domain of more abstract ideas. Freedom is achieved as one approaches that dialectical ground of unity, whether it is God, pure reason, or the voice of united humanity.

History also enters into dialectic (or perhaps more properly dialectic into history) through a rational movement that seizes upon periods, trends, or epochs to characterize the traits and aims of historic groups, like elites, religious movements, or even racial groups (usually defined by dialectical characteristics and not by biological features)—ultimately to attain the comprehensive meaning of history itself. Thus, Marx, a dialectician of the nineteenth century in whose tradition Habermas partly stands (not the Marx as generally discredited in vulgar adaptations of his work), has characterized history as displaying a world historical conflict between bourgeoise and proletarians, a conflict driven by underlying economic or material conditions whose dynamic relation to human life produces these groups and their inevitable conflict. History, however, drives beyond these forces of opposition, first to the victory of the proletariat and then ultimately to a utopia of classless society, since by then—according to Marx—even the material forces of production will cease their underlying disruption of human freedom.

Jürgen Habermas engages in this general spirit of dialectic, certainly in his absorption of political and social conflicts into a dialogical process in which the underlying arguments supporting the conflicts are transformed, without coercion or any other fetters on the free play of human rationality, into comprehensive norms fit to be law.

A PRELUDE TO HABERMAS

A preliminary word to the reader: Habermas is known for using abstract terms freighted with special meanings, along with a distinctive syntax and style, resulting in obscurity, even in English translation. This brief section is intended to make his thought more comprehensible by stating essential points needed in this inquiry to follow his role in it.

In using the abstractions described, Habermas is in company with other dialecticians, who *must* use broad, analogical (rather than precise, univocal) terms to capture and reconcile the essential oppositions and contradictories that can only be understood and set into practice, from the dialectical point of view, when they are collected within these broader terms. Some dialecticians, such as Hegel in the last century and Whitehead in this, have placed transcendent ideas or elements of being in juxtaposition to illumine a greater whole of meaning. Habermas differs because he treats elements of a human discourse of probabilities and opinions (not eternal ideas or truths) as those that must be assimilated, through dialogue, to produce the comprehensive truths and values—ultimately embodied in law—to guide society. But he still uses the basic method of dialectic.

One might well seize the basic meaning of Habermas needed to apprehend the role of his thought in the arguments about diversity by casting that thought in terms of the fundamental dialectical problem of the one and the many.[2] In the words of Whitehead, "The many become one, and are increased by one."[3] The "one" is a new, distinct, richer reality; yet it does not obliterate the identities of the "many" that form it, because their identities remain represented in the synthesis of the whole. (For example, our country is a unity of fifty states, each distinct, yet forming a more enriched whole than if the country were not entirely undifferentiated, and were it not different in kind from a mere composition of states as only parts.) Habermas's thought resembles this mode of thinking in the area of our general concern, the field of law, through what I call "the discursive unity of consociates (or participants in the discourse) under law"—a comprehensive principle that through uncoerced dialogue (that is, dialogue in which the only "force" is rational persuasion) is able to guide the emergence of rational, universal norms fit to be law. Yet this process does not obliterate the individual beliefs of the "consociates," whose diversity *and* autonomy are respected.

These diverse beliefs do not reach a unity simply through studied coincidence, as in the "overlapping consensus" reached by John Rawls.[4] Rather, they are gathered together as a manifold and then *transformed* into valid and binding norms through a process that Habermas calls the proceduralist paradigm of law. Unlike the ostensible debate among hypothetical interlocutors behind the "veil of ignorance" in Rawls's self-styled "original position," this process is expressly meant to involve real dialogue among real interlocutors. "This clearly suggests a dialectical model of legitimacy: legitimate law is *at once* a realization of universal rights [the 'one'—at a higher level of abstraction] and an expression of particular self-understandings and forms of life [the 'many'—concrete and diverse—opposed to and yet embraced by the 'one']."[5] Habermas thus has a dynamic *and* a transformative relation between his particular participant citizens and his abstract norms—plainly a dialectical approach that retains both the abstract and the concrete, the one and the many, in a sustainable tension.

Habermas's dialectical, discursive process would be directly furthered through actual adoption and implementation, in concrete institutions, of Justice Powell's holding in *Bakke* in favor of diversity in the academic world; or stated the other way around, Habermas's principle and method of uncoerced discourse fully undergird Justice Powell's *Bakke* opinion on diversity, because Habermas's form of discourse supports and requires diversity to facilitate its comprehensive norm and law formation—just as Justice Powell's embrace of diversity in academic discourse supports public values. But Habermas does not essentially stop at the boundary of the academic world—because he places no limits on the extension of his procedural paradigm of law to *all* citizens engaged in the law-formation process. *Piscataway* and now the D.C. Circuit in *Lutheran Church*[6] have denied, on *stare decisis* grounds, such an extension to the workplace, and thus they implicitly cut against Habermas and his rational world of dialogue.

But now I must plunge the reader into a more technical excursus of Habermas's thought. This prelude should be considered as a map of the main features of what is to come. Concrete examples illustrating Habermas's thought are occasionally provided, but the reader who desires such examples must be patient until we canvas the case law of diversity in action, in affirmative action—the real testing ground of the relevance of Habermas's ideas to the concrete application of law for social and racial justice.

HABERMAS: PRAGMATIST OR DIALECTICIAN?

It may seem odd to some readers that I call Habermas a dialectician. As I have already indicated, he propounds no *ontological* principle that resolves all conflict and contradictions into an abstract, englobing whole representing all of being or of thought.[7] Instead, he is concerned with the tangible, actual deeds and words of human beings in the course of their living together. His conclusions about valid norms for human life in society and community, though often cast in abstractions that reflect the broad scope of his thinking, are rooted in the most concrete source of all—individual human lives in their collective dimension. Truth and moral norms are a function of association and communication, not openly of a preexisting transcendent or rational ground.[8] Valid norms and their essential relation to truth depend upon the outcome of human discourse and dialogue; one cannot know the truth until the conditions of collective discourse have been purged of self-interested motives and of other "strategic" influences that exercise force.[9] Only then can the community, or "lifeworld," speak with freedom—with speech undistorted by barriers to communication.

Some would on these accounts label him a pragmatist.[10] I might have no quarrel with this characterization in some other context. I offer him here as a dialectical thinker, one whose consequentialist emphasis on speech and action indeed does make him attentive to the pragmatist bent, which he himself views as a method of pure expediency for realizing preferences already given.[11] But his focus on discourse and dialogue reveals a distinctive dialectical drive going beyond pragmatism (as he understands it) to the ideal of pure discourse in search of *moral* norms.[12] He is dialectical in this sense, moreover, because, for him, discourse has within its very structure the power to include that total diversity of human perspectives necessary to create universally valid norms.

HABERMAS'S DIALECTIC OF DISCOURSE

Thus Habermas's approach is neither ontological nor pragmatic. His selection of subject matter for inquiry and dialogue is one of facts and words—not of eternal ideas, external things, or objective natures. Words and facts become the aperture for the descriptive and the normative in his thought.

When dialectic was the method of metaphysics or epistemology, the assimilation [of opposites] was to being or ideas, but the *dialectic of discourse* is an assimilation to concrete facts and contextual statements structured as *process* rather than in essences or in concepts. Facts have their meaning and existence in structured wholes of which they are interpreted parts. Statements have their references in structured discourses of which they are constituent parts. Facts reflect or approximate the ordering principle[] which gave them form; they are orderings in a *manifold*. . . . They are formulated in lawlike statements.[13]

Habermas is forced to turn to a rhetorical dialectic because, as he sees it, supersensible qualities and eternal objects, contained in metaphysics and religion, no longer provide a convincing ground for the morals of individuals nor for the legitimation of political and legal action in the modern world.[14]

Between Facts and Norms is Habermas's application of his theory of discourse to the recognition and legitimation of modern law. Discourse itself is

that form of communication that is removed from the contexts of experience and action and whose structure assures us: that the . . . validity claims of assertions, recommendations, or warnings are the exclusive object of discussion[;] that no force except that of the better argument is exercised; and that, as a result, all motives except that of the cooperative search for truth are excluded.[15]

In this ideal, rational discourse, "the only thing that counts is the compelling force of the better argument based on the relevant information"—"lead[ing] to convincing positions to which all can agree without coercion."[16] Legal discourse is a more limited but equally powerful process for development of *the law*, a type of discourse that focuses on specific communities rather than on more abstract norms for humanity in general.[17] The principle or ground supporting the law-creating validity of Habermas's dialectical discourse I call *the discursive unity of the consociates under law*.[18] This formulation is gleaned from Habermas's own words. The unity supported by this comprehensive principle is related to, but not directly derived from, a transcendent, universal reason in the Kantian sense. Rather, "[i]t is based on fundamental norms of rational speech that we must presuppose if we discourse at all—a transcendental character of ordinary language."[19] Thus while Habermas rejects classical metaphysics with its empasis on abstract being or reason, neither is he a nominalist who finds authentic values only in the words of the individual "consociates." Their very discourse among themselves instead presupposes an authentic reality beyond their particularness, and it is on this view of a social basis for values illumined by speech that Habermas builds his discourse theory.

Transformation of Diversity into Unity

The unity promoted through Habermas's principle is developed through his dialectical method, in which "the needs, wants, and interests of participants . . . are subject to evolution and transformation pursuant to dialogical exchanges . . . not simply to finding overlapping interests [but subject rather] to harmoniz[ing] [their] interests through *dialogical transformation*."[20] " 'Dialectical' methods . . . permit the comparison of things different in kind and [thus] the reconciliation of opposites."[21] Habermas's dialectic satisfies these criteria of harmonization, comparison of the disparate, and reconciliation. It does so through the inclusion of all ideas, beliefs, and opinions expressed in dialogue, where they are both retained in their diversity and yet transformed in the dialectical interchange among the "consociates," the interlocutors in discourse and dialectic.

Dialectical Tensions in Law and Society

Normative versus Factual

Further, the very title of Habermas's book—*Between Facts and Norms*—suggests a tension between two terms requiring, yet defying, reconciliation. "Law borrows its binding force . . . from the alliance that the [coercive, positivistic] facticity of law forms with the [normative] claim [of law] to legitimacy—[an 'alliance' reflecting] a [dynamic] tension between facticity and validity."[22] "Within [the] sphere of adjudication, the immanent tension in law between facticity and validity manifests itself as a tension between legal certainty and the claim to a legitimate application of law."[23] In common practice this tension arises whenever a court renders a decision and opinion through the proper adjudicative[24] framework, and the opinion subsequently appears in the official reporter. There is no doubt that it is the authoritative law of the jurisdiction; but parties and persons peculiarly affected by the decision may be skeptical of the judges' learning or impartiality, doubts that detract from the acceptance of the legitimacy of the decision.

"Lifeworld" versus "Systems"

Analogues to this facticity/validity tension internal to law occur in the tension or opposition between other related, basic terms. The most important of these are the tensions between strategic and communicative action and between "systems" and the "lifeworld." Communicative action or discourse uses general language through which "the only norms that may claim generality [can be expressed. These norms] are [thus] those upon which everyone affected agrees (or would agree) without constraint."[25] In strategic action, however, " 'the actors are interested solely in the success, *i.e.*, the consequences or outcomes of their action, [and] they will try to reach their objectives by influencing their opponent's definition of the situation, and thus his decisions or motives, through external means by using weapons or goods, threats or enticements.' "[26] The lifeworld is that "place" where authentic discourse occurs and where "[t]he conscious life conduct of the individual person finds its standards in the expressivist ideal of *self-realization*, the deontological [rights-based] idea of freedom, and the utilitarian maxim of expanding one's life opportunities."[27] Systems, in contrast, are those economically productive and administrative structures that communicate only in code or through specialized jargon. They are generally identified with the market sector of the private economy and with the governmental bureaucracy. In typical situations "lifeworld communication [embodying universal norms in general language] is interrupted at the points where it runs into the media of money and administrative power, which are deaf to messages in ordinary language."[28] Systems thus are an ever-present threat to the language of personal development and autonomy.

Law as the Dialectical Bridge between the "Lifeworld" and the Bureaucracy of "Systems"

The severance of discursively attained norms from influence over systems functions is particularly critical because " '[i]ncreasing[] . . . bureaucratic control [over] the activities of everyday work and life' " are promoting " 'colonizing tendencies' " of systems over the lifeworld.[29] In this situation, law itself (partially or fragmentarily) dissolves the strong contradiction between lifeworld and systems (embodying discursive and strategic thinking, respectively) by becoming, as it were, the *lingua franca* that can translate the discursive norms of the lifeworld into the codes or jargon of systems language. "Law thus functions as the 'transformer' that first guarantees" unity in communication for society as a whole. [30] Habermas by this means would use discursively generated law and its processes to overcome in dialectical fashion a fundamental conflict.[31] Judicial or administrative procedures that are structured by principles attained through wide public discussion, open to complete participation by the parties in each case, and freed from private sector control through bans on corporate campaign contributions (in those jurisdictions where judges and administrators are elected) would be one area where his discourse method might to some extent resolve the facticity/validity tension in law and its related communicative/strategic and lifeworld/systems tensions.

Such a "place" for public discussion would transcend the banal "candidates' forums" and "town hall meetings" that are manipulated and "spin-doctored" by candidates, their operatives, and the media. Such discussions exhibit only externally imposed, strategic norms. Such "places" consistent with Habermas would be the workplace and educational venues.

THE THREE PARADIGMS OF LAW

Habermas's discourse theory of law also satisfies another criterion of dialectic: For in his discursive process "the varieties of meanings [of law] emerge relative to particular stages and phases of evolution or of argument,"[32] and these meanings are embodied, through assimilation and exemplification, in models or paradigms.[33] As dialectical terms, "model" and "paradigm" do not have a literal signification but are more symbolic and analogical in their communicative impact. In keeping with this dialectical mode of discourse, Habermas propounds three models or "paradigms" of law, two of which are "still competing today[—] bourgeois[-liberal] formal law [and] welfare-state 'materialized' law. [An emergent] third legal paradigm . . . tak[es] the perspective of discourse theory."[34] This last is "the proceduralist paradigm of law[, meant to] take us [dialectically] beyond the opposition between the social models that underlie the [bourgeois-liberal] formalist and the welfarist concepts of law."[35] The proceduralist paradigm is still largely aspirational, but it is the centerpiece of Habermas's treatment of law pursuant to his discourse principle.

The Bourgeois-Liberal Paradigm

The bourgeois-liberal notion of law, still very much in existence, proclaims that "social rewards should be distributed on the basis of individual achievement. . . . The market[, however,] has lost its credibility as a fair (from the perspective of achievement) mechanism for the distribution of life opportunities conforming to the system."[36] Moreover, "bourgeois ideologies . . . offer no support . . . in the face of the basic risks of existence (guilt, sickness, death)."[37] Thus, because of their failure to address basic human needs, the "core components of bourgeois ideology, such as possessive individualism and [the] achievement orientation, are being undermined by changes in the social structure."[38] Nonetheless, so long as this stage retains potency, the liberties of citizens continue to consist mostly of *negative* rights against action by the state.[39]

The bourgeois-liberal paradigm is well represented by the constitutional case of *DeShaney v. Winnebago County Department of Social Services,*[40] in which a young child was severely beaten by his father even after local social workers were put on notice that the father was abusive and violent toward the child. The mother brought an action under the Due Process Clause against the local governmental agency whose social workers had done nothing to prevent the child's abuse; but the Supreme Court held that the suit was groundless. "[N]othing in the language of the Due Process Clause itself requires the State to protect the life, liberty, or property of its citizens against invasion by private actors. The Clause is phrased as a limitation on the State's power to act, not as a guarantee of certain minimal levels of safety and security."[41] Thus, under this paradigm there is no right to affirmative governmental aid, even of the most rudimentary nature—protection of the life of a helpless child from a known danger.

The Social-Welfare Paradigm

The social-welfare paradigm has become associated with the " 'crisis of the welfare state' [and its widely experienced attribute of] the 'insensitivity' of the growing state bureaucracies to restrictions on their clients' individual self-determination."[42] This paradigm emerged to meet the defects of the bourgeois-liberal model by more nearly equalizing the material positions of *all* citizens and to cure the vagaries of the market. "A welfare-state with such . . . paternalistic provisions . . . however, almost invariably tends to impose 'normal' patterns of behavior on its clients,"[43] thus depriving them of their autonomy and their collective diversity.

The contemporary case that fits this paradigm is *Mathews v. Eldridge*,[44] which sets up a utilitarian formula for deciding the scope of due process procedure in disputes over entitlements between a claimant and the government. Professor Jerry Mashaw, who has studied this procedure carefully, concludes:

> The utilitarian calculus is not . . . without difficulties. The *Eldridge* Court conceives of the values of procedure too narrowly: it views the sole purpose of procedural protections as enhancing accuracy, and thus limits its calculus to the benefits or costs that flow from correct or incorrect decisions. No attention is paid to [intrinsic or deontological, rights-based] "process values" . . . or to the demoralizing costs that may result from the grant-withdrawal-grant-withdrawal sequence to which claimants like Eldridge [who had a Social Security disability benefit subject to periodic review] are subjected.[45]

So the social-welfare approach tends to submerge the humanity of its clients in a bureaucratic system without structures to allow those clients to participate rationally and discursively as persons in the system's processes.

The Proceduralist Paradigm

Out of a search for meaning and credible legitimation for law has come "the *search for a new paradigm* beyond the familiar alternatives."[46] Habermas remarks that "so far the contours of the proceduralist legal paradigm . . . have remained vague"; but also that, at a minimum, "the key to a proceduralist understanding of law . . . [links its] legitimacy [directly to] undistorted forms of communication."[47] "The law receives its full normative sense neither through its legal *form* per se, nor through an a priori moral *content*, but through a [dialectical] *procedure* of lawmaking that [*ipso facto*] begets legitimacy."[48] "At the post-traditional level of justification [*i.e.*, beyond the bourgeois and welfare-state paradigms of law] . . . the only law that counts as legitimate is one that is rationally accepted by *all* citizens in a discursive process of opinion—and will—formation."[49]

In the proceduralist paradigm of law, the vacant places of the [bourgeois-liberal] economic man or welfare-state client are occupied by a public of citizens who participate in political communication in order to articulate their wants and needs, to give voice to their violated interests, and, above all, to clarify and settle the contested standards and criteria according to which equals are treated equally and unequals unequally.[50]

In other words, only the proceduralist paradigm of law is fully legitimate because only it gives meaning to law by supporting the citizens' rational discourse, and their rational discourse alone, to determine law and make it binding morally.

A contemporary case, *Romer v. Evans,*[51] provides an example. The Supreme Court, under minimum rationality or scrutiny, struck down as violative of equal protection a statewide voter-approved amendment to the Colorado constitution prohibiting local governments from granting homosexuals and lesbians legal protection against civil rights violations animated by homophobia. The amendment would have voided all such preexisting laws and ordinances and prevented those citizens from seeking their reenactment. Thus the amendment did, and would have continued to, ban deliberative discourse (in the sense that the aim of such discourse would have been futile) by a group of citizens seeking redress because of governmental and private discrimination. The Court's action gave them the power "to give voice to their violated interests, and . . . to clarify and settle the contested standards and criteria according to which equals are treated equally."[52] The case also satisfies Habermas's procedural dictum that "a legal order *is* legitimate to the extent that it equally secures the co-original private and political autonomy of its citizens."[53] After the amendment but before the Supreme Court's action, the gay and lesbian citizens had neither sort of autonomy, because discussion about a most vital aspect of their lives was, as noted above, futile. The amendment barred effective discussion of their civil rights. After the Court's decision, discussion was again legitimized, together with the citizens' powers of autonomy to be free from private and public coercion, through law both imposed and legitimated through dialogue.

Historical Grounds of the Paradigms of Law

A final point needs to be mentioned here: Habermas's discussion of "paradigm shifts"[54] as a result of underlying social changes, together with his reference to "generally accepted ways of referring to a social epoch's paradigmatic understanding of law,"[55] shows that he has a sense of movement in the development of law and of the importance of insight into the meaning-sustaining role of law in a historical age.[56] These are characteristically dialectical ways of viewing law and other social and moral phenomena. But what has all this to do with diversity as a justification for affirmative action?

UNITY IN DIVERSITY

Dialectic represents an all-inclusive mode of thought in which "hindrances in the way of freedom are removed by . . . education and by development of knowledge leading to wisdom."[57] "[E]nglobing truths are approximated"[58] as " '[d]ialectical' methods employ words in broad analogical meanings which permit the comparison of things different in kind and the reconciliation of oppositions."[59] Under this approach "language is adapted to reflect a truth which is found only in system and which cannot be expressed literally."[60] Diversity, or the inclusion of all things or perspectives—even and especially the most dissimilar—into the dialectical vortex, enriches the power, and ultimately the freedom, that emerges from the process. As Charles Hartshorne, a dialectician of being and of esthetic, puts it: "[H]armony [among elements or experiences] is not . . . a sufficient condition of great value. There must be intensity. And intensity depends upon contrast, the amount of *diversity* integrated into experience."[61] By analogy to the sociolegal realm, Hartshorne's intensity through diversity means a greater freedom, both personal and public, for those who participate in political and legal discourses. And the laws and their legitimacy enjoy a greater intensity, that is, a greater power and justice.

For Habermas, "the *dialectic of discourse* is an assimilation to concrete facts and contextual statements structured as *process* rather than in essences or in concepts. Statements have their references in structured discourses of which they are parts. . . . They are orderings in a *manifold*."[62] This manifoldness, or diversity—combined with the procedure or process of discourse—acutely describes Habermas's essential aim:

[A]s participants in [the processes of] rational discourses, consociates under law must be able to examine whether a contested norm meets with, or could meet with, the agreement of *all* those possibly affected.[63]

[In this practice] we presume that we sufficiently approximate the ideal conditions . . . immunized against repression and inequality. . . . [W]hether norms and values could find the rationally motivated assent of *all those affected* can[, therefore,] be judged only from the intersubjectively enlarged perspective of the first-person plural.[64]

There is no going behind the process of discourse itself to find traditional metaphysical objects. When properly orchestrated, this process of social dialogue, *i.e.*, discourse *among* rational creatures and not merely discourse within the individual, will produce laws encompassing the diverse views of the many expressed in a unity containing them all.

In approximating the model of unity in diversity in words and deeds, Habermas is moving toward a realm of freedom through "the victory of persuasion over force"[65]—a victory and unity in which "the pluralism of beliefs and interests is not suppressed but unleashed and recognized."[66] The role of affirmative action in creating and supporting this diversity is *ipso facto* its very justification.

ACKERMAN'S DIALECTIC OF LIBERAL AND CONSTITUTIONAL LEGITIMIZATION

Now that I have examined a more abstract example of the dialectical mode of thought, with Bruce Ackerman's work I now move into a system of thought that deals with American constitutional law, especially the Free Speech Clause of the First Amendment and the Equal Protection Clause. The use of a legal scholar who addresses issues with more concreteness will aid me in ultimately bringing dialectic to bear on the law of affirmative action. Bruce Ackerman expressly utilizes the discursively dialectical philosophy of Habermas[67] to construct a model of distributive justice in *Social Justice in the Liberal State*,[68] as well as to read discursive rationality and purpose into the American Constitution in *We the People: Foundations*.[69] Like Habermas, Ackerman eschews any reliance on transcendent, ontological truths;[70] his reliance, rather, is on his stalwart belief that *"liberalism [must be understood] as a way of talking about power, a form of political culture."*[71] Power is never expressly defined and even has different meanings: On the one hand, power may be understood negatively as domination and compulsion taken "from the outworn husk of 'free market' capitalism";[72] like Habermas, he condemns this equation of power with force. On the other hand, power can have a more beneficent nature when its essence is transformed into rational knowledge, or justified by this knowledge, as is typical in dialectical thought.[73] Understood in this fashion, power generates freedom, not compulsion.[74]

"Undominated Equality"

The arbitrary, compulsive use of power (corresponding here to strategic action in Habermas's work) is itself controlled by "constrained power talk,"[75] which employs three conditions to eliminate the coercive elements from the talk of claimants of unjustifiable power: "Rationality," which restrains the power holder by requiring her to give reasons in defense of her power;[76] "Consistency," which requires the power holder not to vary her proffered justifications irrationally;[77] and "Neutrality," which promotes both equality and diversity by barring the questioned power holder from arguing either her own personal superiority or that her conception of the good is better than others'. Those last positions, which tout superiority of self and of that self's life values, would—if not barred by Neutrality—present a threat that would virtually destroy the notion of recognition and respect for diversity among equal citizens and deny the grounds for public discussion about the plurality of versions of the good life.[78] The upshot of such "constrained power talk"—and especially the power through Neutrality to affirm equality and diversity—is that "the practical implications of liberal conversation . . . can discipline the concrete power struggle of our everyday lives."[79] Power is tamed and thus transformed from irrational force into a rational capacity supportive of diversity and equality, and freedom. Thus constitutional free speech and equal protection benefit. We begin to see that the line between philosophy and law is not always a bright one.

This process of constrained conversation yields what Ackerman calls "the dialogic theory of liberal legitimacy,"[80] a conception of dialogue that, when applied to lawmaking, would be the analogue to Habermas's proceduralist paradigm of law, which itself also operates under conditions designed to remove force from deliberations.[81] Ackerman's is a dialogue promoting "a liberal conception of equality that is compatible with a social order rich in *diversity* of talents, personal ideals, and forms of community."[82] Ackerman calls "this distinctive conception of equality . . . *undominated* equality."[83] "[T]he harmony, generate[d] [by] the liberal method of dialogue [together with the principle of undominated equality] . . . bids us glimpse a deeper harmony in the dialogue that provides the social foundation for all subsequent disagreements, [contradictions, and diversities]."[84] And so undominated equality, harboring extensive diversity within "a deeper harmony," is Ackerman's foundational principle, and liberal dialogue or constrained conversation is the method by which compulsion (or force) is controlled, allowing diversity and reason to be seen and heard. Constrained conversation, producing undominated equality, is Ackerman's analogue to Habermas's discursive process.

In his treatment of the technique of constrained conversation, Ackerman uses a rhetorical device that is as old as dialectic itself—*"constrained silence"*: "Whenever nothing intelligible can be said of a power, its exercise is illegitimate."[85] "Any [proposed] rule [of law] that fails to be supported in this way is to be struck from the agenda under [the condition of] Rationality."[86] Such a stratagem absolutely restrains the interlocutor without any use of force. Plato, the inventor of dialectic, has the student Meno respond to Socrates:

If I may be flippant, I think that not only in outward appearance but in other respects as well you are exactly like the flat sting ray that one meets in the sea. Whenever anyone comes into contact with it, it numbs him, and that is the sort of thing you seem to be doing to me now.[87]

The aggrandizer of power feels this "numbness" when he is confronted with a piercing question about the legitimacy of his power but is unable to make more than a babbling response, if even that. The speaker rendered unintelligible is powerless because he has lost the ability to speak. Both Habermas and Ackerman hold that speech (logos) is directly related to power and its legitimate use. A society is free or not to the extent that speech—generally intelligible speech and not jargon, which carries the stigma of force—is practiced rationally and openly without appreciable restraint.

Ackerman's Conception of Affirmative Action

Ackerman, unlike Habermas, has a *definite* conception of affirmative action directly related to his speech/equality ethos. The purpose of affirmative action is to achieve or to restore undominated equality—a status among persons requiring respect for their diversity. The need for affirmative action arises because of gross inequalities among persons or groups vis-à-vis the five social conditions (or "power domains," as Ackerman later calls them), which, when taken together positively, are the *prima facie* elements of undominated equality (they are listed in the note).[88] The problem arises when "imperfection costs" appear because of flaws in the social, biological, or technological determinants of distributing goods, resources, and services in each of the five "power domains" corresponding to the five conditions of undominated equality. The ideal resolution of the problem would be to require the "[a]ccommodat[ion] [of] imperfection [by] *each* [citizen's] mak[ing] an equal sacrifice of [her] ideal rights,"[89] but some citizens may contrive to make others "bear the brunt of the burden of imperfection,"[90] leading with a certain probability to exploitation of those subjected to the inequalities. The actual forms of discrimination as they exist against blacks, persons with disabilities, or even the poor are all examples of what Ackerman means by this systematic description of exploitation.

Exposing exploitation does not depend on the perception of an unequal power distribution between persons or groups in merely one "power domain"; offsetting advantages in another domain may, for example, even the distribution and restore, on balance, equivalent sacrifice.[91] Rather, "the exploitation of one group by another . . . [requires] add[ing] up each [of the] particular disadvantage[s] into one outrageous violation of the principle of equivalent sacrifice."[92] Thus the conception of exploitation turns on proof of the phenomenon of systematic disadvantages, in which "equal[ity] [of] sacrifice in one power domain cannot compensate for [aggregated deficiencies] encountered in other domains."[93] In other words, the general distribution of social goods is systematically and persistently imbalanced against certain groups in society (groups that might well be referred to as "castes"[94]), and the imbalance is not amenable to redress through normal dialogue. This is an example in which encrusted social practices having substantial force block authentic dialogue.

The nub of the resolution of this problem of exploitation depends on the distinction between negative compensation and affirmative compensation. Negative compensation is designed to make up for a deficiency in *one* domain by granting the subject or group some compensation directly to that deficient domain or by the provision of other compensation to another domain that restores the overall balance. To illustrate this latter instance, Ackerman poses the example of a (genetically) blind child's being assured of a liberal education,[95] presumably an *intellectual* opportunity not secure to a person of that or comparable disability, though such a person may cultivate self-esteem and other *existential* traits as well as, or better than, any other person. The blind child will never have her sight restored and thus will always suffer genetic domination in the corresponding domain because of this fact, although at least she will be spared the additional suffering of not having a liberal education—a benefit found in another domain. But Ackerman goes on to say that such negative compensation, even when flowing into a domain of no injury (*i.e.*, the one of universal liberal education), is not enough: "I aim to prove that a liberal statesman cannot settle for a negative compensation policy. He must move beyond and *act affirmatively* on behalf of those, like [persons with disabilities], who suffer from irremediable domination. Like its negative counterpart, affirmative action will engender a *ceaseless good faith debate*."[96] Thus "[t]o end exploitation, it is not enough to eliminate one or another form of illegitimate dominion."[97] The blind child may need *more* than simply the assurance of a liberal education, to which she was entitled anyway. "A blind citizen has a right to insist that others make a *greater* sacrifice of their rights in nongenetic domains if overall equivalence is to be achieved."[98] *"Exploitation continues so long as the remaining patterns of advantage favor the same group."*[99]

Accordingly, for Ackerman, affirmative action is not simply corrective justice[100] but rather a type of distributive justice[101] crafted to restore a properly equal balance among the *prima facie* components of undominated equality through adjustments in the degrees of social sacrifice. Because undominated equality arises from a system of distributed resources, goods, and services, his method of crafting the scope and of identifying recipients of redirected distribution lies in "the overall public dialogue"[102]—the locus of power. The importance of implementing such affirmative action is evident because when "a unified doctrine of initial endowments . . . [including] *equal* material resources, *liberal* education, [and] *undominated* genetic equality . . . are taken together[,] they describe a power structure that supports a thoroughly liberal form of political discourse."[103] The liberal position, as Ackerman sees it, must be committed to a form of affirmative action that addresses the conditions of exploited groups through revisions in the patterns of distributive justice.

The Dialectics of the American Constitution

Ackerman then goes further than Habermas (as considered here) and—in *Social Justice in the Liberal State* and in *We the People: Foundations*—offers a historically grounded outlook on the American Constitution, an outlook that can be understood in dialectical terms of growth, assimilation, and synthesis of constitutional developments—with novel constitutional elements produced in the most recent constitutional age or epoch and then combined synthetically with elements fashioned in earlier ages. On his understanding, American constitutional history has had three great moments that have decisively shaped our foundational law: the Founding, Reconstruction, and the New Deal. During these moments or times, the populace has actively participated, through public dialogue and discussion, in critical constitutional decisions. In between these moments, however, Ackerman believes that the populace has repeatedly become somnolently private and has left the governance of the nation to politicians whose narrowly interested actions have been restrained primarily by a vigilant judiciary adhering to the authentic constitution and not simply to the latest *modus vivendi* of the day. Because of this characteristic alternation between constitutional (and public regarding) politics and normal (or private interest) politics, Ackerman calls his constitutional doctrine "dualist."[104]

Yet Ackerman might appear to perceive these patterns between more active public and more passive private levels of popular involvement as merely static repetition, not productive of novel growth in constitutional meaning.[105] If Ackerman were truly convinced that "American history has a *cyclical* pattern . . . of normal politics . . . [and] constitutional politics" *simpliciter,*[106] he would accept the view of the ancient Greek world that "[t]he same ideas . . . recur in men's minds not once or twice but again and again."[107] Ackerman is plainly enamored of the Greek tradition of politics,[108] but he rejects any static Greek belief about history in favor of the dynamic view that has prevailed in the West, of both secular and—I would submit—Christian origins.[109] In his view of history the drive toward the new, through the creation of new structures of governance found in the moments of constitutional politics, has dominance over the arguably static pattern of maximum-minimum-maximum participation of the population in politics. His approach, then, *does* point to the new and not simply to the constantly recurring.[110] Ackerman's three great moments and the "constitutional regime[s]" or "epoch[s]"[111] that they define resemble the dialectical unfolding of trinitarian meaning in eschatological doctrines of Christian thinkers.[112] He, finally, at the end of *We the People: Foundations*, proposes a "creative synthesis" between "two great Western traditions [struggling] for hegemony over the modern spirit"[113]—Christian and Greek. Thus despite protestations and some contradictions, Ackerman ultimately adopts a dialectic of history that might well be characterized as a form of secular providence, where the end (purpose) of history is equality and freedom without struggle or strife.

The Dialectical Ground of Legitimacy in Diversity

The people ultimately are the legitimate source of power—and their discursive unity (together with undominated equality), the organizing principle of his work—under Ackerman's dualist constitution. The very title *We the People* gives the point away. During a time of creative or revolutionary change in the Constitution (*i.e.*, a constitutional moment), "the leadership's claim to legitimacy must be validated by the *concrete assent* of fellow citizens, who recognize them as the true representatives of the people."[114] In this sense, only the leaders of the revolution—the "wise men"—are genuinely free because only they truly understand the transformative nature and right use of political power—but participating citizens through exercise of their corresponding powers can approximate this freedom.[115] In a dialogue among participating citizens during a time of constitutional politics, "liberal theory invites [citizens] to pierce their substantive disagreements and achieve a deeper unity—in the fact that they are all seeking to find themselves through a common process of dialogue."[116] This process stands in contrast to one that would "us[e] political power to subordinate people to a single common good" or "to convert people to a single common understanding."[117] Even in these times of dialectical ferment by the people themselves, "[t]he *diversity* of life choices [continues to be recognized as] a positive good, symbolizing the inexhaustible fecundity of human freedom."[118]

When the people do not actively speak, the judiciary faces the task of preserving the people's prior constitutional legacy both through judicial review to prevent contemporary politicians from breaching that legacy and—for our purpose here—through the process of dialectical synthesis. This process Ackerman calls "the problem of multigenerational synthesis"[119] because it describes the judiciary's duty to preserve essential and viable constitutional elements from all times, through a process of reconciliation of opposites and adjustment of compatibles, into a coherent body of law. For example, Republicans of the Reconstruction Era had to "put together a constitutional whole out of . . . discordant parts—their proposed [Civil War] amendments [and the] Federalist world of the eighteenth century,"[120] "identifying these [amendments] as fragments of an evolving whole that began in 1787, not 1866."[121] In Time Three—the New Deal—the Supreme Court was "left . . . to codify the constitutional meaning of New Deal democracy in a series of transformative judicial opinions."[122] It is clear enough by now that Ackerman has adopted dialectical or " 'epochal' history, since [his work] depends on discovering traits which characterize organic wholes—peoples . . . or periods—and which apply to all activities of the group or of the time, including the characteristic form of morals [and] political practices."[123]

The dialectical epochs of Ackerman are analogous to the dialectical models or "paradigms" of law set forth by Habermas.[124] Certainly both, typically of dialectic, have that form of progression, through increasing knowledge and perception, pointing toward an ideal of wisdom or rationality whose application leads to the right use of power and thus to freedom.[125]

Note, however, that *each* of Ackerman's constitutional moments (leading to an epoch or regime of constitutional law) resembles the last of Habermas's paradigms—the proceduralist paradigm of law. Here the resemblance is more than analogical, for at each of these moments the citizenry have been actively engaged in uncoerced dialogue that has turned out to furnish the legitimacy needed for transformative constitutional change. Facticity and validity are held in balance in each of these moments. The degree of diversity in the makeup of the dialectical citizenry *does*, of course, change by increasing from 1787 to 1868 to 1937, Ackerman's three times, because of greater and more inclusive citizen participation; and there can be no doubt that more power and legitimacy have redounded to the Constitution on each successive occasion. This point—that diversity imports renewed and increased vigor, as well as legitimacy and justice, to constitutional decision making—is plainly implied in Ackerman's call for "a new Bill of Rights[, one] that recognizes the *inclusionary* thrust of American history by giving each American an effective guarantee of equal opportunity—in schools, on the job, in public places and public life."[126] Equality may be the guiding principle of this aspiration, but free speech provides the power to attain it, and diversity is the counterpart of equality, without which equality could neither be approached or assured.

RACE AND DIVERSITY

Before I may validly apply Habermas's and Ackerman's respective doctrines of dialectically supported diversity to the law of affirmative action, I must first address a threshold question: Is race *simpliciter* such an appropriate characteristic to the creation of diversity that its enlistment for that purpose is vital? The premise of those who would answer no is that racial characteristics are purely external and thus do not embody or represent in any essential way the intellectual and cultural qualities by which diversity in affirmative action may be furthered.[127] Thus one commentator indicates his skepticism: "The degree to which race or skin pigmentation is a significant part of our experience . . . varies greatly. . . . Race is thus not necessarily a strong clue to genuine intellectual diversity."[128] The court of appeals in a recent important decision rejecting affirmative action—*Hopwood*—stated that "[t]o believe that a person's race *controls* his point of view is to stereotype him," thus making race useless or even harmful as an indicator of diversity.[129]

This viewpoint must be rejected. First of all, no advocate of diversity as a form of affirmative action argues that a person's race—if it is African American or otherwise—"controls" that person's point of view. The organizing principle here, rather, is that the African American race has undergone a long and unique experience since its arrival in America (and even before, in its ancestors' native Africa) that pervasively shapes its view of social reality, especially in light of the history of exploitation that its members have undergone. The fact that skin color and other physical characteristics are associated with African Americans is something of an accident, in the Aristotelian sense;[130] but physical traits have tended, nonetheless, to identify the group members who are the bearers of this culture. "[T]here is a difference between racial identity as a function of skin pigmentation and racial identity as a product of a distinct historical and cultural perspective."[131] The Supreme Court itself has held that scientific evidence supports the conclusion that "racial classifications are for the most part sociopolitical, rather than biological, in nature."[132] We are dealing, then, with a cultural phenomenon that is undeniable, plainly associated with dark-skinned peoples but not an essential outgrowth of their physical traits, and is a culture that is quite different from the mainstream of American culture. These facts are significant because they establish an identifiable segment of the populaton whose inclusion in mainstream institutions will lead to greater cultural and intellectual diversity, with all its benefits.

Indeed, Gunnar Myrdal in 1944 found that "American Negro culture is some-what different from the general American culture . . . and that the difference is significant for Negroes and for the relations between Negroes and whites."[133] The Supreme Court later implicitly accepted this theory of a distinct, intellec-tually formative black culture in *Sweatt v. Painter*[134] in which the Court declared that genuine learning could not take place where a black professional student was kept isolated from white students and teachers, especially when whites predominantly made up the profession and its culture. In *Brown v. Board of Education*[135] the Court found that children of the black race generally suffered from feelings of inferiority caused by educational segregation. Resorting to so-cial psychological studies, the Court declared that such feelings of inferiority were not racially innate but resulted from a culture of prejudice and discrimi-nation.[136]

The cultural diversity that black persons would bring to a dialectic of truth and action is not altogether a culture shaped through the endurance of exploi-tation—though their culture has undeniably been shaped by bigotry and injus-tice—but it is a culture also reflecting a distinct and rich experience on this continent. Individuals, as already noted, are bearers of this culture (though the group is the primary bearer), and their skin color, as a simple matter of fact, tends to identify them. (Not every black individual, however, agrees with the thrust of or the premise of this argument,[137] and this very fact shows that not every black individual will reflect the same perspective.) The truth remains that skin color has an undeniable presence in our society that, for better or worse, seldom goes unnoticed, and a selection of persons on that basis for educational and employment opportunities will tend to produce persons of outlook distinct from white middle-class America. As to the ultimate legitimacy of what factors and perspectives should be the basis for diversity, dialectic itself must be given the task of sorting out genuine from spurious indicators of diversity. "[E]qual consociates under law . . . through communicative action [should] reach agree-ment among themselves as to which factual similarities and differences ought to be taken into account by the law."[138] Again, dialectical discourse is the ul-timate means of sorting the ordinary from the extraordinary, the diverse from the commonplace. And as a prescient observer reminds us, the diverse traits sought from preferential treatment of blacks should, after all, be traits that are associated with their race, not simply interesting but random traits that black individuals may happen to have.

[The] objection . . . that selection on the basis of race . . . wrongly . . . and insultingly . . . assumes that . . . only black students can . . . provide diversity in class, political attitudes, or culture . . . misses the aspect of diversity that is in question, which is not what race may or may not indicate, but race itself. Unfortunately the worst of the stereotypes, suspicions, fears, and hatred that still poison America are color-coded, not coded by class or culture. It is crucial that blacks and whites come to know and appreciate each other better, and if some of the blacks turn out not to have the class or cultural or other characteristics that are stereotypically associated with them, that obviously enhances rather than undermines the benefits of racial diversity.[139]

HISTORICAL FOUNDATIONS OF CONSTITUTIONAL DIVERSITY IN THE SUPREME COURT

The Supreme Court, and the lower federal courts, in their principal cases have addressed racial diversity in the context of education, both primary and secondary and higher education, except for one Supreme Court case, which looked to public broadcasting as an appropriate setting for racial diversity. The high Court, in its education cases, has concentrated on intellectual, cultural, and psychological factors in analyzing the value of diversity. The first three cases to be discussed here concern desegregation of the public institutions of education and not affirmative action as such. That is to say that in them the Court did not rely on any theory of racial preference but rather on a color-blind or neutral theory of racial justice meant to restore or create equal relations between the races, where actual breaches of constitutional equality contemporaneously occurred. Nonetheless, the Court, without—of course—*consciously* adopting his theories as such, followed a position entirely consistent with the conditions needed for the discursive unity of Habermas. This consistency arises from the Court's view, in each case, that the expansion of public dialogue produced by drawing African Americans into this dialogue as it occurs in education (from the primary grades to the postgraduate level) promotes authentic humanity for that race, as it does for other races.

In *Sweatt v. Painter*,[140] the first case directly involving diversity,[141] the Court struck down, as violative of the Equal Protection Clause, a state-supported scheme to keep black law students isolated in an all-black law school, hastily established to evade legal efforts to integrate the University of Texas Law School. The university purported to be following the "separate but equal" doctrine of *Plessy v. Ferguson*.[142] The Court, however, found that the two law schools were inherently unequal.[143]

[A]lthough the law is a highly learned profession, we are well aware that it is an intensely practical one. The law school . . . cannot be effective in isolation from the individuals and institutions with which the law interacts. Few students and no one who has practiced law would choose to study in a vacuum, removed from *the interplay of ideas and the exchange of views* with which the law is concerned.[144]

In a companion case, *McLaurin v. Oklahoma State Regents*,[145] the state *had* permitted McLaurin, a black, to *enroll* in a graduate program in the formerly all-white University of Oklahoma Department of Education; but the authorities restricted his use of the library and remaining otherwise common facilities to areas specially designated for his use as a black. The Court struck down these restrictions, designed to create segregation *within* a school, as unconstitutionally unequal. The restrictions "[impaired] and [inhibited] [McLaurin's] ability to study, *to engage in discussions and exchange views with other students*, and, in general, to learn his profession."[146]

The Court ruled in these two cases that the division of the races into separate facilities or institutions destroys the substantial worth of any such education to minorities by preventing their inclusion into the discourse of that profession— discourse that is of the essence of the profession. By implication, members of the white majority suffer in these situations as well, because their numbers represent less than the whole of society and thus cannot generate the variety and unity of discourse needed to make the legal world unified and legitimized. For Habermas, elimination of the division of the races is essential, especially in law schools where those who will predominantly carry the power of law are trained. "[T]he only law that counts is one that is rationally accepted by *all* [and *a fortiori* by *all* lawyers and students of law] in a discursive process [of *comprehensive* law formation]."[147]

In its famous decision in *Brown v. Board of Education of Topeka*,[148] the Court went further than it had in *Sweatt* and *McLaurin* by declaring that schools— here public primary and secondary schools—segregated by race inherently violate the Equal Protection Clause, with no need for a court to inquire into such schools individually to test their compliance with *Plessy*'s "separate but equal" standard. Rather, the Court substantiated its holding with social scientific evidence, that separation from what otherwise would be a multiracially diverse classroom *ipso facto* destroys the wills and hearts of minority children to learn and to cope with life in their later years.[149] Other Supreme Court decisions have rested on or alluded to diversity to support desegregation measures in the public schools. Such measures have been needed, the Court has found, "to prepare students to live in a pluralistic society"[150] and for them to learn how "to function" in a multiracial society and "to live in harmony and with mutual respect."[151]

Bruce Ackerman makes the *Brown* case illumine his conception of multigenerational synthesis by combining elements of Time Two (the epoch beginning with the ratification of the Civil War amendments) and Time Three (the epoch beginning with the New Deal's interventionist role for government). When *Plessy* was decided in 1896, its "separate but equal" standard reflected the rudimentary state of, and the lack of importance ascribed to, public schools of the day *plus* the generally passive attitude toward the Fourteenth Amendment and its Equal Protection Clause. Both schools and clause were then weak. Against this background *Brown* "is a compelling exercise in two-three synthesis: explaining why *Plessy*'s interpretation of the Fourteenth Amendment is no longer consistent with foundational premises established in the aftermath of the New Deal."[152] "With the New Deal, the *public* schools could take on a new *symbolic* meaning. They were no longer anomalous [*i.e.*, the exception to the educational system], but *paradigmatic* of the new promise of activist government."[153]

By 1954 the major premise of *Plessy*—that public education was "anomalous"—had been completely transformed into a very different model of education through New Deal activism. The Court, using this new historical development, was to fashion in *Brown* a synthesis that would capture both the new essence of citizenship in public education and the destruction of barriers to racial diversity required by the Equal Protection Clause, now perceived to be far more active. The role played here by the Court is prototypical of dialectical thinking in the judiciary. It exemplifies the dialectical mode of thought because of its assimilation of previously disparate ideas and institutions—here, racial equality and public schools—into a new synthesis of racially diverse education.

BAKKE AND THE FIRST AMENDMENT VALIDATION OF DIVERSITY

The Supreme Court first addressed the issue of *affirmative* action in 1978 in the famous case of *Regents of the University of California v. Bakke*.[154] The Medical School of the University of California at Davis was operating an affirmative action program through a special admissions committee. This committee considered *only* the applications of self-designated "disadvantaged applicants." These, in turn, consisted for the most part of members of "minority group[s]" including "Blacks," "Chicanos," "Asians," and "American Indians." "Disadvantaged" whites also applied to this special admissions program, but none succeeded in gaining admission through it. By its separate process the special admissions committee filled a prescribed number of admission slots specifically set aside for these minorities—admissions that were never reviewed by the regular admissions committee (except for extraordinary deficiencies in the minority admittees' academic records).[155]

This procedure was then, and still is, significant because it prompted the idea of "quota"—anathema to opponents of affirmative action and frequently used to label this remedy most pejoratively, because in *Bakke* there was a purely numerical set-aside for minorities immune from revision or encroachment by majority whites.

Allan Bakke was a white man who had applied for admission to the medical school twice, in 1973 and again in 1974. Each time he was rejected after his application had gone through the regular admissions review process while applicants in the special admissions program, with lower objective qualifications than his (including grades, standardized test scores, and interview ratings), were admitted.[156] Bakke brought suit in the California state courts on, among other grounds, the Equal Protection Clause and Title VI of the Civil Rights Act of 1964.[157] The California Supreme Court held the special admissions program unconstitutional on the grounds that *no admissions program* based on the race of applicants could be valid.[158] In a fragmented decision having three major opinions, the Supreme Court both affirmed and reversed.[159]

Thus the Court affirmed the lower court's rejection of the particular plan at the Davis Medical School (Justice Stevens joined by three others plus Justice Powell) but reversed that court's holding that *no admissions plan* based on race could stand (Justice Powell plus Justice Brennan and three others).[160] Justice Brennan stated the basis of this reversal—"Mr. Justice Powell agrees with us that some uses of race in university admissions are permissible and, therefore he joins with us to make five votes reversing the judgment below insofar as it prohibits the University from establishing race-conscious programs in the future."[161] The Court also ordered the admission of Mr. Bakke.

Justice Powell's opinion, though written to express his views only, carries great weight and influence, especially the part on diversity, which can be considered the holding of the case.[162] In the first and less renowned part of the opinion, Justice Powell held that the Davis plan itself failed to meet "the most exacting judicial examination" required by equal protection of "[r]acial and ethnic distinctions of any sort."[163] The second part of the Powell opinion is the soul of the legal and constitutional defense of diversity as a rationale *for* affirmative action. Justice Powell took the significant step of turning from the Equal Protection Clause as a hurdle to affirmative action to the Free Speech Clause of the First Amendment as "a countervailing constitutional interest . . . of paramount importance" in support of affirmative action—at least in the academic world.[164] He went on to add to this holding that "the interest in [racial and ethnic diversity] is compelling in the context of a university's admissions program,"[165] provided that "the diversity that furthers the compelling state interest encompasses a far broader array of qualifications and characteristics of which racial or ethnic origin is but *a single though important element*."[166]

So it is plain that Justice Powell meant for the First Amendment rationale behind diversity to satisfy any compelling interest test imposed by the strict scrutiny required for equal protection whenever racial and ethnic classifications are at issue. His adoption of a free-speech understanding of diversity, though limited in his terms to the relation of diversity to academic freedom, nonetheless is compatible with Habermas's discourse theory as a means to truth and with Ackerman's grounding of freedom and equality in open and unconstrained dialogue. It was not, however, intended to be directly remedial of past discrimination, as Ackerman would seem to support in his affirmative action proposal.[167] Furthermore, the argument from free speech for diversity transcends Justice Powell's *Bakke* opinion and opens up diversity for affirmative action, not simply in higher education but in all places where the discussion of public issues can constructively take place. As we shall note, one such place is the workplace.

Justice Powell's use of free-speech analysis to support academic diversity must also be placed in the context of judicially determined free-speech values. When this step is taken and his opinion in *Bakke* appears in this light, Habermas's and Ackerman's valuation of free speech through diversity can be brought in and directly compared with the judicial values. Such a comparison shows complete congruence between Justice Powell's and the latter two figures' thought on speech and diversity.

Freedom of speech under the Constitution primarily concerns three major values or purposes: democratic participation in political decision making, self-expression and self-realization, and advancement of knowledge and the search for truth.[168] Of these the first (promotion of and participation in self-government[169]) and the last (advancement of truth[170]) are instrumental in nature—they exist for the sake of some other publicly valued good. Thus they tend toward a utilitarian nature. The second (self-realization[171]) is constitutive of and intrinsic in the right to be recognized as an autonomous moral agent. This is a deontological purpose, *i.e.*, it defines a right that must be categorically applied to the individual to protect his own personhood, not simply a good that he may be granted or allowed to participate in for a larger social purpose. All three purposes were reflected in Justice Powell's seminal choice of academic freedom to reflect the First Amendment grounding of affirmative action.[172] Both Habermas's and Ackerman's views on the importance of autonomous discourse free from external restraint fit closely into this approach of diversity and the use of race in admissions to institutions of higher learning; but, again, these two thinkers would not limit the kind of discourse brought about by diversity to the venues of universities and professional schools.

Justice Powell found that his rationale for diversity serves the *democratic form* of government because " 'academic freedom is of transcendent value to all [the] Nation and not merely to the teachers concerned. . . . The Nation's future depends upon *leaders* trained through wide exposure to . . . ideas.' "[173] In *Keyishian*, one of the academic freedom cases cited by Justice Powell, the New York State Board of Regents was charged by statute to require professors and instructors in the state university system to certify their *non*membership in "subversive associations."[174] The Supreme Court struck down the statute, in large part for the reason suggested above: to protect academic dialogue, a process essential to the development of democratic leaders and citizens.[175]

Habermas would view the holding of unconstitutionality in *Keyishian* as protecting the academic world, part of the lifeworld, from the threat of strategic action (here from the bureaucracy of the state legislative body, state executive officers, and the managers of the higher education system).[176] Once strategic action is resisted, "just those norms deserve to be valid that could meet with the approval of *those potentially affected*."[177] "Those potentially affected" are the very citizens whose dialogue is recognized (in the academic world and elsewhere) as vital support for democratic government. The instrument of rule in a democracy—law—links its "legitimacy [directly to] undistorted [*i.e.*, uncoerced] forms of communication."[178] "The law receives its full normative sense . . . through a [dialectical] *procedure* of lawmaking that begets legitimacy."[179]

As for Ackerman, his thought is congruent with the value to democracy of ideas generated through liberal education. In typical dialectical fashion, he assimilates political power to knowledge. "Liberal dialogue[, therefore,] . . . seeks to control the exercise of superior power [Habermas: strategic action] in *all* its forms, insisting that . . . uses of power be justified in a way consistent with dialogic rights."[180] "It is the act of dialogue . . . not the act of voting . . . that legitimates the use of power in a liberal state."[181] Like Habermas, Ackerman views reason, as expressed in dialogue, as public and social, thus embracing in its very dialectical nature the broad diversity in society. Accordingly, all our authorities—Justice Powell, Habermas, and Ackerman—are on record that the academic process of exchanging ideas is protected under the First Amendment rationale of advancing democracy. They all, in addition, embrace diversity as part and parcel of free-speech values—at least in the academy.

That part of Justice Powell's *Bakke* opinion on diversity also appears to meet the First Amendment standard of *self-realization and self-expression*—a *"constitutive* feature of a just political society [requiring] government [to] treat all its adult members . . . as responsible moral agents."[182] His moral and legal support for such autonomy can be inferred from the precise way in which Justice Powell would have allowed race to be used to attain a diverse student body. "The diversity that furthers [First Amendment aims] encompasses a far broader array of qualifications and characteristics of which racial or ethnic origin is but a single though important element."[183] Other qualities or achievements such as "unique work or service experience, leadership, maturity, demonstrated compassion, a history of overcoming disadvantage, ability to communicate with the poor, or other qualifications deemed important" would count toward diversity.[184] Thus an affirmative action program constituted by these widely diverse elements "treats each applicant as an individual in the admissions process."[185] It is not mere race as a biological trait that counts but what it represents in the person. The person is not stereotyped nor objectified but allowed to be spontaneous in her expression.

Except, perhaps, for the Powell opinion's reliance on personal achievements, achievements that Habermas perceives to be of a bourgeois nature,[186] Habermas would support the same kind of attention to personal autonomy and self-realization. *"[A]utonomous will . . .* is freed from the heteronomous features of contingent interests [*e.g.,* external features of race] . . . particular sociocultural forms, and identity shaping traditions. The autonomous will is *entirely* imbued with [pure] practical reason."[187] Law thus promotes self-realization when it reflects the results of dialogue among the diverse citizens of the polity, for such dialogue sheds external forces—"heteronomous features of contingent interests"—that hem in personal autonomy. "The conscious life conduct of the individual person finds its standards in the expressive will of self-realization, the . . . idea of freedom [founded on rights], and [finally] the utilitarian maxim of expanding one's life opportunities."[188] These principles all apply, it should be recalled, where the discourse theory of ethics operates to shape morals from the uncoerced speech of the entire community as lifeworld, not merely as systems.

Bruce Ackerman links his entire scheme of dialogic exchange to the necessity that "each of us describe[] himself as a morally autonomous person capable of putting a value on his life plan."[189] Indeed his formulation of affirmative action is aimed at "provid[ing] each citizen with tools for self-realization."[190] Because (it will be recalled) the decisions about the contours of any affirmative action plan "will engender a ceaseless good faith debate,"[191] autonomy becomes both a precondition of entering into the kind of speech that produces justice *and* an outcome of that very process, since the process promotes self-realization.

In *the search for truth* Justice Powell can be said to have justified academic diversity because it implicitly promotes "the marketplace of ideas" first asserted by Justice Holmes.[192] Specifically and expressly, he affirmed the powerful view " 'that robust exchange of ideas . . . [leads to] discover[y] [of] truth "out of a multitude of tongues [rather] than through any kind of authoritative selection." ' "[193] Habermas would completely support the barring of "authoritative statement[s]" from discourse when they do not depend on the power of rational persuasion alone for their acceptance. "[T]he ideal conditions of a speech situation [are] specially immunized against repression and inequality. . . . [P]ersons for and against a claim . . . [are] relieved of the pressures of action and experience, adopt[ing] a hypothetical attitude in order to test with reasons, and reasons alone, whether [a] proponent's claim stands up."[194] Justice Holmes, though no dialectician in the sense of that word used here,[195] was the father of the idea in American law that coercion (except in the most exceptional of circumstances) should play no role in validating ideas or truths—"[T]he ultimate good desired is better reached by free trade in ideas—that the best test of truth is the power of the thought to get itself accepted in the competition of the market."[196] This view prevailed with him even if an idea in question—like Bolshevism—became generally accepted through speech and by persuasion, with the consequence of gaining for itself the power to sweep away the very foundations of society.[197]

Ackerman takes much the same position. "Liberalism does not depend on the truth of any metaphysical or epistemological system. Instead, liberalism's ultimate justification is to be found in its strategic [not in Habermas's sense of coercive] location in a web of talk that converges upon it from every direction."[198] Ackerman, like Habermas, thus takes a position resembling pragmatism, in which human words and actions replace entities as the subject matter of dialogue. A constraint against otherwise unchecked power claims is imposed by the principle of Neutrality upon conversation and dialogue, not upon postulated ontological ideas or entities. Diversity in viewpoints thus freely emerges in dialogue and in conversation among equals.[199] So Ackerman's position is entirely congruent with Justice Powell's, Justice Holmes's, and Habermas's generally equivalent theses, that ideas must be permitted to compete for the assent of reason, or at least to make themselves available to reason, without any intervention of force by mere undraped authority.

Each of the three rationales supporting academic freedom (and First Amendment free speech) that is asserted in Justice Powell's *Bakke* opinion is also found and elaborated upon in Habermas's and Ackerman's dialectical thought. In other words, Justice Powell's purely legal arguments for First Amendment free-speech functions have corresponding ideas in Ackerman's intermediate position and in Habermas's more nearly pure philosophical thought. To cap my argument, I will show that *diversity itself* is integral to each of these figures' arguments (a matter already accomplished with regard to Habermas[200] and Ackerman[201]).

Certainly there is no doubt about Justice Powell—diversity, together with its raison d'être free speech, is the very capstone of his justification for affirmative action. "The atmosphere of 'speculation, experiment and creation'—so essential to the quality of higher education—is widely believed to be supported by a *diverse* student body."[202] Justice Powell also, in a note, quotes from a statement of the president of Princeton University: " '[A] great deal of learning occurs through interactions among students of both sexes; [and] of different races, religions, and backgrounds . . . and who are able to . . . learn from their differences and to stimulate one another to reexamine even their most deeply held assumptions about themselves and their world.' "[203] Indeed Justice Powell, to support his case for affirmative action still further, strongly relied on the record in support of diversity provided by the Harvard College Program:

"In recent years Harvard College has expanded the concept of diversity to include students from disadvantaged economic, racial and ethnic groups. . . . A farm boy from Idaho can bring something to Harvard that a Bostonian cannot offer. Similarly, a black student can usually bring something that a white person cannot offer."[204]

My philosophical figures support and ground Justice Powell's holding and belief that diversity among the student body results in a fusion of minds and spirits into a unity capable of greater truth and knowledge. Yet this fusion does not destroy or threaten the autonomy or dignity of any person who is part of the unity.

Habermas, when surveying the lawmaking function of legislative bodies, follows and supports with argument the central point of my argument that diversity both enhances dialectical unity and results, through uncoerced discourse, in truth and knowledge both ample and authentic. Thus "the pluralism of beliefs and interests [of the sovereign citizens in discourse] is not suppressed but unleashed and recognized."[205] "This [enlarged] perspective *integrates* the perspectives of each participant's worldview and self-understanding in a manner *neither coercive nor distorting*."[206] This dialectical gathering of perspectives provides the power of a unity that nonetheless preserves the manifoldness gathered. The discursive unity of the consociates becomes a fact.[207]

And Ackerman: "Rather than using political power to subordinate to the pursuit of a single common good[,] liberal[ism] invites people to pierce their substantive disagreements and achieve a deeper unity—in the fact that they are all seeking to define themselves through a common process of dialogue."[208] This dialogue recognizes "[t]he diversity of life choices [as] a positive good."[209]

The case for the support of constitutional diversity in a deeper philosophical view of diversity and dialectics is complete: Justice Powell's *Bakke* opinion, as inquired into here, reveals the first of the four faces of affirmative action—the dialectical approach, which works through diversity and its absorption of the many into a paradoxical unity with the one, to further the processes of human understanding and action. The rationale of diversity also must, despite Justice Powell's view to the contrary, ultimately be judged as one that can support distributive, and not corrective, justice.[210] Any award generated by the operation of diversity, such as a seat in the entering class of a professional school, is not meant to restore a loss to anyone (except in an incidental way[211]) but to recognize and pursue a value that is highly prized in our society—free speech, with all its recognized aims. This process depends on the occurrence of no concrete wrongs (a condition amenable to corrective or compensatory justice) but rather is designed to award one of society's most valuable goods—education—on the basis of the selected value of racial diversity (compatible instead with distributive justice). Certainly the quest for truth through peaceful dialogue is such an aim that serves society as a whole, while the freedom of citizens to enter such dialogue is worthy in itself and needs no further justification.

METRO BROADCASTING—AND THE LOWER COURTS' OPINIONS

Of the Supreme Court cases that follow *Bakke*,[212] only one—*Metro Broadcasting, Inc. v. FCC*[213]—directly faced the diversity issue in an affirmative action program. In a 5–4 majority opinion written by Justice Brennan, with a significant dissent by Justice O'Connor, the Court extended the diversity rationale for affirmative action beyond academia to the public airwaves of broadcasting.

In *Metro Broadcasting* the Court faced the issue of the constitutionality of a Federal Communications Commission (FCC) program of racial preference in establishing more minority owners of broadcast stations.[214] The justification was diversity, connected to the notion that character of ownership or management would strongly influence broadcast content. Black ownership would then perforce increase the number of different viewpoints over the public airwaves. The principal issues were the adequacy of First Amendment support for the program[215] and the strength of the causal nexus between diverse ownership and diversity of viewpoint.[216] Justice Brennan placed his argument that the First Amendment applies to broadcasting squarely upon Justice Powell's *Bakke* opinion:

[W]e conclude that the interest in enhancing broadcast diversity is, at the very least, an important government objective. . . . Just as a "diverse student body" contributing to a " 'robust exchange of ideas' " is a "constitutionally permissible goal" on which a race-conscious university admissions program may be predicated [*Bakke*, opinion of Powell, J.], the diversity of views and information on the airwaves serves important First Amendment values. The benefits of such diversity are not limited to the members of minority groups who gain access to the broadcasting industry by virtue of the ownership policies; rather, the benefits redound to all members of the viewing and listening audience.[217]

The Court relied on studies by the FCC, findings by Congress (which had later enacted a bill supporting the program), and judicial opinions that diversity in broadcast viewpoints would result from the minority ownership program.[218] The decision, however, remains important now for its majority affirmance of Justice Powell's opinion for diversity in *Bakke*. And while, of course, this was no conscious purpose of the opinion or its author, it supported and supports the idea, part and parcel with the thought of Habermas and Ackerman, that dialogue and diversity are worthy of any sphere in which discussion important to the public takes place.

Justice O'Connor, in dissent, attacked what she perceived to be several vulnerabilities in the Court's argument. She made the familiar argument that race does not control viewpoint nor act as its functional equivalent.[219] Thus she disputed the worth of the First Amendment as support for the program.[220] She also questioned the "direct[] and substantial[]" relation of station ownership to the content of a station's broadcasting.[221] These two arguments were of course based on causation (or the lack thereof), meaning that she saw the relation between the agency's program and promotion of diversity in broadcasting as very weak causally.

For my purposes, several of Justice O'Connor's comments are significant because they showed her position to be in conflict with dialectic. "At the heart of the Constitution's guarantee of equal protection lies the simple command that the Government must treat citizens 'as *individuals*, not "as simply components of a racial, religious, sexual or national class." ' "[222] Justice O'Connor intuitively saw only particulars,[223] never wholes (except by construction). Thus she did not begin her reasoning with groups and their unique influence in society. "Dialectical history [in contrast] depends on discovering traits which organize organic wholes—peoples, nations, or periods—and which apply to all of the group or the time, including the characteristic forms of morals, political practices, [or] religion."[224] Justice O'Connor's worldview simply did not permit her to give this dialectical position persuasive force.

She was also dissatisfied with the *measurements* of dialectical diversity: "The interest in increasing the diversity of broadcast viewpoints is clearly not a compelling interest. It is simply too *amorphous*, too *insubstantial*, and too *unrelated* to any legitimate basis for employing racial classifications."[225] But these are *always* the types of criticisms made against dialectic. Justice O'Connor used a method (logistic) that "giv[es] simple terms literal and univocal definitions [and] connects them in[to] long chains of deductive reasoning."[226] In contrast, dialectic uses "language adapted to reflect a truth which is found in system and cannot be expressed literally."[227] Justice O'Connor's assessment that the language of diversity was "too amorphous, too unsubstantial, and too unrelated" belied her logistic demands for scientific precision and proof. While valid on their own terms and within their own mode of thought, these elements of logistic produce a distorted view of diversity when no adjustment or allowance is made for the fact that diversity, as developed in my argument here, emerges from and reflects dialectic.[228]

Other significant statements about diversity in affirmative action have come from Justices O'Connor and Stevens, in opinions not determinative of the Court's holding and judgment in the case at hand. In *Wygant v. Jackson Board of Education*,[229] a case in which a plurality of the Court rejected on equal protection grounds a racial role-model rationale for racial preferences in the retention of public school teachers, purportedly needed to motivate minority students, Justice Stevens, favoring diversity, dissented:

[I]n our present society, race is not always irrelevant to sound governmental decision-making. . . . [I]n law enforcement, if an undercover agent is needed to infiltrate a group suspected of ongoing criminal behavior—and if members of the group are all of the same race—it would seem perfectly rational to employ an agent of that race rather than a member of a different racial class. Similarly, in a city with a recent history of racial unrest, the superintendent of police might reasonably conclude that an integrated police force could develop a better relationship with the community.[230]

In the context of public education, it is quite obvious that a school board may reasonably conclude that an integrated faculty will be able to provide benefits to the student body that could not be provided by an all-white, or nearly all-white faculty. For one of the most important lessons that the American public schools teach is that ethnic, cultural, and national backgrounds that have been brought together in our famous "melting pot" do not identify essential differences among the human beings that inhabit our land.[231]

It is noteworthy that while Justice Stevens supported diversity ("integrated police force," "integrated faculty"), he did not do so on dialectical, discursive grounds. Rather, his primary grounds were socially utilitarian (greater effectiveness of police operations and community relations), or socially egalitarian (diversity among the faculty is grounded in the need of the pupils to learn from experience that no "essential differences" divide them), or both—but neither expressly on the justification of the Free Speech Clause. I shall analyze his position at length in Chapter 4, where I shall treat Justice Stevens's thought as being of the operational mode, designed to advance social *equality* through affirmative action.

Justice O'Connor has not strayed far from her insistence on precision in terminology and causality and from her predilection for primary treatment of individuals rather than groups (as the basic units by which to detect discrimination)—elements of thought that she identified in her *Metro Broadcasting* dissent.[232] In *Wygant*, though, she found that "racial diversity" could be a " 'compelling' " constitutional interest, "at least in the context of higher education," to support racial preferences. She then cited Justice Powell's opinion in *Bakke*.[233] Her concentration here on "higher education" may explain her vigorous dissent in *Metro Broadcasting*—the diversity upheld there was not limited to education, and typically for her mode of thought, she sought to impose preciseness in any extension of affirmative action. I shall explore the primary and highly influential opinions of Justice O'Connor when I reach the next part of this inquiry on the logistic mode of thought and its rationale for affirmative action—compensatory causation.

HOPWOOD AND THE ERUPTION OF ATTACKS ON DIVERSITY

Turning now to recent and instructive lower court opinions, I first take up *Hopwood v. Texas*,[234] the celebrated Fifth Circuit case ruling against affirmative action at the University of Texas School of Law. The court of appeals rejected both the law school's remedial justification as well as its diversity rationale. The decision was a bombshell that asserted that diversity could no longer sustain affirmative action, even among a student body in an institution of higher education. The Fifth Circuit first declined to treat Justice Powell's *Bakke* opinion as binding precedent.[235] The court held that

[w]ithin the general principles of the Fourteenth Amendment, the use of race in admissions for diversity in higher education contradicts, rather than furthers, the aim of *equal protection*. Diversity fosters, rather than minimizes, race [sic—race as a discriminatory factor]. It treats minorities as a group, rather than as individuals. It may further remedial purposes [the only permissible rationale, in the court's view] but, just as likely, may promote improper racial stereotypes, thus fueling racial hostility.[236]

The court perhaps alluded to the free-speech basis for diversity when it referred to "stereotypes" and again later to the same basis when it pointed to the futility of using race "as a proxy for the other characteristics . . . [like] experiences, outlooks, and ideas" that institutions of higher education value but that raise equal protection concerns.[237] Thus the attack was twofold: Diversity is stigmatic (or promotes stigmatic attitudes and stereotypes), and diversity will not work because race *simpliciter* is an inadequate element to the intellectual "mix" and, in fact, injects an unconstitutional element into the operations of the school.

Ironically, in making these arguments against diversity, the two members of the panel who agreed on this point turned their backs on *Sweatt v. Painter*,[238] the very case requiring the Law School to open its doors to black students, so that learning in the law could genuinely take place without isolation of students by race. The Fifth Circuit's decision thus was actually retrogressive—it forced education in the profession of law back to the sterile exclusiveness and separateness of the 1950s by de facto excluding blacks, Chicanos and other Hispanics, and other groups from the premier law school in Texas, the law school whose culture and indoctrination influence more than any other institution the development of law and the legal profession in the state.

My final word on *Hopwood*'s summary dismissal of diversity I give to a commentator who sums up the matter well:

The *Hopwood* court dismisses the role of race as a diversifying characteristic in law school admissions, and holds that race does not affect an individual's point of view. . . . This notion simply ignores the historical fact that sets blacks apart from all other racial groups in the country. Blacks have had the humiliation and injustice of slavery heaped upon them—first, as government policy, and now, as social baggage. . . . *Hopwood* in finding that race does not [affect] an individual's viewpoint, not only ignores the obvious, but also minimizes the savage history of slavery and the degrading saga of segregation in this country.[239]

Accordingly, in *Hopwood*, the Fifth Circuit attacked the dialectically composed, group-based phenomenon of discourse through diversity from the altogether different viewpoint of the primacy of individuals and of redressibility calculated by narrow causality. I take up this view of *Hopwood*—the view held by its authors—in Chapter 2.

In *Taxman v. Board of Education of the Township of Piscataway*,[240] the Third Circuit faced the question of whether Title VII of the Civil Rights Act of 1964[241] permits (or prohibits) an affirmative action plan for employees of a school when that plan is predicated on diversity. The Supreme Court had previously permitted voluntary affirmative action plans under Title VII, so long as these plans were calculated to serve the remedial purpose of "eliminat[ing] a manifest racial imbalance . . . in traditionally segregated job categories."[242] In *Piscataway*, the school board used a standard of racial diversity written into its affirmative action plan—not a standard of manifest racial imbalance in the remedial sense—to decide to retain a black teacher instead of a white teacher. Both were equally qualified, and because of layoff requirements, only one position remained available.[243] This action represented a major extension of the rationale of diversity, for here it was applied to *employees*, not students.

To be sure, teachers are part of the academic world, and so the confinement of this step *within* the school milieu might well have seemed controlling. At least one commentator otherwise hostile to diversity has said (albeit in the context of higher education): "Concern for robust intellectual exchange would appear on the surface to be more a concern in *hiring* faculty than in selecting students. Stimulating one's colleagues and students is the professional task of a . . . teacher."[244] Under this reasoning, diversity would *a fortiori* seem in order for those most responsible for educationally stimulating the students. It *was* in *Keyishian*. The court of appeals, however, viewed the teachers in question as mere employees—not as interlocutors in dialogue—and ruled that the school board had not proven the existence of "manifest imbalance" needed to justify racial preferences under Title VII.[245]

The court further noted that *Bakke* and *Metro Broadcasting* were inapposite. "*Bakke*'s factual and legal setting, as well as the diversity that universities aspire to in their student bodies, are, in our view, so different from the facts, relevant law and the racial diversity purpose in this case that we find little in *Bakke* to guide us."[246] It also found that the discharge of a white to allow a black to take the only available position left, without a showing of the unavailability of reasonable alternatives to racial preference for the selection, trenched on the Supreme Court's long-held opposition to affirmative action plans that *lay off* or otherwise *deprive* an "innocent" employee of an existing job.

In an *amicus curiae* brief filed with the Supreme Court,[247] the solicitor general argued that the *Piscataway* case was rightly decided on its facts, concerned as he was with the white teacher's layoff only because of a racial preference (and not any general opposition to affirmative action), and urged the affirmance of the judgment below on narrow grounds limited to those facts. The solicitor, in fact, went on to argue, though, that a nonremedial "race-conscious employment decision," presumably including a diversity-justified plan, *could* satisfy Title VII if it satisfies the "equal protection standards" of compelling interest and narrow tailoring.[248] Nowhere, though, did the solicitor general or his Justice Department colleagues argue the First Amendment as a justification. Nor did he argue that diversity has intrinsic worth as a means of self-expression: "A simple desire to promote diversity for its own sake . . . is not a permissible basis for taking race into account under Title VII."[249] The government approved societal examples—some of the same ones given by Justice Stevens in his *Wygant* dissent:[250] the assignment of an undercover officer racially matched to the gang that he will try to infiltrate;[251] a racially diverse police force to assuage racial tension and attain public confidence;[252] and "obtaining the educational benefits of a racially diverse faculty" in dispelling racial stereotypes and acquainting students directly with persons of diverse races.[253] This last purpose might seem close to the protective scope of the First Amendment—in support of it the solicitor general spoke of "foster[ing] mutual understanding in a much more powerful and lasting way than imparting those lessons through words alone."[254] But the use of words is not of the essence of this process. The aim depends rather on a togetherness whose function is to permit persons to see and be seen in the same public space—not an objectionable goal on its face but one whose rationale has not been clearly based on diversity as a dialectical means to truth and knowledge, although communication of some sort is arguably involved.[255] Meanwhile, the solicitor failed to argue from *Pickering v. Board of Education*[256] and its progeny that speech on public issues is protected in the workplace under certain conditions.[257] Under *Pickering* it would not be anomalous for an affirmative action program to be bottomed on the free exchange of public ideas.

In a more recent case, one that some observers believed that the Supreme Court would review but to which it ultimately denied review,[258] the Supreme Court of Nevada upheld, in part on diversity grounds, the constitutionality of an affirmative action program for employment in its state's higher education system.[259] The program concerned only the hiring salaries of faculty employees and was not fashioned for deciding the order of discharges of such employees; nor was it an admissions device for students. The court's opinion was eclectic in its grounds to uphold the program. Thus the court's arguments addressed both the Title VII "manifest imbalance" standard and the stricter equal protection standard as well,[260] but the court also strongly relied on "the desirability of a racially diverse faculty as sufficiently analogous to the constitutionally permissible attainment of a racially diverse student body countenanced by the Bakke Court."[261]

The court noted that race was only *one factor* in *hiring* decisions and not in layoffs, but it did not go on to link its point about diversity to the purpose of having enriched dialogue, as it might have more persuasively done. The case might have been a vehicle through which to expand the use of diversity, but the ambiguity of its reliance on diversity, together with its failure to achieve Supreme Court review and the fact that it is from one of the least populous states, should relegate its influence mostly to the state of its origin. Two, more recent, opinions from two U.S. courts of appeals have, notwithstanding the support for diversity and its extension to employment in Nevada, cast still more aspersions on diversity itself and its extension to fields beyond higher education.

RECENT CASES AGAINST THE EXTENSION (AND EXISTENCE?) OF DIVERSITY AS A RATIONALE FOR AFFIRMATIVE ACTION

In *Lutheran Church–Missouri Synod v. FCC,*[262] the D.C. Circuit struck at both the expansion of diversity-based affirmative action to employment and the continued post–*Metro Broadcasting* vitality of diversity over the broadcast airwaves. The court considered the FCC's regulation requiring stations to engage in some preferential hiring of minorities and women, a practice that the Commission defended "by arguing that *all* employees affect programming diversity,"[263] to be in violation of the Equal Protection Clause. The court held that the preferential program failed to provide the compelling interest needed to meet constitutional strict scrutiny.[264] It rejected the authority of *Metro Broadcasting,* holding that that case's precedential value for broadcast diversity was too tightly bound to intermediate scrutiny to have survived *Adarand*'s holding that all federal affirmative action cases, like all state affirmative action cases before them, must meet strict scrutiny.[265] To the extent that the regulation was to promote employment diversity as well as broadcast diversity, the court found that it foundered on the failure to provide the compelling interest required by strict scrutiny and the Commission's having exceeded its public broadcasting responsibilities in addressing antidiscrimination in employment.[266] Indeed the D.C. Circuit arguably rested its decision on its finding that the FCC's EEO regulations too broadly included nonmanagerial employees, who had no influence over broadcast content. The court's most damning attack, however, was on the concept of diversity *simpliciter.*

[In *Metro Broadcasting*] the Court never explained why it was in the government's interest to encourage the notion that minorities have racially based views.... We doubt ... that the Constitution permits the government to take account of racially based differences, much less encourage them. One might think such an approach antithetical to our democracy.[267]

In meeting the court's argument that diversity had been dragged down along with intermediate scrutiny by *Adarand*, it must be stressed that the linkage between the diversity rationale and the subdued standard of review in *Metro Broadcasting* was not indissoluble. At the time that *Metro Broadcasting* was decided, *J. A. Croson Co.* was the controlling precedent, and in it the plurality altogether declined to rule on the standard of review for federal cases.[268] The *Metro Broadcasting* Court acted within this controlling precedent, as well as within the *Fullilove* case, in fixing the standard of review as intermediate scrutiny.[269] Thus intermediate scrutiny was the level of scrutiny then most arguably appropriate to *any* federal plan; it had no essential connection to broadcast diversity and thus could fall without defeating such diversity. The attack on diversity itself is, of course, more serious, because it goes to the heart of what this inquiry concerns. Circuit Judge Silberman's views for the court appear to be of the logistic mode, and these views find general representation in the next chapter.

In *Wessmann v. Gittens*[270] a U.S. court of appeals, ruling on an affirmative action program in public school admissions,[271] struck down such a plan at the prestigious Boston Latin School (BLS) on both diversity and past-discrimination (compensatory causation) grounds. In so doing the court of appeals entered a thicket of contention about the use of racial preferences in the public schools.[272] Here I shall look into the court's holding on diversity (which it accepted as a viable doctrine despite the attacks on it,[273] while applying it to the facts of the case). I will later analyze the court's treatment of remediation of past discrimination in Chapter 2.

Casting aside the Boston School Committee's[274] ("the Committee's") abstract defense of the benefits conferred by diversity, the court, per Selya, C. J., announcing that "the devil is in the details,"[275] found that "the [Committee's] Policy [of racial and ethnic preference in admissions] focuses exclusively on racial and ethnic diversity," despite Justice Powell's warning in *Bakke* not to make race or ethnicity a monolith.[276] Brushing aside the Committee's claim that "BLS historically has been diverse with respect to everything but race and ethnicity [claiming that other forms of diversity were 'prepackaged,' as it were— awaiting only the addition of racial and ethnic diversity],"[277] the court attacked the Committee's methodology as "at the bottom, a mechanism for racial balancing [proportional representation of racial and ethnic groups]."[278] The court reserved its harshest words, indeed, for the practice of promoting diversity, as the court put it, by "racial balancing."

[T]he School Committee has failed to give us a plausible reason why we should believe that racial balancing of any type is necessary to promote the expression of ideas or any other ideas referenced in the Policy. . . . To justify something [racial balancing] so anti-thetical to our constitutional jurisprudence . . . a particularly strong showing of *necessity* would be required.[279] The School Committee has provided absolutely no competent ev-idence that the proportional representation promoted by the Policy is in any way tied to the vigorous exchange of ideas.[280]

Granted that the Committee did have elements of proportional representation in the admissions process, and that it apparently did not make allowance for eval-uating individuals' nonracial or nonethnic factors in an individualized, Powellian fashion—*i.e.*, consider these factors simultaneously with the consideration of race or ethnicity in each person—the court still gave a most daunting standard of proof for the Committee to meet. It would have had to prove under a standard of *necessity* that combining (by a methodology of which the court disapproved) members of different races and bearers of different cultures will produce greater exchanges of ideas. Dialectically such proof is impossible—dialectic's proofs do not submit to the absolute certainty that is tantamount to necessity or to any factor that draws ideas down to the level of mechanistic prediction, where the contingent affairs of men are in issue. The court implies that there are degrees of necessity, but this inference is a logical impossibility—either diversity is necessary to promote the exchange of ideas, or it is not. The best that the Committee could have done would have been to offer proof of the probability—perhaps enhanced—that diversity stands in a favored relation to dialogical exchange.

Of this First Circuit opinion, and from the dialectical point of view, the best that may be made is that it is capable of being read narrowly to have struck down the Committee's affirmative action policy because of the method of ad-missions employed—a method that violated the Powellian standards of individ-ual evaluation that guard against stereotyping and other dangers. Certainly the court's strong reliance on Justice Powell's *Bakke* gave assurance. Yet the court's harsh tone of skepticism about diversity's measure of worth in free speech, and its reliance on a standard of proof gauged in necessity, has left this a somber place to make some conclusions about dialectic and diversity.

COMMENTARY—AND THE CONCLUSION OF DIALECTIC AND DIVERSITY

The commentators tend to revisit the same arguments about *Bakkean* diver-sity. Thus the penchant for particularity is repeated: "A central defect of Justice Powell's decision is its failure to identify a reason for diversity which is suffi-ciently clear and specific that it can be used to design a program for diversity admissions."[281] There remain vehement denials that race is an indicator of in-tellectual temperament or ability, and strong assertions that perhaps those ad-mitted in whole or in part because of race are of even lower-than-desirable aptitude, purportedly leaving the impression with many of these admitted that their selection is a disgrace rather than a merited opportunity.[282] Diversity has been attacked for discarding both "color-blindness" and the requirement of showing past injury to an identifiable racial group.[283] These critics make their points. Diversity *is* vague to *them* because it stands in the tradition of dialectical discourse. Diversity does treat persons *differently*, to a measured extent, because of race, but not *unequally*, because in the reconciliation of differences each person is the end. It recognizes race as an indicator of ideas sociologically and culturally attained, but only on the basis of a known historical and social experience that makes members of such a group bearers of that culture and of its truth.

The grounds for diversity-justified affirmative action have remained the same throughout my discussion. Diversity sets the stage for the dialectical reconciliation of the one and the many. Through dialogue and discourse alone, it assimilates and synthesizes the elements of truth and moral action into an englobing whole—the only "place" where truth and action have authentic meaning, according to dialectic. One leading student of both affirmative action and of the thought of Habermas puts it this way:

[C]ommunicative action taking place under conditions that make it possible for a rational consensus to be reached exclusively on the force of the better argument [follows a] dialectical structure [that] leads to the satisfaction of certain requirements of justice of a universalistic ethics. . . .

[T]he dialogical process is not superfluous, but necessary to produce an optimal balance between *identity* and *difference*, [*i.e.*,] the normative position that allows for the greatest possible *integration* [unity] combined with the greatest possible *differentiation* [diversity].[284]

This quotation from Michel Rosenfeld suggests those qualities of dialectic that have been most prominent here: the assimilation of contraries into greater (and semantically more abstract) wholes, and the corresponding paradox of the unity of the one and the many.

Though it is individuals who enter the dialogue of the diverse, the unique meanings that they thrust into that dialectical vortex are not entirely their own but products of their groups' histories. As one of the leading dialectical figures of this century, Paul Tillich, has said: "[L]ife processes in a community are immediately determined by the historical dimension [of life, because] *the direct bearers of history are groups rather than individuals, who are only indirect bearers.*"[285] This statement would strike many as a paradox, but it directly corresponds to the dialectical vision. It is also true that dialectic generates *symbols* of groups that are richer in power than any literal description of the group or its constituent individuals. "Symbols, although they are not the same as what they symbolize, participate in its meaning and power. The difference between symbol and sign is the participation in the symbolized reality which characterizes the symbols, and the non-participation in the 'pointed to' reality which characterizes a sign."[286] Certainly Bruce Ackerman realizes the dialectical power of symbols when he states that under the New Deal "the public schools could take on a new *symbolic* meaning[—one that carried] the new promise of activist [and more democratic] government."[287] The new and greatly altered status of the public schools thus has unquestionably promoted democratic rule and egalitarianism in a way inexplicable through literal causes.

Diversity and its concrete appearance in academic classes, workforces, churches, within governmental authority, and in all manners of other human association could—beyond simply the discourse that it promotes—become itself powerfully symbolic of the unity of nation and even mankind. It thereby could become the symbolic source of Tillich's "meaning and power," in this instance for the expiation of guilt and bitterness in race relations—a theme touched on in the introduction. "Signs," or the transmitters of literal meaning, do not have this power. They are the instruments of logistic.

Dialectic should now be remembered as the mode of thought that creates truths in system and for this purpose appropriates many elements whose meanings become apparent only within the context of that entire system. Life, here through discourse, is enriched by involvement in the dialectical system. Some of this enriched meaning is created and captured when, under the constitutional protection of the First Amendment, affirmative action is based on the irrepressible discourse of diversity.

NOTES

[1] *Bakke*, 438 U.S. at 313 (opinion of Powell, J.) (citation omitted).

[2] See MORTIMER J. ADLER, "Dialectic," in THE GREAT IDEAS: A LEXICON OF WESTERN THOUGHT 153, 159 (1952, 1992).

[3] ALFRED NORTH WHITEHEAD, PROCESS AND REALITY: AN ESSAY IN COSMOLOGY 21 (1978).

[4] JOHN RAWLS, POLITICAL LIBERALISM 133ff. (1993).

[5] Thomas McCarthy, "Legitimacy and Diversity: Dialectical Reflections on Analytical Distinctions," 17 Cardozo L. Rev. 1083, 1111–12 (1996), reprinted in MICHEL RO-SENFELD AND ANDREW ARATO (EDS.), HABERMAS ON LAW AND DEMOCRACY: CRITICAL EXCHANGES [hereinafter HABERMAS ON LAW AND DEMOCRACY], 115, 141 (1998). The quoted language has been adopted verbatim by Habermas as representing his own views. Jürgen Habermas, "Reply to Symposium Participants," at 400.

The reader may well wonder how the problem of "the one and the many" could be presented when the first term of the topic, "universal rights," is plural in form. This term can be the "one," however, when one remembers that each norm or "right" is an aspect or a result of the principle of discursive unity—which plainly satisfies the criterion of "the one." Habermas's procedure would also satisfy the opposition found in the problem of "the universal and the particular." *Cf.* Richard McKeon, "Philosophic Semantics and Philosophic Inquiry" 12–13, supra Intro., note 40, reprinted in FREEDOM AND HISTORY AND OTHER ESSAYS, at 252–53.

[6] Lutheran Church–Mo. Synod v. FCC, 141 F.3d 344 (D.C. Cir. 1998).

[7] Alfred North Whitehead and Charles Hartshorne have been prominent ontological dialecticians, and a brief review of their thought may give some insight into Habermas and his discourse-oriented dialectic. Whitehead has given us a very broad, very deep ontological glimpse of how diverse entities can combine into an englobing whole:

> The ultimate metaphysical principle is the advance from disjunction to conjunction, creating a novel entity other than the entities given in disjunction. The novel entity is at once the togetherness of the "many" which it finds, and it also is one among the disjunctive "many" which it leaves; it is a novel entity, disjunctively among the many entities which it synthesizes.

ALFRED NORTH WHITEHEAD, PROCESS AND REALITY 21 (1929). Whitehead posits his principle as one of "unity in diversity" and joins it to a method capable of resolving and synthesizing all the given disjunctions into a unity that nonetheless retains the diversity of those entities conjoined. "It lies in the nature of things that many enter into complex unity." Id. Mr. Hartshorne also expresses this dialectical concept of the relation between the one and the many:

> The basic value is the intrinsic value of experiencing. . . . If we know what experience is, at its best or most beautiful, then and only then can we know how it is right to act; for the value of action is in what it contributes to experiences.
>
> [H]armony [among elements or occasions of experiencing] is not, however, a sufficient condition of great value. There must be intensity. And intensity depends upon contrast, the amount of *diversity* integrated into an experience.

CHARLES HARTSHORNE, "The Esthetic Matrix of Value," in CREATIVE SYNTHESIS AND PHILOSOPHIC METHOD 303,303 (1983) (emphasis supplied).

Mr. Hartshorne's principle of diversity is truly comprehensive because it includes within it the power both to direct right action and to project beauty, powers and qualities that are often distinguished into different fields grounded by separate principles rather than by a single englobing principle. Indeed, his principle is so englobing that it supports the highest intensity (or freedom) when the contrast among the constituent parts is greatest. His approach, like Whitehead's, is anchored in the deepest regions of being—in the ontological.

[8] *Cf.* JÜRGEN HABERMAS, BETWEEN FACTS AND NORMS: CONTRIBUTIONS TO A DISCOURSE THEORY OF LAW AND DEMOCRACY 128–29 (1996) [hereinafter B F & N]; Jürgen Habermas, "Morality and Ethical Life: Does Hegel's Critique of Kant Apply to Discourse Ethics?" 83 Nw. U. L. Rev. 38, 46 (1988–89).

[9] HABERMAS, B F & N, at 227–28.

[10] *Cf.* JOHN DEWEY, THE PUBLIC AND ITS PROBLEMS 158 (1927) ("But in fact, knowledge is a function of association and communication.").

[11] See, *e.g.*, HABERMAS, B F & N, at 159, 161, 163, & 165 ("Pragmatic discourses extend only to the construction of possible programs and estimation of their consequences.").

[12] See McCarthy, "Legitimacy and Diversity," at 1089–90, reprinted in ROSENFELD AND ARATO (EDS.), HABERMAS ON LAW AND DEMOCRACY, at 121 (Habermas "followed Kant in distinguishing the types of practical reasoning appropriate to questions about what is practically expedient, ethically prudent, and morally right. . . . Questions of what is right or just . . . call for the adoption of the moral point of view. And like Kant, Habermas regards matters of this last type, rather than specifically ethical matters, to be the proper domain of moral theory.").

[13] RICHARD MCKEON, "Discourse, Demonstration, Verification, Justification," in RHETORIC: ESSAYS IN INVENTION AND DISCOVERY 37, 51 (Backman ed. 1987; orginally published in 1969) (emphasis supplied).

[14] HABERMAS, B F & N, at 33.

[15] JÜRGEN HABERMAS, LEGITIMATION CRISIS 107–08 (1973; Engl. trans. 1975) [hereinafter L C]. See also HABERMAS, B F & N, at 127 ("According to the discourse principle, just those norms deserve to be valid that could meet with the approval of those potentially affected, insofar as the latter participate in rational discourses.").

[16] HABERMAS, B F & N, at 103.

[17] Id. at 152–53.

[18] See, *e.g.*, HABERMAS, B F & N, at 103–04 ("[I]f discourses . . . are the site where a rational will can take shape, then the legitimacy of law ultimately depends upon a communicative arrangement: as *participants in rational discourses, consociates under law* must be able to examine whether a contested norm meets with, or could meet with, the agreement of all those possibly affected.) (emphasis supplied to show the meaning of "consociates under law"); 414 ("Discourse theory explains the legitimacy of law by means of procedures and communicative presuppositions that . . . ground the supposition that the processes of making and applying law lead to rational outcomes. The norms passed by the political legislature and the rights recognized by the judiciary prove their 'rationality' by the fact that addressees are treated as *free and equal members of an association of legal subjects*.") (emphasis supplied).

[19] HABERMAS, L C, at 110; see also 83 Nw. U. L. Rev., supra Ch. 1, note 8, at 41.

[20] Michel Rosenfeld, "Can Rights, Democracy, and Justice Be Reconciled Through Discourse Theory? Reflections on Habermas's Proceduralist Paradigm of Law," 17 Cardozo L. Rev. 791, 812–13 (1996) (emphasis supplied) (footnotes omitted); reprinted in ROSENFELD AND ANDREW ARATO (EDS.), HABERMAS ON LAW AND DEMOCRACY, at 102.

[21] MCKEON, FREEDOM AND HISTORY, at 7, 14, reprinted in FREEDOM AND HISTORY AND OTHER ESSAYS, at 160, 167.

[22] HABERMAS, B F & N, at 38–39.

[23] Id. at 197.

[24] *Cf.* H.L.A. HART, THE CONCEPT OF LAW 97–107 (1961) (application of the rule of recognition establishes authenticity of the decision as law).

[25] HABERMAS, L C, at 89. See also HABERMAS, B F & N, at 103–04.

[26] Rosenfeld, "Can Rights, Democracy, and Justice Be Reconciled Through Discourse Theory? Reflections on Habermas's Proceduralist Paradigm of Law," supra Ch. 1, note 20, 17 Cardoza L. Rev, at 804 n.30 (quoting JÜRGEN HABERMAS, MORAL CONSCIOUSNESS AND COMMUNICATIVE ACTION 66 [Lenhardt & Nicholsen trans. 1990]), reprinted in ROSENFELD AND ARATO (EDS.), HABERMAS ON LAW AND DEMOCRACY, at 94 n.30.

[27] HABERMAS, B F & N, at 98 (emphasis supplied).

[28] Id. at 56.

[29] Id. at 420 (quoting from I.T.M. YOUNG, JUSTICE AND THE POLITICS OF DIFFERENCE 25 [1990]).

[30] HABERMAS, B F & N, at 56. See also id. at 80.

[31] *Cf.* HABERMAS, L C, at 27 ("We can speak of the 'fundamental contradiction' of a social formation when, and only when, its organizational principle necessitates that individuals and groups repeatedly confront one another with claims and intentions that are, in the long run, incompatible. In social class societies this is the case.").

[32] McKeon, Freedom and history, at 26, reprinted in Freedom and History and Other Essays, at 178.

[33] McKeon, "Philosophic Semantics and Philosophic Inquiry," supra Intro., note 40, at 4–5, reprinted in Freedom and History and Other Essays, at 245. See also Habermas, B F & N, at 194 ("A *paradigm of law*" draws on a model of contemporary society to explain how constitutional rights and principles must be conceived and implemented if in the given context they are to fulfill the functions *normatively* ascribed to them [emphasis in original].).

[34] Habermas, B F & N, at 195.

[35] Id. at 7.

[36] Habermas, L C, at 81.

[37] Id. at 78.

[38] Id. at 79.

[39] Habermas, B F & N, at 268.

[40] 489 U.S. 189 (1989).

[41] Id. at 195.

[42] Habermas, B F & N, at 390. These dehumanizing effects are part of systems' "colonization of the lifeworld."

[43] Habermas, "Paradigms of Law," in Rosenfeld and Arato (eds.), Habermas on Law and Democracy, at 17.

[44] 424 U.S. 319 (1976).

[45] Jerry Mashaw, "The Supreme Court's Due Process Calculus for Administrative Adjudication in *Mathews v. Eldridge*: Three Factors in Search of a Theory of Value," 44 U. Chi. L. Rev. 28, 47–48 (1976).

[46] Habermas, B F & N, at 390 (emphasis in original).

[47] Id. at 409.

[48] Id. at 135 (emphasis in original).

[49] Id. (emphasis supplied).

[50] Habermas, "Paradigms of Law," in Rosenfeld and Arato (eds.), Habermas on Law and Democracy, at 18.

[51] 517 U.S. 520 (1996).

[52] Habermas, "Paradigms of Law," in Rosenfeld and Arato (eds.), Habermas on Law and Democracy, at 18.

[53] Id. at 19.

[54] Habermas, B F & N, at, e.g., 390, 391, 397.

[55] Id. at 392.

[56] *Cf.* Michael J. Buckley, Motion and Motion's God: Thematic Variations in Aristotle, Cicero, Newton, and Hegel 215 (1971) ("[P]hilosophic progress is obtained [dialectically] by following through the self-movement of the object of study as it passes through the forms or moments of its self-differentiation."); Habermas, B F & N, at 196 ("*[l]egal theory* moves within the compass of particular legal orders." [emphasis in original]).

[57] McKeon, "Philosophic Semantics and Philosophic Inquiry," supra Intro., note 40, at 8, reprinted in Freedom and History and other Essays, at 248.

[58] Id. at 4, reprinted in Freedom and History and Other Essays, at 245.

[59] McKeon, Freedom and History, supra Intro., note 38, at 14, reprinted in Freedom and History and Other Essays, supra Intro., note 37, at 167.

[60] Richard McKeon, "Dialectic and Political Thought and Action," 65 Ethics 1, 1 (1954).

[61] HARTSHORNE, "The Esthetic Matrix of Value," in CREATIVE SYNTHESIS AND PHILO-SOPHIC METHOD, supra Ch. 1, note 7, at 303 (emphasis supplied).

[62] McKeon, "Discourse, Demonstration, Verification, Justification," supra Ch. 1, note 13 and text (emphasis supplied).

[63] HABERMAS, B F & N, at 104 (emphasis supplied).

[64] Id. at 228 (emphasis supplied).

[65] ALFRED NORTH WHITEHEAD, ADVENTURES OF IDEAS 42 (1933).

[66] HABERMAS, B F & N, at 186.

[67] Personal interview with the author, January 6, 1996, at the AALS Convention in San Antonio, Texas; see also BRUCE ACKERMAN, SOCIAL JUSTICE IN THE LIBERAL STATE [hereinafter S J] 10 n.7 (1980).

[68] (1980).

[69] (1991).

[70] See, *e.g.*, ACKERMAN, S J, at 368.

[71] Id. at 6 (emphasis in original and extended to bracketed material).

[72] Compare Habermas, text at notes 47–49, supra.

[73] ACKERMAN, S J, at, *e.g.*, 36–37 (power holders must show that their power corresponds to knowledge of rationality).

[74] McKEON, FREEDOM AND HISTORY, at 37, reprinted in FREEDOM AND HISTORY AND OTHER ESSAYS, at 189 ("Freedom is . . . a power based on conformity to . . . to truth, wisdom, [or] spirit.").

[75] ACKERMAN, S J, at 8.

[76] Id. at 4.

[77] Id. at 7.

[78] Id. at 11.

[79] Id. at 18.

[80] Id. at 25.

[81] See, *e.g.*, notes and text at Ch. 1, notes 23 & 24, supra.

[82] ACKERMAN, S J, at 18 (emphasis supplied).

[83] Id. at 18 (emphasis supplied).

[84] Id. at 231.

[85] Id. at 9 (emphasis in original).

[86] Id. at 37.

[87] PLATO, Meno 80a, in EDITH HAMILTON AND HUNTINGTON CAIRNS (EDS.), THE COL-LECTED DIALOGUES OF PLATO 363 (1961).

[88] ACKERMAN, S J, at 28, 237. The five conditions or "power domains" are (1) No genetic domination of another; (2) Universal liberal education; (3) Conditions of material equality for all at the beginning of adulthood; (4) Capacity to exchange freely one's initial entitlements under transactional flexibility; and (5) Liberal trusteeship for succeeding generations. Id. at 28.

[89] Id. at 238.

[90] Id. at 239.

[91] Id. at 242.

[92] Id.

[93] Id. at 243.

[94] See notes and text at Intro., notes 8, 10, supra; and at Ch. 3, notes 32–33, infra.

[95] ACKERMAN, S J, at 247.

[96] Id. (emphasis supplied).

[97] Id. at 248.

[98] Id. (emphasis in original).

[99] Id. (emphasis in original).

[100] See ARISTOTLE, ETHICS 1131b25–1132a25, in RICHARD MCKEON (ED.), THE BASIC WORKS OF ARISTOTLE 1005–07 (1968) ("For it makes no difference whether a good man has defrauded a bad man or a bad man a good one. . . . [T]he law looks only to the distinctive character of the injury, and treats the parties as equal, if one is in the wrong and the other is being wronged. . . . Therefore, this kind of justice being an inequality, the judge tries to equalize it.").

[101] Id. at 1131a10–1131b24; 1006–07 ("[A]wards should be 'according to merit'; for all men agree that what is just in distribution must be according to merit in some sense, though they do not all specify the same sort of merit, but democrats identify it with the status of freemen, supporters of oligarchy with wealth . . . and supporters of aristocracy with excellence.").

[102] ACKERMAN, S J, at 248.

[103] Id. at 169 (emphasis in original).

[104] See generally BRUCE ACKERMAN, WE THE PEOPLE: FOUNDATIONS 171 (1991) [hereinafter W P].

[105] Id. at 32.

[106] Id. at 31–32 (emphasis supplied).

[107] ARISTOTLE, DE CAELO 270b20, in MCKEON (ED.), THE BASIC WORKS OF ARISTOTLE, supra Ch. 1, note 100, at 403.

[108] ACKERMAN, W P, at 205, 321.

[109] Id. at 204, 205, 312 (averring that he "do[es] not look to traditional religions for inspiration"; yet advocating "preserv[ation] [of] a spiritual space for matters of ultimate concern"), 321 (proposing a synthesis of secular and Christian ideals of community).

[110] Indeed Ackerman debunks "the myth of rediscovery" of constitutional ideals when he defends the New Deal's authenticity against claims that it had merely revived ideas from the time of John Marshall. Id. at 120 n.†.

[111] Id. at 59.

[112] Compare, e.g., Joachim of Floris, who "spoke about the three dispensations which unfold in history" that reveal "the new . . . in history." PAUL TILLICH, A HISTORY OF CHRISTIAN THOUGHT 176, 179 (1968).

[113] ACKERMAN, W P, at 321–22.

[114] Id. at 170 (emphasis in original) (Ackerman adds "despite their illegality" to indicate that constitutional changes, including the authority of the original Constitutional Convention of 1787 even to meet, have or may have occurred without sanction of existing law); see also 211 ("Like the Federalists themselves, latter-day revolutionaries neither played by the old rules nor ripped up the entire institutional system in a show of disdain. They combined old ideas and institutions in new ways—ways that finally allowed them to gain wide acceptance of their claim that *the People themselves* have endorsed their transformative social initiatives.") (emphasis in original).

[115] MCKEON, FREEDOM AND HISTORY, at 38, reprinted in FREEDOM AND HISTORY AND OTHER ESSAYS, at 189.

[116] ACKERMAN, S J, at 359.

[117] Id.

[118] ACKERMAN, W P, at 312 (emphasis supplied). At the same time, Ackerman rejects

reductionism that would trivialize politics and pare down the scope of diversity in the public world. Id.

[119] Id. at 88.

[120] Id. at 89, 98.

[121] Id. at 93.

[122] Id. at 108–09. One of the most significant of these opinions was United States v. Carolene Products, 304 U.S. 144, 152 n.4 (1938), which was a major synthetic effort to replace earlier concepts of freedom of contract, of property, and of markets with (1) "specific" rights from the Bill of Rights [Time One] and (2) political liberties from the Fourteenth Amendment [Time Two]. These changes were needed because the New Deal Court had transformed those earlier concepts in Time Three.

[123] McKeon, Freedom and History, at 30, reprinted in Freedom and History and Other Essays, at 182.

[124] See text at Ch. 1, notes 72ff.

[125] See McKeon, "Philosophic Semantics and Philosophic Inquiry," supra Intro., note 40, at 8, reprinted in McKeon, Freedom and History and Other Essays, at 248.

[126] Ackerman, W P, at 319 (emphasis supplied).

[127] Gender has also been the ground of affirmative action, see, e.g., Johnson v. Transp. Agency, 480 U.S. 616, and my focus on race here in no way is meant to denigrate gender as a legitimate basis of diversity-supported affirmative action. See id. at 638 (suggesting diversity as a ground for the affirmative action plan in Johnson).

[128] Paul D. Carrington, "Diversity," 1992 Utah L. Rev. 1105, 1143.

[129] Hopwood v. Texas, supra Intro., note 4, at 946 (emphasis supplied) (citing Richard A. Posner, "The DeFunis Case and the Constitutionality of Preferential Treatment of Racial Minorities," 1974 Sup. Ct. Rev. 12 ("[T]he use of a racial characteristic to establish a presumption that the individual also possesses other . . . socially relevant characteristics . . . encourages prejudice and bigotry.").

[130] Aristotle, Categories, 5 2a27–33, in McKeon (ed.), The Basic Works of Aristotle, supra Ch. 1, note 100, at 9 ("With regard . . . to those things which are present in a subject, it is generally the case that neither their name nor their definition is predicable of that in which they are present. . . . For instance, 'white' being present in a body is [accidentally] predicated of that in which it is present, for a body is called white: the [essential] definition, however, of the color 'white' is never predicable of the body.").

[131] Rosenfeld, "Can Rights, Democracy, and Justice Be Reconciled through Discourse Theory? Reflections on Habermas's Proceduralist Paradigm of Law," supra Ch. 1, note 20, 17 Cardozo L. Rev. at 803 reprinted in Rosenfeld and Arato (eds.), Habermas on Law and Democracy, at 93–94.

[132] Saint Francis College v. Al-Khazraji, 481 U.S. 604, 610 n.4 (1987).

[133] Myrdal, An American Dilemma, supra Intro., note 8, at 930.

[134] 339 U.S. 629 (1950). See text and notes at Ch. 1, notes 139ff., infra.

[135] 347 U.S. 483 (1954). See text and notes at Ch. 1, notes 147ff., infra.

[136] Id. at 494 n.11.

[137] See Jenkins v. Missouri, 515 U.S. 70, 121 (1995) (Thomas, J. dissenting) ("Segregation was not unconstitutional [as held in Brown] because it might have caused psychological feelings of inferiority. . . . Psychological injury or benefit is irrelevant to the question whether state actors have engaged in intentional discrimination. . . . The judiciary is fully competent to make independent determinations concerning the

existence of state action without the unnecessary and misleading assistance of the social sciences.").

[138] Rosenfeld, "Can Rights, Democracy, and Justice Be Reconciled through Discourse Theory? Reflections on Habermas's Proceduralist Paradigm of Law," supra Ch. 1, note 20, 17 Cardozo L. Rev. at 806, reprinted in ROSENFELD AND ARATO (EDS.), HABERMAS ON LAW AND DEMOCRACY, at 96.

[139] Ronald Dworkin, "Affirming Affirmative Action," in THE N.Y. REV. OF BOOKS, Vol. XLV, No. 6, 91, 99–100 (Oct. 22, 1998).

[140] 339 U.S. 629 (1950).

[141] Carrington, "Diversity," supra Ch. 1, note 128, 1992 Utah L. Rev. at 1141.

[142] 163 U.S. 537 (1896).

[143] On the recollection of two of my colleagues, Frank W. Elliott and Denny O. Ingram, both of whom were involved in legal education and state politics, respectively, in Austin at the time, the black law school was located in the basement of the state capitol—then a dungeonlike, windowless space thickly platted with steam pipes and electrical wires. Four white' professors from the University of Texas Law School, then about three-fourths of a mile away on the main campus, taught the separate law school at the capitol.

[144] *Sweatt*, 339 U.S. at 634 (emphasis supplied).

[145] 339 U.S. 637 (1950).

[146] Id. at 641 (emphasis supplied).

[147] See text at Ch. 1, note 49, supra (emphasis supplied).

[148] 347 U.S. 483 (1954).

[149] Id. at 493.

[150] Swann v. Charlotte-Mecklenburg Bd. of Educ., 401 U.S. 1, 16 (1971).

[151] Washington v. Seattle Sch. Dist. No. 1, 458 U.S. 457, 472–73 (1982). See generally Brief for Amicus Curiae United States, Piscataway Township Bd. of Education v. Taxman, *cert. granted*, 521 U.S. 1116 (June 27, 1997), October Term 1996, No. 96-679 (case below, 91 F.3d 1587 (3d Cir. 1996) (en banc)), *cert. dism'd*, 522 U.S. 1010 (December 12, 1997), at 22. Accessible at 1997 WL 523854. See Ch. 1, note 247, infra.

[152] ACKERMAN, W P, at 145. *Plessy* was, of course, directly about segregated railway facilities; but its application to public schools was also a fact.

[153] Id. at 148 (emphasis supplied).

[154] 438 U.S. 265 (1978); see also notes and text at Ch. 1, notes 179–88, infra.

[155] Id. at 272–76 (opinion of Powell, J.).

[156] Id. at 276–78 (opinion of Powell, J.).

[157] 42 U.S.C. § 2000d (prohibiting racial discrimination in institutions receiving federal funding).

[158] *Bakke*, 438 U.S. at 279–80 (opinion of Powell, J.) (citing 18 Cal.3d 34, 55, 132 Cal. Rptr. 680, 684, 553 P.2d 1152, 1156 [1976]).

[159] Justice Stevens and three other justices struck down the Davis plan pursuant to Title VI, avoiding the constitutional question. *Bakke*, 438 U.S. at 411–13 (opinion of Stevens, J., concurring in the judgment in part and dissenting in part, joined by Burger, C. J., and Stewart & Rehnquist, JJ.). Justice Brennan and three other justices upheld the Davis plan pursuant to the Equal Protection Clause under a theory of societal discrimination (social causation in this inquiry), *Bakke*, 438 U.S. at 324–26, and also accepted Justice Powell's diversity plan as constitutionally viable (see note 161, infra).

(opinion of Brennan, J., concurring in the judgment in part and dissenting in part, joined by White, Marshall & Blackmun, JJ.). Justice Powell struck down the Davis program pursuant to the Equal Protection Clause because it did not meet the standard of narrow causation (compensatory causation in this inquiry), *Bakke*, 438 U.S. at 307–10 (opinion of Powell, J., affirming in part the judgment below), but he upheld the possibility of an affirmative action plan *in general* through diversity based on the First Amendment. *Bakke*, 438 U.S. at 320 (opinion of Powell, J., reversing in part the judgment below).

[160] See id.

[161] *Bakke*, 438 U.S. at 326 (opinion of Brennan, J.). This is the holding of the case. "When a fragmented Court decides a case and no single rationale explaining the result enjoys the assent of five Justices, 'the holding of the Court may be viewed as that position taken by those members on the narrowest grounds.' " Marks v. United States, 430 U.S. 188, 198 (1977) (quoting from Gregg v. Georgia, 428 U.S. 153, 169 n.5 [1976]). The constitutional permissibility of affirmative action *did* draw five votes under the *Marks* condition. Justice Brennan also dropped a footnote, 438 U.S. at 326 n.1, stating that "[w]e also agree with Mr. Justice Powell that a plan like the 'Harvard' plan . . . is constitutional under our approach, at least so long as the use of race to achieve an integrated student body is necessitated by the lingering effects of past discrimination." This arguably conditional emendation by Justice Brennan indicates that "diversity" is the one ground on which the holding, that race-conscious admissions are constitutionally permissible, itself rests, since the condition would presumptively be met.

The Fifth Circuit, however, has attempted to blunt this reasoning by noting that Justice Brennan did condition his acceptance of Powellian diversity on a remedial purpose, just as quoted above. *Hopwood*, 78 F.3d at 944 (citing *Bakke*, 438 U.S. at 326 n.1 [opinion of Brennan, J.]).

First, this sortie by a lower court on a Supreme Court doctrine inflicts no injury on the unquestionable holding that affirmative action *is* constitutionally permissible—this, from the statement of the holding quoted in the text above. Second, insofar as it seems to split Justice Powell's diversity position from the broad remedial approach of the four justices of the Brennan group, it fails to note that the Brennan condition in the footnote is a *de minimis* statement simply indicating that *some* compensatory purpose should be served under Equal Protection, as well as First Amendment values, when diversity is deployed. Whenever diversity redresses "societal discrimination"—the Brennan standard and goal, not Justice Powell's—the two justifications fit together. Because there is hardly any diversity-based program that would not also remedy societal discrimination as understood by Justice Brennan in his *Bakke* opinion, diversity and the broad *remedial* program advocated by Justice Brennan will inevitably share common ground. This arrangement, too, meets the "narrowest grounds" standard of *Marks*. See also Akhil Reed Amar and Neal Kumar Katyal, "*Bakke*'s Fate," 43 U.C.L.A. L. Rev. 1745, 1752–54 & 1768 n.117 (1996) (arguing that diversity is the holding because passages in the Brennan opinion embrace diversity).

[162] See text of Ch. 1, note 161, supra.

[163] *Bakke*, 438 U.S. at 291 (opinion of Powell, J.).

[164] Id. at 313.

[165] Id. at 314.

[166] Id. at 315 (emphasis supplied).

[167] See text and notes at Ch. 1, notes 91–94, supra.

[168] See, *e.g.*, THOMAS I. EMERSON, THE SYSTEM OF FREEDOM OF EXPRESSION 6–7 (1970), and Geoffrey R. Stone, "Content Regulation and the First Amendment," 25 Wm. & Mary L. Rev. 189, 194–95 (1983).

[169] See, *e.g.*, NAACP v. Claiborne Hardware Co., 458 U.S. 886, 913 (1982).

[170] Abrams v. United States, 250 U.S. 616, 630 (1919) (Holmes, J., dissenting) ("marketplace of ideas").

[171] See Whitney v. California, 274 U.S. 357, 372–80 (Brandeis J., concurring).

[172] Academic freedom is not recognized or protected by the express terms of the First Amendment, but this concept of freedom has been found necessary to create and preserve the conditions for the free exchange of ideas on university and college campuses. Justice Powell in *Bakke*, 438 U.S. at 312–13, cites two leading cases: Keyishian v. Board of Regents, 385 U.S. 589, 603 (1967), and Sweezy v. New Hampshire, 354 U.S. 234 (1957) (opinion of Warren, C. J.) and 260–64 (opinion of Frankfurter, J., concurring in the result).

[173] *Bakke*, 438 U.S. at 312 (quoting from Keyishian v. Bd. of Regents, 354 U.S. at 603).

[174] *Keyishian*, 354 U.S. at 594–95.

[175] Id. at 603. In *Sweezy*, supra Ch. 1, note 172, a similar situation had occurred when the authority of a state attorney general, to conduct investigations into university professors' ideas and beliefs to detect any sign of "subversion," was declared unconstitutional for "impinging [upon] freedom of communication of ideas, particularly in the academic community." Id. at 245.

[176] See text at Ch. 1, notes 28–29, supra.

[177] See text in Ch. 1, note 15, supra (emphasis supplied in text here).

[178] See note and text in Ch. 1, at note 47, supra.

[179] See note and text in Ch. 1, at note 49, supra (emphasis supplied in text here).

[180] ACKERMAN, S J, at 161 (emphasis in original).

[181] Id. at 297. The Supreme Court seems to have treated academic freedom in this sense predominantly (though not altogether) in an instrumental or utilitarian sense. In *Sweezy*, supra Ch. 1, note 172, one of the cases cited by Justice Powell on academic freedom and diversity, the *Sweezy* Court stated: "No one should underestimate *the vital role* in a democracy that is played by those who guide and train our youth." *Sweezy*, 354 U.S. at 250 (plurality opinion of Warren, C. J.) (emphasis supplied). *"For society's good . . .* [p]olitical power must abstain from intrusion into [academic] freedom, *pursued in the interest of wise government and people's well being."* Id. at 262 (concurring opinion of Frankfurter, J.).

In contrast Habermas's thought seems predominantly deontological: "[L]egal validity . . . has the deontological character of a command, and not the teleological character of a desirable good that we can achieve to a certain degree . . . within the horizon of our preferences." HABERMAS, B F & N, at 261; see also id. at 98 & text of Ch. 1, notes 12 & 27, supra; Habermas, "Morality and Ethical Life," supra Ch. 1, note 8, 83 Nw. U. L. Rev. at 45–46.

Ackerman follows a similar tack: Utilitarianism is prevented from playing a role in liberal discourse in large part because of "its self-confident hedonism—its conviction that the good consists entirely in subjective satisfaction. . . . [T]he problem with utilitarianism is its teleological character, its efforts to evaluate . . . rules by how much 'good' they produce." ACKERMAN, S J, at 49.

This difference between the Court's predominant utilitarianism and Habermas's and Ackerman's deontologies seems to have no material effect on the analysis so far. See generally Ronald Dworkin, "The Coming Battles over Free Speech" (Book Review of

Anthony Lewis's Make No Law: The Sullivan Case and the First Amendment), THE N.Y. REV. OF BOOKS 55 (June 11, 1992) (distinguishing between the *instrumental* justification for free speech, and the *constitutive* valuation).

[182] Ronald Dworkin, "The Coming Battles over Free Speech," supra Ch. 1, note 181, at 56 (emphasis supplied).

[183] *Bakke*, 438 U.S. at 315 (opinion of Powell, J.).

[184] *Bakke*, 438 U.S. at 317.

[185] *Bakke*, 438 U.S. at 318.

[186] HABERMAS, L C, at 78–79; see text in Ch. 1, at notes 37 & 38, supra. (The "core components of bourgeois ideology, such as possessive individualism and the achievement orientation" "offer no support . . . in the face of the basic risks of existence.").

[187] HABERMAS, B F & N, at 164 (emphasis in original); see also id. at 418 ("The normative key is autonomy, not well-being. In a legal community, *no one* was free as long as the freedom of one person must be purchased with another's oppression.") (emphasis in original).

[188] Id. at 98; previously quoted in text at note 67, supra.

[189] ACKERMAN S J, at 57.

[190] Id. at 255.

[191] Id. at 247; previously quoted in text at note 136, supra.

[192] See Ch. 1, note 183, supra.

[193] *Bakke*, 438 U.S. at 312 (opinion of Powell, J.) (quoting *Keyishian*, 385 U.S. at 606) (further citation deleted). The concept of a "robust exchange of ideas" is no doubt taken from Justice Brennan's opinion for the Court in New York Times Co. v. Sullivan, 376 U.S. 254, 270 (1964) (upholding "a profound national commitment to the principle that debate on public issues should be uninhibited, robust, and wide-open.") I say "no doubt" because Justice Brennan was also the author of the Court's opinion in *Keyishian*.

[194] HABERMAS, B F & N, at 228.

[195] He was more of the operational type, to be considered last.

[196] *Abrams*, 250 U.S. at 630 (Holmes, J., dissenting).

[197] Gitlow v. New York, 268 U.S. 652, 673 (1925) (Holmes, J., dissenting) (even revolutionary Bolshevism must be accorded the rights of free speech and allowed "to be accepted by the dominant forces of the community.").

[198] ACKERMAN, S J, at 361.

[199] Id. at 37; see also notes and text at Ch. 1, notes 182–83, supra.

[200] See notes and text in Ch. 1, at notes 4, 20, 21 (text after), 49, 63, and 64, supra.

[201] See notes and text in Ch. 1, at notes 78, 82, 118, supra. This claim is made for both Habermas and Ackerman by showing that effective dialogue *and* diversity are essentially interrelated, at least in Habermas's argument for the universality of norms derived from dialogue, and for both in their claims that legitimacy flows from discourse and dialogue.

[202] *Bakke*, 438 U.S. at 312 (quoting from *Sweezy*, supra Ch. 1, note 172, 354 U.S. at 263) (emphasis supplied).

[203] *Bakke*, 438 U.S. at 312 n.48 (quoting from Bowen, "Admissions and the Relevance of Race," Princeton Alumni Weekly 7, 9 [Sept. 26, 1977]).

[204] Id. at 316 (App. to Brief for Columbia University, Harvard University, Stanford University, and the University of Pennsylvania, as amici curiae 2–3).

[205] HABERMAS, B F & N, at 186; see also notes and text in Ch. 1, at notes 62–66, supra.

[206] Id. at 228.

[207] See notes and text in Ch. 1, at notes 20–21, supra.

[208] ACKERMAN, S J, at 359.

[209] ACKERMAN, W P, at 312.

[210] See Ch. 1, notes 100 & 101, supra.

[211] See text of Ch. 1, note 161, supra (showing how diversity can coincide with broad remedial action).

[212] The discussion that follows on Supreme Court affirmative action cases, concerned with diversity, owes much to Akhil Reed Amar and Neal Kumar Katyal, *"Bakke's Fate,"* supra Ch. 1, note 161, 43 U.C.L.A. L. Rev. 1745.

[213] 497 U.S. 547 (1990).

[214] Justice Brennan and the four justices who joined his majority opinion used an intermediate standard of scrutiny to test the FCC's program under the First Amendment. Later, in Adarand Constructors, Inc. v. Pena, 515 U.S. 200 (1995), the Court, per O'Connor, J., required cases of affirmative action developed and justified under federal law to be judged by the same standard of strict scrutiny (here under the equal protection component of the Fifth Amendment) that state cases had already been held to— thus overruling the intermediate-scrutiny part of *Metro Broadcasting*; but the issue of *diversity* was never presented in *Adarand*, leaving that part of *Metro Broadcasting* intact. See *Adarand*, 515 U.S. 258 (Stevens, J., dissenting) ("Fostering [broadcast] diversity [in a case like *Metro Broadcasting*] may provide a sufficient interest to comply with the Court's holding today."). *But cf.* Lutheran Church Mo.–Synod v. FCC, supra Ch. 1, note 6, 141 F.3d 344 (finding diversity rationale in *Metro Broadcasting* weakened by its tie to intermediate scrutiny).

[215] *Metro Broadcasting*, 497 U.S. at 567, 568, & 577.

[216] Id. at 569, 570, 570–71, 577, 578, 579, & 589–90.

[217] *Metro Broadcasting*, 497 U.S. at 567–68 (citation omitted). Note that five members of the *Metro Broadcasting* Court cited Justice Powell's *Bakke* most favorably. The issue of authority for Powell's *Bakke* surfaces in the Fifth Circuit's treatment in the *Hopwood* case, notes and text at Ch. 1, notes 235–37, infra.

[218] Id. at 569–71.

[219] Id. at 617 (O'Connor, J., dissenting); see text at Ch. 1, note 138 (setting out the dialectical method of resolving this issue).

[220] Id. at 616 (O'Connor, J., dissenting).

[221] Id. at 626 (O'Connor, J., dissenting). Presented here as an empirical question, the question of causal nexus necessarily rests on certain principles that I in the next part will characterize as logistic. Logistic principles support a strict and direct form of causation that is associated with scientific proof. From a dialectical point of view, causation is viewed far more broadly than Justice O'Connor's argument would seem to permit. See, *e.g.*, text at notes 46–49, supra.

[222] *Metro Broadcasting*, 497 U.S. at 602 (O'Connor, J., dissenting) (further citation omitted).

[223] She is of the logistic type, to be taken up in my next chapter.

[224] McKEON, FREEDOM AND HISTORY, at 30, reprinted in FREEDOM AND HISTORY AND OTHER ESSAYS, at 182.

[225] *Metro Broadcasting*, 497 U.S. at 612 (O'Connor, J., dissenting) (emphases supplied).

[226] McKEON, FREEDOM AND HISTORY, at 14, reprinted in FREEDOM AND HISTORY AND OTHER ESSAYS, at 167–68.

[227] McKeon, "Dialectic and Political Thought and Action," supra Ch. 1, note 60, at 18.

[228] This is not to say that Justice Brennan in *Metro Broadcasting*, nor Justice Powell in *Bakke*, used language that is prototypical of dialectical expression. That is not the point. Rather, the point is that their writings in defense of free-speech-based diversity can be supported and understood by the dialectical presuppositions found in the work of Habermas and Ackerman. These sources, taken together, exhibit a worldview or mode of thought that is distinct in its own terms. Justice O'Connor, having a different mode of thought, must also be understood on her own terms—as I shall endeavor to make possible in the next chapter.

[229] 476 U.S. 267 (1986) (plurality opinion).

[230] These two arguments, plus the need for diverse racial role models among the faculty of a public school, were presented in the Government's Amicus Curiae brief to the Supreme Court in *Piscataway*, infra notes and text in Ch. 1, at notes 250–54, at 21, 22.

[231] *Wygant*, 476 U.S. at 315 (Stevens, J., dissenting).

[232] See text at Ch. 1, notes 222–28, supra.

[233] *Wygant*, 476 U.S. at 286 (O'Connor, J., concurring) (citing *Bakke*, 438 U.S., at 311–15 [opinion of Powell, J.]).

[234] Supra Intro., note 5, 78 F.3d 932.

[235] *But cf.* text Ch. 1, in note 161, supra, arguing, *inter alia*, that Justice Powell together with the Brennan group provided the needed support to make *Bakke* on diversity a binding precedent. At any rate, Judge Weiner of the Fifth Circuit, while joining the court of appeals on other issues, declined to join his brothers' would-be extermination of *Bakkean* diversity. *Hopwood*, 78 F.3d at 962, 964.

[236] *Hopwood*, 78 F.3d at 945 (emphasis supplied).

[237] Id. at 949.

[238] Supra Ch. 1, note 134, 339 U.S. 629.

[239] Roscoe C. Howard, Jr., "Getting It Wrong: *Hopwood v. Texas* and Its Implications for Racial Diversity in Legal Education and Practice," 31 New Eng. L. Rev. 831, 854, 859 (1997).

[240] 91 F.3d 1547 (3d Cir. 1996) (en banc), *cert. dism'd*, 522 U.S. 1010 (1997).

[241] 42 U.S.C. §§ 2000e (1994).

[242] *Johnson v. Transp. Agency*, supra Intro., note 14, 480 U.S. at 630.

[243] *Piscataway*, 91 F.3d at 1550–52. See also deposition testimony of Board President Theodore H. Kruse, at 1551–52 (describing the Board's plan to make groups under its aegis "diverse" but without citing a free-speech purpose).

[244] Carrington, "Diversity," supra Ch. 1, note 128, 1992 Utah L. Rev. at 1145 (emphasis supplied). See also *Wygant*, 476 U.S. at 288 n.* (opinion of O'Connor, J., concurring in part and concurring in the judgment) ("The goal of providing 'role models' . . . should not be confused with the very different goal of promoting racial diversity among the faculty.").

[245] *Piscataway*, 91 F.3d at 1559–60.

[246] Id. at 1561, 1562.

[247] Brief for Amicus Curiae, United States, before the Supreme Court in the Case of Piscataway Township Board of Education v. Taxman, October Term 1996, No. 96–679 (filed Aug. 22, 1997), at 10–11. Accessible at 1997 WL 523854.

[248] Brief for Amicus Curiae, United States, supra note 247, at 10–11.

[249] Id. at 8, 16.

250 See text at Ch. 1, notes 230–31, supra.

251 Brief for Amicus Curiae, United States, supra Ch. 1, note 247, at 20 (Hardly a diversity measure, this is a commonsense tactic of ordinary police work!).

252 Id. (An outcome likely to be attained through existing devices used under Title VII, *e.g.*, to combat systemic disparate treatment in pattern and practice cases. See Hazelwood Sch. Dist. v. United States, 433 U.S. 299 [1977]).

253 Brief for Amicus Curiae, United States, supra Ch. 1, note 247, at 21, 22.

254 Id. at 22 (citing Justice Stevens's dissenting opinion in *Wygant*, 476 U.S. at 15).

255 The Supreme Court dismissed the *writ of certiorari* in *Piscataway* when a coalition of civil rights groups furnished the funds to pay the white teacher's damages and to pay her lawyers' fees. 522 U.S. 1010 (December 12, 1997). The groups were reportedly concerned that the facts and the posture of the case could have led to an opinion of the Court harmful to affirmative action. See Barry Bearak and Linda Greenhouse, N.Y. TIMES, §A, p. 1, col. 5–6, "Settlement Ends High Court Case on Preferences," Nov. 22, 1997.

256 391 U.S. 563 (1968).

257 See my "Public and Private Speech: Toward a Practice of Pluralistic Convergence in Free-Speech Values," 1 Tex. Wesleyan L. Rev. 1 (1994).

258 See Steven A. Holmes, N. Y. TIMES, §A, p. 11, col. 1–6, "Major Ruling on Affirmative Action Is Likely Sooner or Later," Dec. 1, 1997.

259 University and Community College System of Nevada v. Farmer, 113 Nev. 90, 930 P.2d 730 (1997), *cert. denied*, 523 U.S. 1004 (1998).

260 *Farmer*, 930 P.2d at 734–35.

261 Id. at 735.

262 Supra Ch. 1, note 6, 141 F.3d 344.

263 Id. at 350 (emphasis in original).

264 Id. at 354.

265 Id. *But cf.* text of Ch. 1, note 214, supra, arguing that the diversity element of *Metro Broadcasting* did survive *Adarand*.

266 Id. at 354.

267 Id. at 355 (footnote and citation omitted). For the FCC's attempt to create an affirmative action program that would pass the D.C. Circuit's standards, see Revision of Broadcast and Cable EEO Rules and Policies, 65 Fed. Reg. 7448 (February 15, 2000) (to be codified at 47 C.F.R. pts. 0, 73 & 76).

268 *J. A. Croson Co.*, 488 U.S. at 487–91 (opinion of O'Connor, J.) (section 5 of the Fourteenth Amendment requires that Congress be given special deference in framing affirmative action).

269 *Metro Broadcasting*, 497 U.S. at 563–66 (citing Fullilove v. Klutznick, 448 U.S. 488 [1980]).

270 160 F.3d 790 (1st Cir. 1998).

271 Tamar Lewin, N.Y. TIMES, §A, p. 1, col. 1, "Court Ruling Blocks Affirmative Action at a Public School," Nov. 20, 1998.

272 Tamar Lewin, N.Y. TIMES, §A, p. 1, col. 5–6, "Public Schools Confronting Issue of Racial Preferences: Growing Number of Parents, Mostly White, Challenge Policies They Deem Unfair," Nov. 29, 1998.

273 *Wessmann*, 160 F.3d at 796.

274 Of which respondent Gittens was the chairperson.

275 *Wessmann*, 160 F.3d. 798.

[276] Id. at 799 (citing *Bakke*, 438 U.S. at 315 [opinion of Powell, J.]).

[277] *Wessmann*, 160 F.3d at 798.

[278] Id. at 9–10. The methodology allowed half of the available seats for an entering class to be assigned strictly on the basis of composite test/grade scores. The remaining half of the seats, however, were assigned on the basis of proportional representation of race and ethnicity in the remaining applicant pool. Thus it was possible for a white applicant in this second group of applicants to be passed over for a black or other ethnic applicant with a lower composite score, when his proportionate share of the remaining applicants was larger than the white share. Id. at 793. This is precisely what happened in this case, when a father, Mr. Wessmann, brought this suit for his rejected daughter.

[279] *Cf. J. A. Croson Co.*, 488 U.S. at 521 (Scalia, J., dissenting) ("[O]nly a social emergency rising to the level of imminent danger to life and limb . . . can justify an exception to the [color-blind] principle embodied in our Fourteenth Amendment.").

[280] *Wessmann*, 160 F.3d at 799 (emphasis supplied); see also Ho. v. San Francisco Unified School District, 147 F.3d 854 (9th Cir. 1998) (holding that school district's use of racial/ethnic categories to maintain diversity was unconstitutional enforcement of racial classifications and quotas). See generally Jeffrey Rosen, N.Y. TIMES, §A, pp. 1, 5, "The Lost Promise of School Integration," April 2, 2000.

[281] Gabriel J. Chin, "*Bakke* to the Wall: The Crisis of *Bakkean* Diversity," 4 Wm. & Mary Bill of Rights J. 881, 890 (1996). *But cf.* text and Ch. 1, notes at notes 226–27, supra (pointing out that dialectic does not require such precision).

[282] Jim Chen, "Diversity and Damnation," 43 U.C.L.A. L. Rev. 1839, 1879 (1996) ("In academic callings as well as in criminal ones, '[w]e must start with the presumption that people of *all* races' pursue all types of interests, 'not with the premise that any kind of [interest] is the exclusive province of any particular racial or ethnic group.' " (citing United States v. Armstrong, 48 F.3d 1508, 1516–17 (9th Cir 1995), *rev'd*, 517 U.S. 456 [1996] [emphasis in original]).

[283] RICHARD D. KAHLENBERG, THE REMEDY: CLASS, RACE, AND AFFIRMATIVE ACTION, at 28 (1996) ("[T]he new advocates of diversity argue that the color-blind ideal [and the aspirations to achieve it through compensatory strategies] w[ere] wrong all along. [To such advocates] race is not just skin color but also a substantive cultural characteristic.").

[284] MICHEL ROSENFELD, AFFIRMATIVE ACTION AND JUSTICE: A PHILOSOPHICAL AND CONSTITUTIONAL INQUIRY [hereinafter AFFIRMATIVE ACTION AND JUSTICE] 266, 267, 245 (1991) (citation omitted) (emphasis supplied).

[285] 3 PAUL TILLICH, SYSTEMATIC THEOLOGY 308 (1963).

[286] PAUL TILLICH, "The Nature of Religious Language," in THEOLOGY OF CULTURE 53, 54–55 (Robert C. Kimball ed. 1959, 1970).

[287] ACKERMAN, W P, at 148 (emphasis supplied). See also notes and text at notes 122–23 (emphasis supplied). See also note and text Ch. 1 at note 152, supra.

2

Logistic and Compensatory Causation

THE NATURE OF LOGISTIC

"[T]he 'rights created by the . . . Fourteenth Amendment are, by its terms, guaranteed to the individual. The rights established are personal rights.' . . . [A] generalized assertion that there has been discrimination in an entire industry provides no guidance . . . to determine the precise scope of the injury it seeks to remedy [through affirmative action]. It 'has no logical stopping point.' "[1] That is, on this view, no such stopping point exists because the injury cannot be definitely linked to known individuals but would continue along an infinite chain of causation. With this vision of the context of affirmative action, Justice O'Connor in the *J. A. Croson* case stakes out a controlling viewpoint that is at once mechanistic and individualistic—a view with constitutional principles that rely heavily on causation and deduction to reach its conclusions. In this inquiry her view goes under the heading of logistic.

Logistic constructs knowledge and the rationale for political society—with its corrective form of justice—from simple, irreducible units or "simples," which maintain their ontological priority even when they are built into vast systems or wholes intended to explain or support the cognitive or political world as though it were a mechanism. Thus in ancient times, Democritus and Lucretius used for these purposes the motion of postulated but unseen atoms, whose concatenations determined events in the world; while in modern times Newton explained the movement of the universe by adding together the natures and consequences of simple motions and efficient causes into a whole explicable because of its constituent parts; and John Locke, beginning with the simple unit of "man in the state of nature," built up as an artifice the state, making its existence depend upon the (hypothetical) agreements and conventions of individual men and not upon any organic or "natural" relations among them.

Indeed, logistic grasps reality through the methods of "scientific" proof, whether these proofs involve the deductive methods of mathematics, geometry, or physics. Great stress is laid on causation—causal nexuses among the simples serve as links in deductive reasoning—but causation consists entirely of *efficient causes* and not *final causes*. The former follow Hume's paradigm of the customary conjunction of antecedent and consequent; they consist of only the bare and uniform connections between phenomena. The latter deal with the distinctive teleological or purposive development in a phenomenon. With final cause (or a comprehensive social goal) eliminated, the reasoning of logistic takes a markedly quantitative direction. Literalness is also a factor; terms that are not univocal are resisted—indeed, cannot be absorbed or fathomed by the system.

Logistic history is causal history. Because the causes acting upon all classes of phenomena are uniform (differing perhaps in their *degree* of force upon perceptibly reaching the mind but not in *kind*), human history at all times and in all places can be explained by the same scientific, irreducible causal principles. We have knowledge of the past either because of the regularity and consistency of these causal principles, and the causally perceived competence with which past events, under a given regime or other controlling influence, have been recorded; or by the convergence of different sources of the same events. History does not divide itself into ages or epochs, nor does it have an end or telos, but is marked by the steady and uniform appearance of causes in time sequence. There is, however, a recurring tension between the *determinism* imposed by the causal mechanism and *freedom*, or man's self-determination in a place where unimpeded, unfettered human motion is possible. In *Anarchy, State, and Utopia*,[2] Robert Nozick lays out a logistic scheme of causation and corresponding freedom highly relevant to understanding the prevailing form of affirmative action.

NOZICK AND THE LOGISTIC VIEW OF FREEDOM AND JUSTICE

The whole of Robert Nozick's libertarian enterprise need not concern us here. My concern is primarily with his emphasis on the artificial nature of the state, whose genuine powers are merely derived from the powers and rights of its individual components—its citizens; and with the causally linear nature of those citizens' rights and powers vis-à-vis themselves, the state, and their history. "[T]he fact," he says, "that we are 'social products' in that we benefit from current patterns and forms created by the multitudinous actions of a long string of long-forgotten people, forms which include institutions, ways of doing things, and language . . . does *not* create in us a *general floating debt* [to the principle of cooperation in the existing social order] which the current society can collect and use at will."[3]

Such a principle of causation "would be so complex and involuted" that "it would not obviate the need for other persons' [specifically] *consenting* to cooperate and limit their own activities."[4] "[H]istory [thus] tends to become the account of the *actual operation* [not a "general floating debt"] of . . . causes in past events."[5] "Logistic history . . . finds its basic laws in a science of human actions which is the same for all men, at all times, and in all places."[6] The uniformity of causation in the scheme before us is bolstered by the fact that "Nozick's operative conception of individuation—'the fact of our separate existences'—is sufficient only to numerical individuation and thus is short of the requirements of a true individualism."[7] The causal literalness and uniformity, together with the corresponding unidimensional nature of the persons whom he views as possible citizens, determine the state that Nozick is bound to construct, together with its justice.

Nozick's philosophical goal is to describe and orchestrate the construction of a state from the (hypothetical) state of nature—though not from a "social compact view[]," which "conveys nothing like [the] unanimous joint agreement [claimed for it]"—but rather from within an "invisible-hand structure" where "the process of accumulating sole effective enforcement and overseeing power may take place without anyone's rights being violated."[8] Those rights derive from the prepolitical period and primarily include Kantian "side constraints," which forbid the subordination of another to one's purely self-regarding or utilitarian goals, and the generally inferable prohibition of physical aggression against one another.[9] Consistent with the operation of side constraints, no one (*e.g.*, a utilitarian) may "violate [sic] persons for the greater social good[.] . . . [T]here is no *social entity* with a good that undergoes some sacrifice for its own good. There are only individual people, different individual people, with their own individual lives."[10] Nothing could emphasize more strongly that in the logistic mode of thought the individual is favored ontologically and that the state and society are subordinate entities and artifices, whose worth is measured in convenience but not as a source of ethical grounds for human action. "What persons may and may not do to one another limits what they may do through the apparatus of a state, or to establish such an apparatus."[11]

Justice in Nozick's state is conditioned by the equation of power with coercion or force and by the identification of freedom with unimpeded motion.[12] The "[c]ommunity and right and wrong are grounded in convention and agreement by [simples], and no inference is possible from what is to what ought to be."[13] The citizens' expectations of justice from the state are thus very minimal, centering on their protection from physical forces and external constraints on their movements. Protection of a citizen's physical integrity is accordingly a major state function.[14] Perhaps *the* major function, though, is protecting citizens' rights to their property.

"Justice in [property] holdings is historical; it depends on what actually has happened."[15] One legitimately obtains property by "*original acquisition*" and by "*transfer*" from another person.[16] This process is called the *entitlement theory of property,* and it is contrasted with what Nozick calls current "time-slice" principles of property—later denominated as end-result or "patterned" principles.[17] "Patterned" or "time-slice" principles disrupt the just distribution of property. The latter two principles (but not entitlement), both illustrated by utilitarianism, cannot "be continuously realized without continuous interference with people's lives."[18] For "lives" one can easily read "movements"—for life *is* motion, and movement without "continuous interference" is the very essence of logistic freedom. According to this view of freedom, whatever a person originally acquires or receives in a transfer, over or during the course of "history" or the simple duration of time, is *ipso facto* his property under the entitlement theory.[19] The process alone of historical entitlement, as noted, normally results in a just distribution of property. *R*edistribution of property, on the other hand, is not just, because it "involv[es] . . . the violation of people's rights."[20] "[P]atterned principles of distributive justice involve appropriating the actions of other persons" and "confront [opponents of entitlement] with the question of whether the actions necessary to achieve the selected pattern don't themselves violate moral side constraints [protecting rights to historically obtained property]."[21]

Because, however, "not all distributions actually take place in accordance with the two principles" of acquisition and transfer, a third principle, one concerned with the rectification of injustices, "will be required in actual societies."[22] Rectification is not redistributive but, rather, is compensatory to victims of violations of their property rights.[23] The injustices rectified typically involve previous unjust violations of one or both of the principles of acquisition and transfer.[24]

And whatever difficulties [an entitlement theorist] has in applying the principle of rectification to persons who did not themselves *violate* the first two principles are [simply] difficulties in balancing the conflicting considerations so as correctly to formulate the complex principle of rectification itself; he will not violate moral side constraints by applying the principle [to persons who have no direct relation to the initial victims].[25]

The person or persons whose entitlement rights *are* violated, *mutatis mutandis,* do not necessarily have to be the persons who are *compensated* for injury, provided (of course) that the causal nexus between injury and ultimate compensation is not attenuated.[26] The causes linking one wrongdoer with another (or with a proxy) would not be preferred in logistic to the causes linking a victim of the injustice to a successor. Causal links justifying rectification can be forged in either case, although Nozick does not expressly take up the latter case here.

Thus, while "patterned" or "time-slice" systems of distribution often encounter side constraints in their operation,[27] distribution according to rectification, measured by precise calculation of the causal linkage of the past injury to the present objects of benefaction, will rarely violate anyone else's rights. "[B]y Nozick's exclusively historical conception, [o]nce distribution has been set right [through rectifying injustices in the causal chain of entitlement,] it shall ever remain right as long as justice in transfer obtains."[28] It follows that, to set the inexorable chain of causation in property rights back into proper motion, successors to victims as well as proxies for violators may have to be benefited, or enveloped, respectively, in the process of rectification. This is Nozick's model of compensatory causation as justice.

EPSTEIN'S VISION OF RACE AND CAUSATION

Richard A. Epstein, in his recent book *Forbidden Grounds: The Case against Employment Discrimination Laws*,[29] starts out from the model proposition that "[t]he rules of acquisition for personal liberty and external property [rest on] a set of original rights which can be transformed and recombined through *voluntary transactions*."[30] This model, he finds, has been championed best by Robert Nozick in *Anarchy, State, and Utopia*.[31] But of the principles introduced by Nozick, Professor Epstein gravitates toward the freedom to transfer property: "Within a libertarian framework, freedom of contract becomes the central issue."[32] While this statement marks no material break with Nozick, Epstein's apparent movement *away* from the Kantian-style side constraints advanced by Nozick[33] and *toward* utilitarianism[34] *are* different. The upshot is a brand of libertarianism that relies on a self-governing market and its subjective preferences to bring forth the good.[35]

The capstone is that Epstein is opposed to antidiscrimination laws *simpliciter*[36] and, *a fortiori*, to affirmative action (in the public sector, at least, though private employers, in keeping with libertarian principles, might do as they please in the matter).[37] Affirmative action, like direct enforcement of the antidiscrimination laws, interferes with employers' (and employees') exercise of their "taste[s] for discrimination,"[38] through which "persons can sort themselves out in[to] the environment[s] that they like best, free of external constraint."[39] If racial (or racist) preferences interfere with fair consideration of persons of color or other stigmata, in the employment decisions of some employers (or the reverse, employers' being shunned because of race or other marks of prejudice), no issue of justice—especially of freedom—is raised. "[T]he . . . economic and social consequences of allowing the private use of force and allowing private discrimination are so different that it becomes indefensible to treat ostensible wrongs in the second category [discrimination] as though it were akin to the former [force]."[40]

This *distinction* between force and race discrimination reflects an extreme even within the logistic mode of thought, for it reduces to insignificance a phenomenon that surely could not withstand a Kantian-style side constraint wielded by Nozick, nor could it avoid the atomistic criticism about the internal effects of racial repulsion and its touching and moving the mind and spirit of one who experiences racial discrimination.[41] It is a more extreme position than that of Epstein's former colleague at the University of Chicago, Antonin Scalia, who views racial discrimination as a real but illusive phenomenon, often proven up fallaciously on speculative or even nonsensical evidence but, when properly detected, is nonetheless capable of exerting force because it sometimes justifies the award of damages for race-motivated acts.[42]

Then why would I want to use Epstein as a figure to justify affirmative action, when he is totally turned against its purpose and logic? The answer is that I shall use his views as a quite important aspect of logistic thought to explain, not justify, this legal issue of affirmative action within the schema that I have set out. His lucid and provocative style commends his writings for analysis. His position is, in my opinion, the most extensive contemporary development of logistic as applied to current general and antidiscrimination law, and its dissection of recent affirmative action cases provides further insight into logistic. Finally, the book is preceded by a number of articles, written in the 1970s by Epstein and published in the *Journal of Legal Studies*, in which he discusses *his* conception of "corrective justice" (the same concept, of course, as compensatory justice and Nozick's rectification) and argues that his conception should be established and measured by a carefully refined form of causation, as it could operate in the common law of torts. Such analysis is quite material to understanding compensatory causation as a justification for affirmative action.

Epstein's "assumption [is] that all cases should be decided solely with reference to principles of corrective justice: rendering to each person whatever redress is required because of the violation of his *rights* by another."[43] "[T]he concept of causation . . . [is directly] relevant to the ultimate question [of] who shall bear the loss [in cases of harm to person or property]."[44] Cause is a unitary concept, not split in two as necessary condition ("but-for" cause) and "proximate" cause but modeled after commonsense notions of the necessary relation between antecedent and consequent in the public space.[45] Liability is imposed upon a defendant, regardless of whether he had any intention to harm or his reasonableness or lack thereof, whenever the plaintiff establishes a causal connection between the plaintiff's harm, or violation of his rights, and the defendant's volitional conduct (motion)—conduct that calls for redress because it has upset the preexisting legal status of the plaintiff and especially the balance of legal rights of the plaintiff vis-à-vis the defendant.[46] This, of course, is a form of strict liability.

Taken at face value, this system could never produce the corrective justice needed to support an affirmative action program—even if it relied on *intentional* harms (or violations of rights) and not simply on strict liability[47]—because for Epstein racial discrimination does not produce the quasi-physical force necessary to violate one's rights or freedom.[48] This view, once again, is nonsense, rejected even by Epstein's former colleague, Justice Scalia.[49] But assuming *arguendo* that rights amenable to violation through Epsteinian force *were* at issue in race discrimination—including affirmative action cases—I want to examine the implications of his causal principles for affirmative action built on a logistic view.

Early in his enterprise of linking tort liability to corrective justice through mere causation, Epstein sets out four models or paradigms of causation to narrow the scope of his arguments and protect them from a charge of advancing a unitary theory of causation far too generalized in its application. The four paradigms are "force, fright, compulsion and dangerous conditions."[50] Of these, harm may be "immediately" caused through the operation of the first three— force, fright, and compulsion. But of the fourth—creation of a dangerous condition—"the harm to the plaintiff can be completed only upon the occurrence of some subsequent act or event that works upon the condition that the defendant created," and thus the resultant harm is "best regarded as [an] instance[] of *indirect* (but not *remote*) harm."[51] While at least one of the first three causal paradigms is capable of intermediate or indirect causation,[52] the fourth paradigm creates the most complex causal nexus that Epstein seems able to tolerate in his system—it is the most complex, by degree, of all the paradigms.[53] "The last of these paradigms[—*viz.*,] A created a dangerous condition that resulted in B's harm[—]demands a detailed analysis of, first, the kinds of conditions that should be regarded as dangerous, and, second, the impact of the actions or events that intervened between A's conduct and B's harm."[54] Of all the paradigms this last probably most resembles the typical situation in which a school or university, an employer, or a government must justify its affirmative action as corrective justice designed to redress the "dangerous condition" of a previous, historical instance of discrimination.

If A is the government (or university, *etc.*), trying to justify an affirmative action plan, it must first somehow show that an invidious condition created by it in the past presented a dangerous condition that was activated by some other event (layoffs? discriminatory actions by persons in supervisory or management positions? an economic downturn?). It must then be shown that this condition, together with its activating event, has produced a discriminatory impact (harm, injury to rights) on a class of protected employees, B, that requires corrective justice to restore their rights or undo the harm. The right to corrective justice accrues at the time of the activating event and (at least for the time being) belongs only to that class B.

Second, if the employer is to have a *real* affirmative action plan (and not simply a system of individualized compensation for the most direct victims), the right to corrective justice, once established in B (the group of most direct victim[s]), must also accrue successively and causally in affected groups C, D, E, or even F, who are causally linked to the original harm through B. This, though, is surely what Epstein means by "remote" causation.[55] There are too many intervening parties beyond the point that the dangerous condition reacts to the initial event, yielding immediate harm only to B. The paradigm of compulsion permits one intervening party without breaking the causal chain,[56] and the dangerous conditions paradigm may be activated by a third party.[57] But the notion that the dangerous condition would be activated and *then* carried forward as justification for corrective action by successors to the first victim(s), who subsequently are said to suffer actionable harm derivatively despite ostensibly weaker and weaker linkages to the original discriminatory event, places an ontologically impossible strain on Epstein's theory. As a logistic thinker, Epstein requires exactness, particularity, and sustained force without substantial interruptions in causal connections. Because these conditions tend to diminish greatly once the initial causal surge has passed very far beyond its initial recipient, and further because the objects of causation are individuals in atomistic flux rather than in group modality, a typical affirmative action plan that purports to trace its pedigree to past group-related injustices would almost certainly founder on Richard Epstein's causal requirements[58]—if he favored affirmative action at all.

A return to *Forbidden Grounds* amply illustrates that Epstein has consistently applied his causal principles developed in the journal articles of some twenty years before, this time not just in the common law but in the statutory and constitutional law of affirmative action as well. For example, he attacks Justice Brennan's broad allowance of relief in the pattern and practice action of *Sheet Metal Workers v. EEOC*.[59] The controversy turned on the proper construction of section 706(g) of Title VII,[60] which is Title VII's major provision for fashioning relief once liability has been established. Justice Brennan found that because of the particularly egregious character of the union's discrimination and its recalcitrance to reform, Title VII permitted the fashioning of "affirmative race-conscious relief which may incidentally benefit individuals *who are not identified victims of unlawful discrimination*."[61] Epstein finds such relief to be outside his causal world: "[S]trangers to the discrimination are entitled to *no* remedial protection. . . . [My] 'victims only' approach [shared and argued for here by the Reagan era EEOC (Equal Employment Opportunity Commission)[62]] seeks to fit Title VII into the standard *corrective justice* mode of adjudication. Only [direct or nonremote] victims can initiate actions against wrongdoers."[63] Epstein shows his strong proclivity for unmediated causation in mainstream antidiscrimination actions as well. "The disparate treatment [intentional] Title VII cases involve a shorter chain of inference than the disparate impact [strict liability] cases[, which almost always involve multiple or class action plaintiffs]."[64] The theory of disparate impact eschews employer discriminatory intent and looks strictly to the systemic discriminatory consequences of employment practices that are not necessary for the employer's operation of its business. "Disparate impact opens up a far wider vista of potential liability than disparate treatment, given that disparate impact is a virtual universal consequence . . . of many . . . employer practices."[65] Epstein's adverseness to disparate impact (despite its strict liability) is a strong indication that his "dangerous conditions" paradigm, which on its face seems to fit the potentiality for liability that disparate impact factors pose, rests instead on individual, identified causes of limited scope. His idea of a causal paradigm, it turns out, cannot encompass the multiplicity of causes and the generality of proofs that a disparate impact case may present.[66]

Nozick, in contrast, and as it will be remembered, has some tolerance for tracing the chain of causation through a complex web of transactions in order to identify both the perpetrator and the victim of injustice, so that rectification may be done.[67] And Nozick's adoption, even in the minimal state, of deontological side constraints to protect the dignity and integrity of all persons against exploitation provides a basis in liberty and especially property interests to invoke the device of affirmative action. This device may be used as a form of rectification or redress, even if only narrowly and specifically after precise proof of desert by the beneficiaries. Epstein does not offer any comparable alternative.

THE LOGISTIC APPROACH TO AFFIRMATIVE ACTION

The logistic point of view, when incorporated into the reasoning of the cases, presents or requires a typical pattern: Once the plaintiffs (usually white males) have made a *prima facie* case of discrimination against them, produced by preferences for other groups by the employer, school, or government, that latter entity, as defendant, must show past intentional, invidious harm to the benefited class (minorities, women) that has causally carried forward to the present in its invidious effects, resulting in tangible harm to members of the benefited class (some or all of whom may or must be among the actual victims in the past). Supreme Court justices whose work on affirmative action is closely related to the logistic point of view apply their notions of equality and redress to those entities whom they conceive to be individuals (or to be constructed of individuals) and not to groups or to individual persons *qua* their group characteristics, which these justices frequently regard as stereotypes. They "link equal treatment to the strict scrutiny test [of the Equal Protection Clause][68] and [further link their] acceptance [of affirmative action] as constitutional only when it serves narrowly compensation goals."[69] That is, when a wrongdoer has injured the constitutional rights of direct or actual victims, only they—or perhaps their most immediate successors in the causal chain—are entitled to redress, as affirmative action, from that wrongdoer for the precise injury inflicted.[70] By the same token, affirmative action can be viewed a kind of defense to the plaintiffs' initial complaint of discrimination against white males, discrimination *ipso facto* required to justify affirmative action in the first place. That this is a mechanistic and atomistic approach should be evident.

Proponents of this logistic approach—led mainly over the years by Justices Powell and O'Connor—have completely eschewed any effort to provide distributive justice. The aim of distributive justice is to award the "goods" of society *in a comprehensive way* according to some basic principle or belief—in a democracy, *e.g.*, by the belief in freedom for the *many*, achieved through reductions in disparities of wealth.[71] Distributive justice, which requires no finding of wrongdoing, apportions social goods in geometric proportion, generally gravitating toward equality of *result*; but the proponents of logistic favor equality of *opportunity*. This latter form of equality, rather than aiming at reapportionment of the distribution of wealth and power in a global or comprehensive way, is aimed instead at particular injustices and at the restoration of injured parties to their rightful or *status quo ante* conditions. "[R]ectificatory [justice] looks only to the distinctive character of the injury, and treat[ing] the parties as equal" employs a judge to identify the wrongdoer and to "tak[e] away from the gain of the [wrongdoer]" so that the injured party can be made "equal," that is, restored to his previous condition, according to arithmetic proportion.[72] The distinction between distributive and corrective justice thus becomes critical. For by settling on corrective justice as the right aim of affirmative action, Justice Powell and Justice O'Connor and their followers, who have controlled the most crucial decisions under the Equal Protection Clause, have hemmed in the justification for affirmative action to this rationale (excepting, perhaps, for that part of Justice Powell's own *Bakke* opinion concerned with diversity). They have hemmed it into a causally and remedially narrow space, which is bounded by limitations on causation and by a nearly exclusive concern with giving individuals who have suffered personal harm their appropriate measure of justice—all so closely identified with logistic.

JUSTICE POWELL'S INVENTION OF COMPENSATORY CAUSATION IN *BAKKE*

In that part of his *Bakke* opinion that does not address diversity,[73] Justice Powell closely examined the Davis Medical School's special admissions program to see whether its racial classifications could withstand an attack under the Equal Protection Clause.[74] On the precise issue of whether reserving definite numbers of spaces for minority students could be valid, Justice Powell found the constitutional answer to be no. In so doing, he set the basic perimeters for a compensatory causal rationale for affirmative action that have been refined but never replaced since.[75]

The first element established by Justice Powell is the familiar one of the primacy of the individual, both as victim and as wrongdoer, as the focus of analysis. Groups and their distinctive histories are pushed into the background. The medical school, for example, had argued that any whites harmed by the program were not members of "a discrete and insular minority"[76] and thus were entitled only to lesser constitutional protection than minorities, because only the latter suffer invidious discrimination—and *that* because of their race or class.[77] Justice Powell emphatically denied the validity of the school's group-based premise: "The guarantee of equal protection cannot mean one thing when applied to one individual and something else when applied to a person of another color."[78] "Racial and ethnic distinctions of *any* sort are inherently suspect and thus call for the most exacting scrutiny."[79]

The upshot of this reduction of the problem of racial justice to one of individuals subject equally to discriminatory harm meant that the so-called standard of "color-blindness"—and not a guide of color preference to be adjusted to various circumstances of discrimination—would govern the legality of affirmative action under a compensatory rationale. Justice Brennan, and his three colleagues joining his opinion, had, however, stated that the *Carolene Products* footnote[80] *did* apply to the case and that white males were obviously *not* members of a "discrete and insular class" meant for heightened protection (as *were* minority races discriminated against). Moreover, no *stigma* attached to individuals of the majority when minority members were preferred over them.[81] This theory of lesser harm to whites from discrimination became known as "benign" discrimination. Justice Brennan predicated it directly on the primacy of group characteristics and used it to justify a shift in the level of equal protection scrutiny from strict to the less demanding intermediate when whites claim harm,[82] a shift that would have made compensatory (perhaps even distributive) affirmative action much more readily justifiable. Justice Powell demurred. "The guarantees of the Fourteenth Amendment extend to all persons."[83]

Mr. Justice Brennan[] [views] . . . the pliable notion of "stigma" [as] the crucial element in analyzing racial classifications. . . . The Equal Protection Clause is not[, however], framed in terms of *stigma.* . . . It reflects a subjective judgment that is standardless. *All* state-imposed classifications that rearrange burdens and benefits on the basis of race are likely to be viewed with deep resentment by the individuals burdened. The denial to *innocent persons* of equal rights and opportunities may outrage those so deprived and therefore be perceived as *invidious.* These *individuals* are likely to find little comfort in the notion that the deprivation they are asked to endure [here, a seat in the entering class] is merely the price of membership in the dominant majority and that its imposition is inspired by the *benign* purpose of aiding others.[84]

Not only must the victims be individually identified, but the alleged wrongdoers—the source of the causal impetus eventually requiring compensation—must also be seen, said Justice Powell, as individual persons, firms, and government agencies and not as undifferentiated society. This latter fact is so and must be accepted to avoid deliberately or inadvertently expanding causal blameworthiness to "innocent victims" whose jobs, lives, or careers may be sacrificed with "no relationship to [their] worth" because they are made to "bear the burdens of redressing grievances not of their making."[85]

In *Bakke* Justice Powell established a second element, one of causation, that is narrow and direct, intentional in origin, and specific as to scope. "[W]e have never approved preferential classifications in the absence of [past] constitutional or statutory violations . . . by the respondent [putative wrongdoer] in that case."[86] There was "no determination by the [California] legislature or a responsible administrative agency that the University [of California at Davis] engaged in a discriminatory practice."[87] Thus the Davis Medical School had not laid the necessary predicate of specific acts of discrimination to trigger the causation necessary to justify affirmative action.

Justice Brennan, however, had argued in support of the Davis program that "a state government may adopt race-conscious programs if the purpose of such programs is to remove the *disparate racial impact* its actions might have and if there is reason to believe that the *disparate impact* is itself the product of past discrimination, whether its own or that of *society at large*."[88] Justice Brennan found these conditions to exist and, specifically, to justify the Davis program under intermediate scrutiny.

Justice Powell's response was twofold. "Disparate impact" can never give rise to even "a presumption of causation."[89] Thus predicate discriminatory acts must—by inference—be intentional. Otherwise, discrimination by "society at large" (and its concomitant disparate impact) necessarily "involves a speculative leap" when that general term is used to explain the cause of minorities' failure to qualify for admission under regular procedures.[90] Justice Powell's objection to this "societal discrimination" appears to have had the same grounds as Epstein's objection to disparate impact under Title VII: a strong predilection for particular, identified causes of limited range and force.[91] "[S]ocietal discrimination[, in contradistinction, involves] an amorphous concept of injury that may be ageless in its reach into the past."[92]

The intentional harm caused by a specific wrongdoer must be proportionately linked to the relief granted; this standard was first established in earlier school desegregation cases: "[T]he scope of the remedies [must] not [be] permitted to exceed the extent of violations."[93] Furthermore, as I indicated earlier, relief must be carefully correlated to officially documented evidence by the institution or other wrongdoer.[94] This insistence on a very strict correlation, as though the proper relief (causal consequent) will appear only if the injury (causal antecedent) is vivid and distinct enough to produce it, has clear affinities with logistic causation as illustrated by Nozick and Epstein. The former rejects "a general floating debt," which might be likened to "societal discrimination" in the present inquiry in favor rather of the *familiarity* of literal causes that operate uniformly and particularly upon individuals.[95] The latter position of Epstein means that causation is directly relevant to ascertaining the scope of required redress, arising from the violation of one's rights by another; and cause itself is nothing more than the necessary relation between antecedent and consequent that we all *customarily and normally assume* without questioning.[96] "We only find, that the one [the consequent] does actually, in fact, follow the other [the antecedent motion]. The impulse of one billiard ball is attended with motion in the second."[97] So in a sense Justice Powell's requirements of causation (apart from his discussion of diversity) stemmed from little else (and no less) than commonsense observations applied to the complexities of race relations. With simple (but not unsophisticated) ideas he constructed a framework of racial justice.[98]

FULLILOVE: A DIFFERENT TACK?

In the next constitutional affirmative action case to come before it, *Fullilove v. Klutznick, Secretary of Commerce,*[99] the Court (albeit fragmented, again without a majority) seemed to retreat from that equal protection analysis presaged by Justice Powell in *Bakke.* "This opinion does not adopt, either expressly or implicitly, the formulas of analysis articulated in such cases as [*Bakke*]. . . . [O]ur analysis demonstrates that the [contested statutory] provision would survive judicial review under either [equal protection] 'test' [in *Bakke*, Justice Powell's strict scrutiny or Justice Brennan's intermediate scrutiny]."[100] Thereby arose the belief that a congressionally mandated affirmative action plan was subject only to intermediate scrutiny and a laxer causality—a belief that was not punctured until *Adarand* over fifteen years later.

The contested provision was section 103(f)(2) of the Public Works Employment Act of 1977,[101] which provided that "no grant shall be made under this Act for any local public works project unless the applicant gives satisfactory assurance to the Secretary that at least 10 per centum of the amount of each grant shall be expended for minority business enterprises [MBEs, a term of art referring to firms the controlling interest of which lay in minority hands]."[102] Thus two essential things were different from *Bakke* in this case: First, it stemmed from a congressional condition placed on the issuance of federal public works grants, not a provision originating in a state or its subdivision to promote diversity or corrective justice in higher education; and second, though couched in the terms of a remedial program, it was at best a prophylactic one, at least from the prospective of logistic—aimed at the prevention of racial anomalies never shown by strict proof to have existed in the past.

Although it was said that "Congress enacted the program strictly as a remedial measure [that is, to restore victims of past discrimination to their rightful places],"[103] there was little specific evidence, in the logistic sense, of actual discrimination to rectify or to redress. Introduced as a floor amendment to an already pending bill, the proposed minorities set-aside provision (as contained in the entire Act) never received any extensive committee hearings, markup, or other consideration.[104] Both the amendment's sponsor and later the plurality of the Court had to rely on the histories of other legislation to establish and to trace the existence of remediable discrimination in federal grant procedures.[105]

The upshot of the three-member plurality's opinion was that "[i]t is not necessary that these prime contractors [the grantees] be shown responsible for any violations of antidiscrimination law."[106]

The program was designed to ensure that, to the extent federal funds were granted under the Public Works Employment Act of 1977, grantees who elect to participate would not employ procurement practices that *might result in perpetuation of prior discrimination* which had impaired or foreclosed access by minority businesses to public contracting opportunities.[107]

The background of this justification and its express terms show with little doubt that it could not pass logistic standards. The primary ground of logistic rejection would be that this form of justification leans heavily toward the model of societal discrimination. By effectively adopting this model, the plurality showed no tight causal nexus between some definite harm and definite victims who required compensation to redress the impact of that harm on them. The logistic mind resists any finding of causation that either does not proceed directly from a concrete antecedent to a definite consequent or at least is not composed of an identifiable (and relatively short) chain of antecedents and consequents.[108] The MBE plan was also designed "to place . . . selected minority groups . . . on a more equitable footing" and thus more nearly resembled distributive than corrective justice—anathema to proponents of logistic, because the set-aside aimed more at the redistribution of wealth than at a redress of individual harm.[109] The question thus arises: Why did Justice Powell vote to approve this plan, considering his *Bakke* principles?[110]

Justice Powell supported the plan apparently both because he was willing to defer to the predicate (though scanty) findings of past discrimination by Congress and because he found enough limitations on the scope and duration of the plan to satisfy his requirements that causation be restricted. "Implicit [he found] in its holding was the Court's belief that Congress had the authority to find, and had found, that members of this minority group had suffered governmental discrimination."[111] "Congress [had accordingly] reasonably concluded that private and governmental discrimination had contributed to the negligible percentage of public contracts awarded minority contractors."[112] Having so found, the Congress had a wide variety of allowable options to redress the harm: "[T]his Court has not required remedial plans to be limited to the least restrictive means of implementation. We have recognized that the choice of remedies to redress racial discrimination is a 'balancing process.' "[113] Justice Powell did not indicate which interests would be balanced, but he must have intended that the congressional interest in ameliorating discrimination in government contracting be very great; it was obviously greater than that of the medical school in *Bakke*, "in reducing the historic deficit of traditionally disfavored minorities."[114]

As to causal limitations on the program, such as would prevent the mindless injury of "innocent" third parties, the greatest was the limitation on its duration—"As soon as the [public works] program concludes, this set-aside program ends."[115] The choice of a ten percent set-aside bore an equitable relation to the deficit in minority contractors.[116] The effect of the set-aside on potential "innocent" third parties had actually been calculated and found to be limited fairly.[117]

These limiting factors, plus his constitutional faith in the power of Congress to make findings, in its own way, to set the compensatory causal chain in motion, evidently led Justice Powell to accept an outcome fairly at odds with his *Bakke* version of compensatory causation. Never again, though, would this view of affirmative action, which he founded in *Bakke*, be in such disarray.

Though *Fullilove* has never been expressly overruled, its influence in federal set-aside cases has been strongly eroded. Justice Powell, for one, returned to his more rigorous formulation of the compensatory grounds for affirmative action in the next case.

JUSTICE POWELL'S VIEWS IN *WYGANT*

Causation and Remediation

Mr. Justice Powell, in his plurality opinion in *Wygant v. Jackson [, Michigan,]* *Board of Education,*[118] refined and perfected his theory of compensatory causation, leaving an impression that his concurrence in *Fullilove* was indeed something of a sport. For the first time he clearly identified two constitutional standards, compelling interest and "narrow tailoring," which—although touched upon before—were now cast as standards that must be satisfied with particularity in defending an affirmative action plan resting on racial or ethnic preferences.

The *Wygant* case took place in the context of a public school and its teacher employees, who were represented by a union and governed, vis-à-vis the school administration and themselves, by a collective bargaining agreement (CBA). The CBA had a provision designed to maintain a "racial balance" in the teacher workforce in the event of layoffs.[119] Layoffs became necessary. After protracted litigation by the union and minority teachers to force its adherence to the CBA, the Board followed the CBA and began to lay off some nonminority teachers "while minority teachers with less seniority were maintained."[120] Then the Board faced legal opposition from the other side of its workforce, when the displaced nonminority teachers brought a federal lawsuit pursuant to the Equal Protection Clause to stop the racial preferences in layoffs. The U.S. district court held for the Board. It found both that the Board did not need to justify its use of preferences through proof of specific acts of prior discrimination and that, instead, the compelling purpose for retaining more minority teachers than seniority alone would permit could be the need to remedy "societal discrimination" by providing " 'role models' " for minority schoolchildren.[121] The court of appeals affirmed.

Justice Powell first reaffirmed his "color-blind" approach to treatment of the races by stating that *all* individuals may suffer discrimination, whatever their past history, group affiliation, or physical characteristics.[122] He then launched an attack on the Board's claim to have followed a compelling purpose, based, as it were, on the construct of societal discrimination and its concomitant need to provide racially selected "role models" to alleviate the effects of such discrimination on minority pupils. "This Court never has held that societal discrimination alone is sufficient to justify a racial classification. Rather, the Court has insisted upon some showing of prior discrimination by the governmental unit in order to remedy such discrimination."[123] Justice Powell relied heavily on the Title VII systemic disparate treatment case of *Hazelwood School District v. United States,*[124] where—in a non–affirmative action case—the Court had held that the federal courts must rely on statistical evidence, as proof of intentional discrimination, only as generated from comparison of populations composed of the employer's workforce and the "qualified" portion of the general labor pool, each having the closest similarity to the other in skills and other work traits. The local labor market, a supposedly racially neutral mechanism for sorting workers into jobs matching their qualifications, is a classic logistic device. A comparison of the racial compositions of these otherwise similar groups—one inside, one outside the employer's employment—would yield proof of employment disparities, if any. These disparities, if measured within certain statistical levels of probability, would show the required "prior discrimination," interpretable as a dysfunction of the employer's workforce composition in relation to the labor market. More important, such a finding would serve as a causal basis for, and a *limitation on*, race-based remedies.[125] A finding of basis for limitation of the causal grounds or prior discrimination would be just as important as finding a basis for proof of the *existence* of discrimination itself. This *Hazelwood* doctrine provided an exemplar of demonstrating discrimination and its necessary causal basis.

Unlike his approval of the reasoning and results in *Hazelwood*, Justice Powell's opinion in *Wygant* condemned the role model theory as a kind of societal discrimination that "has *no logical stopping point*."[126] It had no "logical stopping point" because it could or would benefit persons who had not suffered harm (or benefit them out of proportion to the harm suffered), and it could or would harm "innocent" employees. Missing from his analysis, typically, was any sense of benefit or harm to society.

The societal discrimination rationale, with its role model remedy, failed, in Justice Powell's view, for the same reason that the Davis Medical School's plan for "reducing the historic deficit of traditionally favored disfavored minorities in medical schools"[127] failed: lack of causation, either concerning the very existence of prior discrimination or any limitation on the scope of its remedy. "[T]he role model theory does not necessarily bear a relationship to the harm caused by prior discriminatory practices."[128] There must be "evidentiary support" of specific discriminatory acts, and in the instant case, none was documented, despite the extensive litigation that both sides in the controversy initiated.[129] Thus, because no causal nexus could be shown with particularity between a definite wrongdoing affecting them and their beneficial layoff treatment, the minority teachers (through their school board) were not sheltered from strict constitutional scrutiny. Only a closely woven causal linkage can confer the compelling interest in compensation or remediation that provides such a shelter.[130]

Causal Intermediaries/Causal Chain Ending in the Victim

Interestingly, however, Justice Powell strongly intimated that the causal linkage tying wrongdoer to victim might have causal intermediaries. "Respondents also . . . argue that their purpose in adopting the layoff provision was to remedy *prior* discrimination against minorities by the Jackson School District in *hiring* teachers."[131] Minority teachers unlawfully not hired would necessarily not have been among the class of existing black teachers seeking relief and thus would have no direct causal linkage to that prior illegal act; yet the Board's action against the former could have had indirect deleterious effect on the latter. Subject to countervailing equal protection concerns and the existence of "convincing evidence that remedial action is warranted [*i.e.*, that prior discrimination affecting the prospective beneficiaries did occur through the initial job applicants as causal intermediaries] . . . race-conscious remedial action may be necessary."[132] While no such evidence was adduced here, the upshot is that "a voluntary affirmative action plan . . . implemented by a wrongdoer [*may* include] beneficiaries . . . *who are not actual victims.*"[133] Justice Powell in this respect followed (though not by design, of course) the moderately attenuated causal linkage theory of Robert Nozick for rectification;[134] but whether Justice Powell and Epstein are in conformity is very doubtful. For although Epstein develops some taste for accepting a causally compatible intervenor in the causal chain of tort actions,[135] his denunciation of Justice Brennan's having reached beneficiaries not directly harmed, in establishing an involuntary judicial decree for class-wide relief in *Sheet Metal Workers,*[136] seems quite conclusive on his nonacceptance of such causal compatibility in affirmative action.

"Innocent Victims"

Justice Powell's fashioning and application of the second constitutional prong, "narrow tailoring," turned on causation, to be sure, but more strongly on the principle of individualization. Here that principle manifests itself in respect for the dignity and worth for the individuals caught in compensatory measures brought down upon them without their individualized fault. These are the "innocent victims" (whites) who, not having committed voluntaristic acts in furtherance of racial discrimination, were (in the instant case) laid off because blacks junior in seniority were preferred and protected. Other cases, including *Fullilove*, had only *hiring* preferences[137]—where generally the most one might have to lose would be a comparatively uncertain opportunity for a job.

While hiring goals impose a diffuse burden, often foreclosing only one of several opportunities, layoffs impose the entire burden on particular individuals, often resulting in serious disruption of their lives. That burden is too intrusive [and therefore] is not sufficiently narrowly tailored[, because o]ther, less intrusive means of accomplishing similar purposes—such as the adoption of hiring goals—are available.[138]

Here Justice Powell establishes a deontological element of this theory—much as he established a deontological element in his theory of diversity by recognizing the participants as persons with strong, if not unconditional, rights of self-expression and self-realization.[139] While the rights of "innocent" persons are not absolute,[140] they are given so much weight that they probably protect persons in this position from subjection to a mere utilitarian calculus—crudely put, being laid off for the "good of the school." In this respect, these rights are, interestingly enough, more protective of the incumbent employee in the path of a program of corrective justice potentially destructive of his job than the protection pre-scribed by the most preeminent of contemporary libertarians, Robert Nozick. Nozick counsels that a doer of rectificatory justice need not concern himself with "violat[ing] [deontological] moral side constraints by applying the principle . . . of rectification . . . [unless he is a] [p]roponent of patterned conceptions of justice."[141] Since Justice Powell is hardly a proponent of patterned [or distrib-utive] justice or the wholesale redistribution of wealth,[142] it is hard to avoid the conclusion that his concerned solicitude for the rights of the unexceptional work-ers caught up in an exceptional situation is quite strong, perhaps too strong.

JUSTICE O'CONNOR'S EARLY VIEWS

Justice Sandra Day O'Connor made her debut in the affirmative action field in *Firefighters Local Union No. 1784 v. Stotts*,[143] with a concurrence in the Court's opinion and judgment that a district court's order modifying an affir-mative action consent decree—to protect the original purpose of the decree by shielding minority firefighters in a time of layoffs—was in violation of section 703(h) of Title VII[144] because it disrupted a bonafide seniority system and caused whites, whose generally longer seniority was protected under that system, to be laid off. Justice O'Connor agreed with the Court and, although in comments made on purely statutory issues, began to mark out her positions in later cases.

Even when its remedial powers are properly invoked, a district court may award pref-erential treatment only after carefully *balancing* the interests of the discrimantees [here, minority firemen], innocent employees, and the employer.[145]

To be sure . . . respondent[] [minority firemen] could have gone to trial and *established illegal discrimination in the [City's] past hiring practices*, identified its specific victims, and possibly obtained retroactive seniority for those individuals[, a step that would have avoided the effect of section 703(h)]. . . . But respondents did none [of this].[146]

Here she showed both her concern for identifying all the interests and their weight and her taste for exactitude and concreteness in the evidence.

Now in a case directly concerned with the constitutionality of affirmative action, Justice O'Connor joined most of Justice Powell's plurality opinion in *Wygant*. Settling on strict scrutiny as the proper standard of review under the Equal Protection Clause, she also agreed that "remedying 'societal' discrimi-nation, that is, discrimination not traceable to [the governmental agency's] own actions, cannot . . . pass constitutional muster [*i.e.*, serve as a compelling state interest]."[147] She pointed out, though, that requiring agencies to prove their il-legal past discrimination poses a very real hazard to them: exposure to civil liability under the antidiscrimination laws. This exposure would in turn deter them from engaging in affirmative action.[148] Thus public employers have the practical dilemma of avoiding "the competing hazards" of liability to minorities if affirmative action is *not* taken as a kind of defense to charges of discrimination, or to their white employees (under a color-blind standard of racial non-preference) when these employers act affirmatively to prefer minorities, without a sufficient causal basis in the past to justify discrimination against white workers. These risks are so great that she would not have increased them by requiring proof of contemporaneous discrimination,[149] lest these employers be exposed to overwhelming litigation risks.

Both following his doctrine and bending Justice Powell's thought to support her own course of thought, she characterized the quality and quantum of proof needed as a predicate for affirmative action as a *"firm basis* for determining that affirmative action is warranted." She used Justice Powell's example of statistically proven racial disparities in the *Hazelwood* case as one "reliable benchmark" for making this determination.[150] She noted a final safeguard for protecting the employer from liability for unwarranted affirmative action: the allocation of the burdens of proof. Plaintiffs (*i.e.*, white attackers of the plan) would have the initial burden of production and the ultimate burden of persuasion.[151] The employer need only meet a burden of production ("a firm basis"), while the attackers must offer a preponderance of the evidence that the plan is invalid.[152] This meticulous care in looking at the corners of Justice Powell's plan, and rounding them off (here, by showing how public employers can be left in a bind and how to get them out of it), is typical of Justice O'Connor's approach to logistic.[153] Thus at this early stage of her attention to this subject, she firmly committed herself to the elements of corrective justice, mechanistic causation, precision in proof, and an equal protection of the laws that is kept color-blind through strict scrutiny—all elements of logistic that she later led the Court in formulating more firmly and precisely.

INTERLUDE: AFFIRMATIVE ACTION AS ATONEMENT FOR SIN

This is a good place to make an interlude in the case analyses, because it marks the end of Justice Powell's major contributions to the theory of compensatory causation and the beginnings of Justice O'Connor's. Kathleen Sullivan at this very time (1986) wrote an insightful article using the powerful religious metaphors of sin, penance, and atonement to characterize the prevailing Court rationale for affirmative action.[154]

[T]he Court has approved affirmative action only as a precise *penance* for the specific *sins* of racism a government, union, or employer has committed in the past. Not surprisingly, this has invited claims, such as the Solicitor's last term, that nonsinners [nonsinners?]—white workers "innocent" of their bosses' . . . past discrimination—should not pay for the "sins" of others of their own race, nor should nonvictims benefit from their sacrifice. The Court has never answered these claims from within a *sin*-based paradigm, as it might have either by viewing the category of black "victims" of past discrimination expansively [through "societal discrimination"] or by discounting claims of white "innocence." But neither has the Court ever broken out of *sin*-based rationales to elaborate a paradigm that would look forward rather than back, justifying affirmative action as *the architecture of a racially integrated future.*[155]

Of course, the Court has failed to limit relief to direct or actual victims in *Sheet Metal Workers* and two other cases.[156] Professor Sullivan would surely point beyond these cases and their implications about the causal range of "sin" and emphasize rather that it was only *fortuitous* probabilities operating in two of them, at least, that linked the ultimate beneficiaries to definite, prior wrongdoing. Corrective justice, as "atone[ment]" for sin, by employers or unions for past discrimination,[157] is all well and good, but its reasons and rationale based on "sin" are not enough for her to build an "architecture of a racially integrated future."[158] The causation that goes with this version of sin is also too flimsy, too much dependent on chance for her taste. The real problem, however, may lie in Sullivan's conception of sin *itself* (or the conception that she attributes to the Court and against which she is ultimately combative), a conception as singularly logistic as it is misdescriptive of the human predicament (from the dialectical mode of thought, as stated by Paul Tillich):

If one speaks of "sins" and refers to special acts which are considered sinful, one should always be conscious of the fact that "sins" are the expression of "sin." It is not the disobedience to a law which makes an act sinful but the fact that it is an expression of man's estrangement from God, from men, and from himself.[159]

It seems as if Professor Sullivan, because her critical view contains an unduly cramped version of "sin," has failed therefore to adopt a more comprehensive view of "sin" as the occasion of racial discrimination. Indeed she did not. She herself stated, "Casting affirmative action as penance for particular sins of discrimination . . . has appeal at first glance. Limiting [the application of] affirmative action to those [employers, unions, *etc.*] who have specifically wronged blacks or other racial minorities in the past steers neatly between two courses: that all must pay or none."[160] The prevailing view of the Court, she claims, "rejects any notion that the original sin of American slavery so taints everyone in our current society" that affirmative action would be justified: "But [the Court] likewise rejects the notion that all must be equally absolved."[161] Thus *some* employers and white workers (but not all) will be required to "atone" for injustices of the past through affirmative action. This situation leads, however, to all the judicially created terms and distinctions that Sullivan so dislikes: They include terms such as "innocent third parties," "actual victims," and the like. These terms carry the imagery of measured responses to sin and reflect the decidedly constricted view that there are shades of difference in "the extent of personal participation and guilt in a [single] sinful act [that require] weighing the differences in guilt. . . . [From another perspective t]here is only 'the Sin,' the turning away from God, and from 'the Grace,' or reunion with God."[162] Judicial decisions alluding to sin—viewed from Professor Sullivan's perspective—become a hindrance to affirmative action because they remain focused on that aspect that, ironically, *she* remains focused on (at least in her understanding of sin): matching remedies to the degree of preceived wrongdoing or sin. No one pays attention to sin spread through society.

In a final section entitled "Alternatives to Sin"[163] Professor Sullivan argues for "different forward-looking reasons for affirmative action."[164] She quotes Justice Stevens's dissent in *Wygant* approvingly for supporting the proposition that heavy white teachers' support for the layoff provision through their union should have been grounds to blunt these white teachers' later legal attack on the integration and retention of black teachers. The white teachers had suffered, at most, "benign" discrimination—discrimination without animus. Indeed, they had participated democratically in the very decision that had adversely affected them. Thus "as Justice Stevens stated and no Justice disputed, the white teachers' layoff[s] [were] *'not based on any lack of respect for their race, or on blind habit and stereotype.'* "[165]

By opting for this position, Professor Sullivan drops her metaphorical references to sin and looks toward a vision of future race relations to be devised apart from a rationale attached specifically to wrongdoing through racial animus. By doing so, she begins to reveal that she has had no genuine place for "sin" at all, other than as a trope or metaphorical placeholder. It was a rhetorical device to attack the particularistic kind of causation that I have called endemic to the logistic approach. The conception of "benign" discrimination, which is part of her forward-looking approach, is also designed to break free from the bondage of sin, whether perceived metaphorically or as bondage to the past.

The last question thus to be asked about Ms. Sullivan's article on sin is whether she has read the concept of sin and atonement therefore altogether out of her own resolution of the problem posed by affirmative action. For many liberals, of whom she seems to count herself one, believe that sin can be avoided through exercise of an uncorrupted power of decision between good and evil— in this context, the power to avoid racial animus. "Here . . . we are speaking only of the propensity [not predisposition] to genuine evil, that is, moral evil; for . . . such evil is possible only as a determination of the free will [*i.e.*, by decision or choice]."[166] Thus Kant states the position that we can choose against sin. This would seem to be Ms. Sullivan's position: that one is truly free to avoid dealing with evil, *i.e.*, free not to reintroduce the old racial problem of past guilt into contemporaneous, forward-looking solutions. But Reinhold Niebuhr has stated that we are not so free to choose:

Sin is to be regarded as neither a necessity of man's nature nor yet as a pure caprice of his will, for which reason *it is not completely deliberate*; but since it is the will in which the defect is found and the will presupposes freedom the defect cannot be attributed to a taint in man's nature.[167]

Professor Sullivan is surely not an adherent of the logistic, mechanistic view of sin, which she invented for her rhetorical purposes but which may actually represent the popular notion of sin's "workings." Sin is a more comprehensive concept, as affirmed in the quotations from the two great dialectical theologians Paul Tillich and Reinhold Niebuhr. On their views, both of which have their roots in Saint Augustine, sin is a pervasive condition of human estrangement that arises neither from choice nor necessity and yet stains human kind with guilt. Professor Sullivan rejects this comprehensive view of sin as well, intellectually if not morally and spiritually. By so doing, she unfortunately impoverishes a means to explain the working out of racial justice through an understanding of society that has depth and insight into the human predicament. Affirmative action then need not be bottomed on the belief that guilt for racism is divisible.

Rather, Professor Sullivan has taken the position that I pluck from Kant: "[S]uch evil [sin] is possible only as a determination of the free will [and thus can be avoided by rational creatures]."[168] This certainly places her in esteemed company but also excises the possibility of a powerful extension of her metaphor to include an understanding of sin that includes suffering to overcome guilt and estrangement. This rejected understanding is one in which affirmative action becomes the symbolic (and perhaps actual) expiation for the tragic and unavoidable guilt for racial injustices of the past and present.

Seen in this light, there are no "innocent victims" because racial discrimination is a comprehensive evil that has stained society as a whole and can only be rectified through the unavoidable suffering of the many and not only of a few. Professor Sullivan is implicitly correct to the extent that her argument excudes expiation of sin from the views of Justices Powell and O'Connor that might justify affirmative action. To the end of carrying through my explanation of the prevailing view that Professor Sullivan and I both attack from somewhat, but not entirely, different angles, I return to the developing thought of Justice O'Connor.

JUSTICE O'CONNOR AND THE TURNING POINT: *CITY OF RICHMOND V. J. A. CROSON CO.*

In 1989 Justice O'Connor and the Court were faced with deciding whether the city of Richmond, Virginia, was justified in imposing an affirmative action plan on its "public contracting market."[169] In *J. A. Croson*[170] the Richmond City Council, relying heavily on the similar federal affirmative action plan approved in *Fullilove v. Klutznick,*[171] voted a thirty percent set-aside of the aggregate dollar amount of the city's contracting awards to minority business enterprises (MBEs). Demographic statistics stood at the center of the controversy:

Proponents of the set-aside provision relied on a study which indicated that, while the general population of Richmond was 50% black, only 0.67% of the city's prime construction contracts had been awarded to minority businesses in the 5-year period from 1978 to 1983. It was also established that a variety of contractors' associations, whose representatives appeared in opposition to the ordinance, had virtually no minority businesses within their membership.[172]

Justice O'Connor thrust aside *Fullilove*—largely because in it the Court had relied on unique *federal* power under section 5 of the Fourteenth Amendment requiring the Court to grant " 'appropriate deference to Congress' " without the more demanding and specific findings needed by " '*other* governmental entities before undertaking race-conscious measures,' "[173] She put this case, which turned on the validity of municipal (and thus state) power, on standards of proof and review that considerably exceeded those in *Fullilove*. She thus formulated grounds for belief that congressionally created affirmative action plans were more easily justified.

Requirements of Proof of a Sufficient Causal Relation between the Initial Discrimination and Compensation

Justice O'Connor wrote an opinion (not always for a majority of the Court) that affirms practically every major tenet that logistic and compensatory causation have to offer. The heart of her reasoning lies, it seems to me, in Part III B, when she was writing for the Court and using statistical analysis from Title VII cases to make her point. In the absence of any appreciable direct evidence,[174] she was obliged to consider, as a null hypothesis implicitly adapted from the *Teamsters* case, that "[t]he [city's] theory of discrimination was simply that the [city, in earlier times], in violation of [the Equal Protection Clause], regularly and purposefully treated Negro [contract bidders] less favorably than white persons."[175] Justice O'Connor directed her attention, however, to the methodologically different systemic disparate treatment case of *Hazelwood*,[176] which shifts the basis for identifying minority workers and persons in the general population, for comparison with the workforce, from the *un*skilled, as in *Teamsters*, to the smaller and more select group of the skilled, as in *Hazelwood*.[177] This shift ultimately made it possible for her to reject the city's implicit hypothesis and contention of past discrimination by focusing her attention away from the very large black population of the entire city (fifty percent) as the appropriate comparison group and onto instead the select group of fully qualified MBEs.

The *Hazelwood* approach employed is an outgrowth of the classic logistic mechanism of the market. Here in *J. A. Croson* Justice O'Connor assumed the assignment of contracts to prime contractors and subcontractors through a market that is neutral as to race and that takes into account only proper qualifications vis-à-vis the bidding process.[178]

Accordingly, her application of the law and statistical assumptions from Title VII—together with her reliance on the premise of a neutral market mechanism described above—enabled Justice O'Connor to hold that "[r]eliance on the disparity between the number of prime contracts awarded to minority firms [0.67 percent] and the minority population of Richmond [50 percent] is . . . misplaced."[179] Because only special qualifications to be contractors and not discrimination against minorities in the labor pool at large (comparable to societal discrimination) were, in her view, at issue, the general population could not be "the relevant statistical pool for purposes of demonstrating discriminatory exclusion."[180] "The city does not even know how many MBE's in the relevant market are qualified to undertake prime or subcontracting in public construction projects."[181] Thus Richmond had only conclusory evidence at best to support its putative remedial action of affirmative action and could not meet Justice Powell's standard of review in *Wygant* of a "strong basis in evidence for its conclusion that remedial action was necessary."[182] The implicit null hypothesis of prior or even contemporaneous discrimination was rejected. Even if the city had used the correct comparison group and not its general population, there was no evidence of a statistically significant disparity between minority contractors whose bids were accepted and the percentage of qualified minority contractors passed over.

It is noteworthy that Justice O'Connor traces the present effects of antecedent causes of discrimination only to direct victims. Generally these may be considered to be the inchoate group of qualified black managers and workers (if any) who had not been awarded contracts through the system. Not only does she not look for or recognize contiguity between multiple, temporally linked subjects of harm in a causal chain begun by an original cause of harm, but—and this is the nub—she also apparently sees no causal linkage between any antecedent "actual" or direct victims in the past and related successors entitled to relief in the present. She does not look for any causes *behind* the low numbers of qualified minority contractors in the Richmond market. She is interested in only one layer or stratum of causation; how or why that contemporaneous layer has come to be as it is, through several layers of causation, is not part of her calculus. " [A] generalized assertion that there has been past discrimination in an entire industry provides no guidance . . . to determine the *precise scope* of the injury it seeks to remedy. It 'has no logical stopping point.' "[183] In other words, generalized causation could extend backwards or forwards through time with a potential infinity of wrongdoers or victims, but it would not be actionable.

In contrast, however, the social causation approach does look for the causes of the causes, and it *does* so in a broad way to include even the role of the government in promoting discrimination. Justice Marshall, dissenting in *J. A. Croson*, explained:

In my view, the interest in ensuring that the government does not reflect and reinforce prior private discrimination in dispensing public contracts is every bit as strong as the interest in eliminating private discrimination. . . . The more government bestows its rewards on those persons or businesses that were positioned to thrive during a period of private racial discrimination, the tighter the deadhand grip of prior discrimination becomes on the present and future.[184]

This is the position that Justice O'Connor is dead set against.

Passively Extending the Causal Reach of Logistic—A Unique Cause?

Justice O'Connor, however, did make a concession to lengthening the causal chain between wrongdoer and victim—from a linkage forged temporally *behind* or *next to* the putative original, active wrongdoer, not from a causal extension of that wrongdoer's action temporally *beyond* the first actual victim.

[I]f the city could show that it had become a "passive participant" in system of racial exclusion practiced by elements of the local construction industry [the active wrongdoer], we think it clear that the city could take affirmative steps to dismantle such a system. It is beyond dispute that any public entity, state or federal, has a compelling interest in assuring that public dollars . . . do not serve to finance the evil of private prejudice.[185]

Justice Marshall, of course, would have found such a connection, involving use of the municipal fisc, between the city and the predominantly white contracting industry to be an *active* causal promotion of a privately discriminatory contracting market.[186] Justice O'Connor evidently saw the matter from the other direction. Because there were no documented and probative *Hazelwood* disparities between the actual percentage of MBEs under contract and the percentage of MBEs that qualified minority persons could form to become acceptable subcontractors, she found no harm and thus saw no need to probe the causal relations of the city and the majority contractors.[187]

One commentator finds this move by Justice O'Connor to be a causal innovation, because the causal chain can originate with a putative nonwrongdoer that meets certain conditions—here, dispensations or appropriations from the fisc under color of law, in tandem with a second, active or actual wrongdoer. This view is said to differ from Justice Powell's because he required causation to originate, and affirmative action to issue, from one wrongdoer *simpliciter*.[188] This same commentator also finds that Justice O'Connor has even, by this "passive" connection, opened the door to the possibility of distributive justice—beyond compensatory justice.[189]

But did Justice O'Connor truly recognize a new or even unique cause, leading to a difference in the kind of justice it demands, or did she simply extend the causal chain, when her view is combined with Justice Powell's idea that causation can pass among victims (and even nonvictims)?[190] Logistic frowns on the idea of unique causation,[191] because causes are nothing more than the universally perceived regular connections among simples.

The first time a man saw the communication of motion by impulse, as by the shock of two billiard-balls, he could not pronounce that the one event was *connected*: but only that it was *conjoined* with the other.... [Thus] [i]n all single instances of the operations of bodies or minds, there is nothing that produces any ... idea of power or necessary connexion. But when many uniform instances appear, and the same object is always followed by the same event; we then begin to entertain the notion of cause and connexion.[192]

One can see the difference between Justice O'Connor's reaction to causal transmission in a case like *Sheet Metal Workers* and in *J. A. Croson*. In the former a court-ordered remedy imposed "racial preferences in employment to individuals who have not been subjected to unlawful discrimination."[193] There was no contiguity or logistic connection in the mind between those persons—the "non-victims"—and the union wrongdoer; and she accordingly opposed relief to them.

But in *J. A. Croson* the possibility of a connection between the city's spending of its funds and a whole industry financed through this fiscal activity was more than the onetime "shock of two billiard-balls"—it had already been established by the Court that governmental units may not evade direct constitutional restraints "[by] induc[ing] ... private persons to accomplish what [the governmental unit] is constitutionally forbidden to accomplish."[194]

In this latter context—reinforced by an earlier opinion of the Court—an impression of such force and vivacity may readily arise, suggesting a vividly corrupt connection between city funding and private discrimination; and the concept of a "passive" city participant would not diminish this vivacity. Passivity in a city government may be likened to a cue ball (or other ball on the table) struck in such a way to produce motion in others while itself remaining (apparently) motionless. No one familiar with gaming at billiards or pool will likely deny that there are such "motionless" causes of motion demonstrated in almost every game. Thus arguably Justice O'Connor has invented nothing unique; her *passive* city officials will simply join the causal chain in the most regular way, leading to the uniformity of perception of Richmond or other cities as causal agents in the chain of causation. Nor does this result conflict with her opinion in *Sheet Metal Workers*, because here the connection is between two indisputed wrong-doers (one active and one passive), and their connection meets the logistic test of causation.

Renewed Emphasis on the Individual

Interestingly this case is an instance in which logistic uses the relation between large aggregate bodies to reach conclusions about causation and the requirement of past discrimination. But the statistical aggregates remain just that—large collections of individuals, collections that are constructed through principles of logic and that have no organic character. Certainly the small percentage of MBEs in the general population, and their inchoate parallel business organizations, did not form an organized community with a genuine history as the city of Richmond itself did. The use of statistics, furthermore, did not change the Court's "view[] of racial discrimination as if it were simply a matter of individual harm."[195] In *J. A. Croson* Justice O'Connor, writing now for a plurality, once again emphasized the logistic position that the rights protected in these cases are those of "the individual."[196] Moreover, she reemphasized that review "under the Equal Protection Clause is not dependent on the race of those benefited"[197]—thus confirming that the theories of individualism and of the so-called color-blind constitution operate in tandem. Finally a large part of her affinity for the individual approach to understanding racial discrimination and her adverseness to group understandings lay in her fear that the latter has in it the roots of serious social conflict. "Classifications based on race carry a danger of stigmatic harm [that] may in fact promote notions of racial inferiority and lead to politics of racial hostility."[198] Thus the inevitable focus on the individual.

Revision of the Standard of Review to Include a *"Prima Facie Case"* and Its Chilling Effect

In her separate opinion in *Wygant*, Justice O'Connor had propounded a standard of a "firm basis for determining that affirmative action is warranted," as the quality and quantum of proof required of an employer of its own prior discrimination, to meet its burden of production as a defendant/respondent.[199] The upshot of her reasoning there seemed to have been the need for a flexible standard to protect an employer considering affirmative action from a litigation whipsaw between minorities seeking relief from a dearth of jobs for themselves and their comrades in the workforce and employees, predominantly white males, pursuing a cause of action for "reverse discrimination."[200] Now she refined her standard for the allocation of the burden of proof and her seeming purpose for it with this pregnant statement: "There is nothing approaching *a prima facie case* of a constitutional or statutory violation by anyone in the Richmond construction industry."[201] A virtual showing of evidence of a *prima facie* case of straightforward discrimination against minorities under Title VII or the Fourteenth Amendment thus became what an employer, public school, *etc.*, would have to adduce, in effect, *against itself* as its burden of production to rebut white workers' initial proof of "reverse discrimination" against them.[202] With the standard of proof revised to this more definite level—from "a firm basis," without explanation for the change—more state and local government employers would quite arguably be deterred from initiating affirmative action. Such employers would be faced with a dilemma: lest they be sued *first* by minority workers (because a *prima facie* case of discrimination against them could materialize before an affirmative action program settles in place), or lest they be successfully sued by white workers because they (the employers) were not able to prove the requisite level of discrimination against minorities.

Strict Scrutiny and "Smoking Out" Impermissible Racial Classifications

The *prima facie* case standard of allocating the burdens of proof is designed to meet the compelling-interest component of the standard of review of strict scrutiny. Strict scrutiny imposes the strongest constitutional presumption against the validity of a legal phenomenon—here a facially racial classification (normally construed against whites, but here against minorities under the color-blind standard). Strict scrutiny tends to reinforce emphasis on the individual by "smok[ing] out . . . what classifications are in fact motivated by illegitimate notions of racial inferiority [presumably to protect blacks[203]] or simple racial politics [presumably all races, but needed in this case to protect whites]."[204] Strict scrutiny also includes the concept of a close "fit" or narrow tailoring to assure that the remedy justified by the compelling interest presents "little or no possibility that the motive for the classification was illegitimate racial prejudice or stereotype."[205]

The sum total of *J. A. Croson*'s parts (as written by Justice O'Connor) places an exacting justification on the creation of any affirmative action plan. The state or city must be able to demonstrate past, identifiable discrimination involving *individuals*—who, at least in principle, must normally have features distinguishing them from the general minority population, features that must frequently show merit, initiative, or special qualifications. That nonfederal unit of government must show a short, plain causal nexus between antecedent discrimination and consequent injury. Strict scrutiny encompasses all this, and more.

Yet Justice O'Connor could say: "Nothing we say today precludes a state or local entity from taking action to rectify the effects of identified discrimination [in a case such as this, if the city had shown] a significant statistical disparity between the number of qualified minority contractors . . . and the number of such contractors actually engaged by the locality or the locality's prime contractors."[206] In these circumstances the city might have taken some limited group-based action—"some form of narrowly tailored racial preference . . . necessary to break down patterns of deliberate exclusion."[207] Such an approach would have operated to create hiring *goals* and not *quotas*. Even so, were no group- or aggregate-based discrimination found, Justice O'Connor noted that ample avenues of relief are available for minority *individuals*, whether they had been victims of discrimination or not.[208] The danger is that, otherwise, "the deviation from the norm . . . to assure all citizens . . . of equal treatment [will deteriorate into] unthinking stereotypes or a form of racial politics."[209] Her strong insistence on not unnecessarily classifying on the basis of race, with emphasis on the individual as the ultimate locus of racial justice, has—however—been presented in a more strident, extreme sense by another member of the Court.

JUSTICE SCALIA'S STERNER STANDARDS

Justice Scalia has embraced a more draconian form of logistic in his view of affirmative action. His view normally envisages a greatly attenuated causal connection between racial wrongdoing and injury in a broadly societal setting. Thus relief in the form of affirmative action would only rarely—if ever—be appropriate. "[O]nly a social emergency rising to the imminent danger to life and limb—for example, a prison race riot, requiring temporary segregation of inmates" can justify such broad, group-based racial classifications.[210] The only exception to this rule exists where the government itself has maintained past discrimination in public institutions, such as in the public schools, and now may act by racial classification to eradicate the present effects of that past officially sanctioned segregation or other discrimination.[211] Justice Scalia would therefore make the granting of affirmative relief turn on necessity itself and not on a balanced allocation of burdens of proof that would allow an employer or a university to rebut charges of "reverse discrimination" brought by disgruntled whites.[212]

In fact, Justice Scalia evidently views the mode of individual disparate treatment from Title VII cases and their analogues under equal protection as the only truly justified mode of relief from racial injustice. "In my view, government can never have a 'compelling interest' in discriminating on the basis of race in order to 'make up' for past racial discrimination in the opposite direction. . . . *Individuals who have been wronged should be made whole*; but under our constitution there can be no such thing as a creditor or debtor race."[213] Thus he has opposed "racial or sexual discrimination [through affirmative action, which] is [wrongfully] permitted under Title VII when it is intended to overcome the effect, not of the employer's own discrimination [found largely in individual disparate treatment cases], but of societal attitudes [against certain races or a particular gender]."[214]

Justice Scalia placed his stamp on the law of employment discrimination in the Title VII individual disparate treatment case of *St. Mary's Honor Center v. Hicks*.[215] While letting stand an individual's right to recover for racial discrimination, the Justice, in a measure opposed by four dissenters, adjusted the allocation of the burdens of proof to make it harder for a plaintiff to prevail, while expressing in dictum his view of the illusory and misleading evidence commonly offered for racial discrimination.[216] So there is considerable similarity between the views of Justice Scalia and his former colleague at the University of Chicago, Richard Epstein. Both have very strict views requiring direct or largely unmediated causation between wrongdoer and victim, both believe that such causation is seldom (or never) found in a form permitting broad group racial classification by organs of the government, both believe in the primacy of the individual over group dynamics, and both view force as a preeminent factor in shaping legal and social relations. The principal difference is that Justice Scalia accepts the fact that racial discrimination can embody force, *ipso facto* because it can cause harm requiring legal compensation. Epstein, of course, has denied this connection between discrimination and force.[217] Justice Scalia would permit redress in limited circumstances of direct harm, mostly to individuals, but no affirmative action.

FINAL ISSUES IN *J. A. CROSON*

Kathleen Sullivan, skeptical of Justice O'Connor's assurances that affirmative action *is* permissible with the proper proof, has suggested that *J. A. Croson* is symptomatic of a "societal backlash . . . against affirmative action . . . that . . . has touched the Supreme Court."[218] "*Croson* culminated the Court's long-mounting trend toward limiting the justification for affirmative action to a narrow band of corrective justice . . . [needed] to root out the identified sins of the past."[219] This assessment descriptively fits the logistic approach and its two champions selected for their usefulness in analyzing affirmative action: Robert Nozick and Richard Epstein. What *J. A. Croson*, surprisingly perhaps, left unsettled was the standard of review, under the equal protection component of the Fifth Amendment, for congressionally enacted affirmative action programs.[220] Only a year before *Metro Broadcasting*,[221] which had given majority approval to intermediate scrutiny for federal programs, the *J. A. Croson* Court, in a plurality opinion penned by Justice O'Connor, had vacillated on this point by failing to close up this seeming exception to strict scrutiny—indeed, by even seeming to legitimize a lower, intermediate standard for federal set-aside programs by extensive reference to section 5 of the Fourteenth Amendment, the peculiarly congressional enforcement provision included in the amendment.[222]

ADARAND AND UNIFORMITY IN THE STANDARD OF REVIEW

Unlike *J. A. Croson, Adarand Constructors, Inc. v. Peña*[223] concerned an affirmative action program, using subsidies to improve the bids of minority bidders and aimed at *federal* subcontractors. A substantial part of the program was aimed at " '[t]he Government-wide goal for participation by small business concerns owned and controlled by *socially and economically disadvantaged individuals*' at 'not less than 5 percent of the total value of all prime contract and subcontract awards for each fiscal year.' "[224] But most federal agency contracts contained the rebuttable presumption that racial and ethnic minorities *were* such disadvantaged individuals.[225] Adarand Constructors was a majority-owned highway subcontractor, which—having submitted a low bid on guardrail work—nonetheless lost the job to a minority subcontractor whose higher bid was offset by an additional subsidy payment to the prime contractor from the government.[226] Adarand thereupon sued the U.S. Secretary of Transportation.

Justice O'Connor, now speaking for the Court on all issues, once again rejected the distinction between racially " 'benign' " classifications and those

" 'motivated by illegitimate notions of racial inferiority or simple racial politics.' "[227] A lower standard of review against such "benign" discrimination would flout the

> basic principle that the Fifth and Fourteenth Amendments protect *persons*, not *groups*. It follows from that principle that all government action on race—a *group* classification long recognized as "in most circumstances irrelevant and therefore prohibited"[—] should be subjected to detailed judicial inquiry that the *personal* right to equal protection of the laws has not been infringed.... [H]olding benign ... state and federal racial classifications to different [intermediate] standards does not square with [equal protection].[228]

Finally, Justice O'Connor added a postscript: "[W]e wish to dispel the notion that strict scrutiny is 'strict in theory, but fatal in fact.' ... The unhappy persistence of both the practice and lingering effects of racial discrimination against minority groups in this country is an unfortunate reality, and government is not disqualified from acting in response to it."[229]

The latter statement mirrored her assurance at the end of her opinion in *J. A. Croson* that "a state or local entity [is not] precluded from taking action to rectify the effects of discrimination."[230]

In the arena of higher education this promise of the availability of logistic racial justice had already been tested at the University of Maryland and was about to be tested at the University of Texas in a case, *Hopwood*, that caused much anguish nationwide to believers in the power of affirmative action to assuage racial suffering.

PODBERESKY AND *HOPWOOD:* THE LOWER COURTS TIGHTEN CAUSATION

The U.S. Court of Appeals for the Fourth Circuit, in *Podberesky v. Kirwan, President of the University of Maryland at College Park*,[231] used a strict interpretation of *J. A. Croson* and its line of cases to rule unconstitutional a program of scholarships limited to black students "as a partial remedy for past discriminatory action by the University of Maryland."[232] The court purported to follow *J. A. Croson* to find that there were no continuing effects palpably caused by the claimed past discrimination.[233] The nub of the court's argument was that there must be a " 'strong basis in evidence' "[234] of past discrimination, properly documented and linked to present discriminatory effects (if any), as well as the same evidentiary basis to support the efficacy of the proposed remedy for addressing them—all by the most exacting standards of causation.[235]

Under this standard the university's efforts to use the scholarship program to improve and alter the racial environment on its campus failed. The court of appeals found the connection between improvement of the university's *reputation among blacks* and its past practices to be ethereal. De facto segregation at the university had been declared ended in 1970, and such racial incidents as existed in the present could not necessarily be attributed to past and causally spent discrimination on the part of the university, as distinguished from any causal influence of present societal discrimination (which, of course, would not serve as supporting proof, either).[236] The university's further claim of justification, to be using the scholarship program to improve the underrepresentation of black students in its student body, foundered on similar considerations. The court, following *J. A. Croson*'s teaching "that the selection of the correct reference pool [for statistical analysis and comparison] is critical,"[237] denied that the university's goal of improving minority representation could justify lowering "the effective minimum criteria needed to determine the applicant pool [because, in part] any intergenerational effects of segregated education are the product of societal discrimination."[238] The disqualification of "intergenerational effects" as an admissions enhancement meant that the university could not take into account the fact that a minority applicant might be disadvantaged because he was the latest link in a causal chain reaching into the past, through which his parents and ancestors had passed on the effects of educational discrimination. The implication is that discrimination can live through one life span only.

The remainder of the second *Podberesky* opinion largely uses the narrow-tailoring prong of the strict scrutiny standard of review to reinforce its insistence on exact causation.[239] The *Podberesky* case thus takes logistic standards and uses them to restrict dramatically and mechanistically what an institution of higher learning can do to improve its relations with minority students. In this case, for example, the Office of Civil Rights (OCR) of the (presently denominated) U.S. Department of Education notified the entire State of Maryland in 1969 that it was grossly in violation of Title VI[240] (though the university itself was not subjected to formal proceedings). Since then the state and OCR had mutually pursued plans and means to eliminate the vestiges of segregation in postsecondary education—through discussions that included the university and, at times, references to its black scholarship program.[241] The court of appeals rejected the OCR's findings of past discrimination, perhaps because it believed that the kind of discrimination documented by OCR was not the kind needed specifically ("narrowly tailored") to support the black scholarship program and its outreach and remedial purposes.[242] As the Fourth Circuit claimed to demonstrate in its second opinion, "[T]he district court did not sufficiently connect the problems the University purports to remedy to the [black scholarship p]rogram."[243]

This situation is typical for the entire standard of review in this case and not simply for the portion discussed above. Here judicial practitioners of logistic have managed to break the simples of that mode of thought into even smaller and smaller parts; and they now demand a causal analysis of greater precision than ever before—linking the most discrete events occurring in the recent past at the university, through exact cause, to the most closely related and pulverized phenomena about racism now coming to light at the university.

The U.S. Court of Appeals for the Fifth Circuit, in *Hopwood v. Texas*,[244] followed and even tightened the *Podberesky* conception of exact causation, in emphatically rejecting the remedial justification[245] set out by the University of Texas Law School for its affirmative action program. The parallels between *Podberesky* and *Hopwood* are striking: The State of Texas had entered into a consent decree with the U.S. Department of Education in 1983, a decree that provided for minority recruitment subject to federal oversight;[246] and the district court found that Texas had a "long history of racially discriminatory practices . . . in the not-too-distant past . . . in its primary and secondary schools" that had certain deleterious effects in the present—a bad reputation of the Law School with minorities as a "white" school, underrepresentation of minorities in the student body, and a public perception that the school was a "hostile" environment for minorities.[247] As a result it found that the Law School's admissions program gave separate and preferential remedial treatment to minorities.[248] The district court upheld the Law School's affirmative action program from equal protection attack because, in its view, the record of minority discrimination in Texas education and its present effects at the Law School supported and composed a compelling interest for the remedial program.[249] The Fifth Circuit, in a decision that has dramatically altered the prospects for affirmative action in untold institutions of higher education, not only in the states of the Fifth Circuit but all over the nation, reversed.[250]

Quoting from *Wygant* that there must be " 'some showing of prior discrimination involved before allowing limited use of racial classifications in order to remedy such discrimination,' "[251] the panel held that the discrimination relied upon by Texas and its university's Law School was too weak, attenuated, and unfocused to justify the program, even if the appropriate governmental unit for collecting past data were not the school (as was really, in the court's view, the case) but the state instead. *J. A. Croson* and *Wygant* controlled, with a strong nod to *Podberesky* as well.

[W]e conclude that the district court erred in expanding the remedial justification to reach all public education in the State of Texas. The Supreme Court repeatedly has warned that use of racial remedies must be carefully limited, and a remedy reaching all education within a state addresses a putative injury that is vague and amorphous. It has "no logical stopping point."[252]

Thus the court's parry to the Law School's case was causation: No train of causation acceptable to the court could connect the deficient state of public education for minorities in Texas to the dearth of their numbers in the state's flagship public university and its Law School.

That a deplorable disparity existed in Texas between whites or so-called Anglos, on the one hand, and blacks and Hispanics, on the other, is hardly open to serious dispute. As I have alluded to, the Office of Civil Rights of the U.S. Department of Education had been monitoring deficiencies in Texas public education, including higher education, for some time.[253] Other evidence of race and ethnic disparity abounds. In *San Antonio ISD v. Rodriguez,*[254] the state made no serious effort to deny enormous gaps in the public funding of geographically distinct and racially and ethnically disparate school districts; and in *Plyer v. Doe*[255] the Supreme Court struck down restrictions that barred undocumented resident alien children (mostly Mexican and Central American) from attending the public schools. Finally, protracted litigation in the state courts, directed at something known derisively as the "Robin Hood" plan (to equalize school funding), has featured for years a struggle about these fiscal disparities—a struggle that all knew had strong overtones about the levels and layers of racial and ethnic discrimination in the schools.[256]

The court of appeals, borrowing from the *Podberesky* case, set out a strict standard of proof: " 'To have a present effect of past discrimination sufficient to justify the program, the party seeking to implement the program must, at a minimum, prove that the effect it proffers is caused by the past discrimination and that the effect is of sufficient magnitude to justify the program.' "[257] Can this formulation and its repercussions state a valid and believable standard for causation in these cases, judging from both the philosophical figures analyzed and particularly from the precedents provided in key Supreme Court cases? The answer is plainly no—it denies ordinary and strong perceptions of causation previously accepted as the basis for logistic.

The Fourth and Fifth Circuits deny that "[a]ny thing may produce any thing,"[258]—the basic tenet of universal causation found in logistic[259]—by making many distinctions between the efficacious and ineffective sources of causative harm.[260] Thus they deny the effect of deficient public school education but allow for closely related and highly similar effects in the university and particularly at its Law School. They further disregarded the causal import disclosed in the Humean statement that "the shock of two billiard-balls" does not, at its first instance, allow us to "*infer* one [ball's being struck] even from another['s]: [but] we are enabled to do so at present, after so long a course of *uniform experience.*"[261] Certainly, evidence has been adduced of so many instances of the poor education (through state institutions) of younger minority students that it is "customary" in Hume's epistemological sense to ascribe a cause and effect relation between this antecedent condition and their—the students'—consequent efforts to enter the state's elite schools.

If there is not a powerful direct causal connection by which minorities' preparatory education and entrance levels can be *intuitively* grasped, there are certainly ways to demonstrate causal chains from the past discrimination against them and the present effects of that discrimination, legally required as proof, needing remediation. Robert Nozick has demonstrated that an injustice perpetrated anywhere, upon anyone in the chain of acquisition, may be rectified at any point, even if causal intermediaries are involved in the transmission of the harm or its corresponding rectification.[262] Richard Epstein, while keeping a tight hold on causal chains, nonetheless has accepted the principle of intermediate causation, especially when—in one of his paradigms—a dangerous condition is activated by a third party.[263] Here the conditions of primary and secondary public education may be considered to be a "dangerous condition," created by others in state and local government besides the Law School. The Law School may then activate liability for itself and/or the state, if it simply treats the minority applicant pool as if the applicants' collective condition is normal instead of pitted with deficiencies, like allowing traffic on a street with no warning signs but that is rough and filled with potholes. The school thus activates the "dangerous condition"—by denying admission to and excluding the minority from a fair opportunity to join the state's educated elite. Corrective justice *is* available, though, to counter the "dangerous condition."

From the cases of the Supreme Court, we know that benefit or harm (1) need not be direct but may be transmitted (or its legal protections or liabilities transmitted) by intermediaries; and (2) need not mirror initial causes of the cause of the ultimate harmful effects. Consider *Sheet Metal Workers v. EEOC*.[264] There, some workers, not harmed at all, received relief simply because of some involvement—minimally, if at all, causally generated—with an errant union.[265] Thus the effect on them need not have closely reflected the initial harm at all. Further, Justice Powell strongly intimated in *Wygant* that intermediaries could be the bearers of causation in a causal chain.[266] And, of course, Justice O'Connor held that a governmental entity might have responsibility for the harm of racial discrimination caused more directly by others if that entity remains passive while discrimination proceeds apace in a domain that it administers, oversees, or customarily relies upon to support its very functioning.[267]

As these examples show, the existence of a causal linkage between the state of public education in Texas for minorities and a deficiency to be remedied at the University of Texas can be inferred: Poorly educated blacks and Hispanics cannot meet the entrance requirements. One does not even need a dozen shocks of two billiard-balls to grasp this point. One explication of the situation is enough, because it intuitively represents the universal. The causal principle of the court in *Hopwood* (and in *Podberesky*) is too formal, too direct, and is mechanistically applied. One is reminded of the judicial controversy in the New Deal era between formal causes and their required direct (as opposed to indirect) relation to interstate commerce and the more fluid, empirical causes that finally prevailed.[268] Something similar to the New Deal era controversy over causation in interstate commerce is happening here: The lower courts are fracturing or squeezing the concept of causation *beyond* ordinary understanding. Their notions of causation extend beyond the common, everyday ideas of cause and effect. On the other hand, Hume, Nozick, and Epstein all comply with the common convictions about causation that we have traced to logistic, convictions that depend, as we have seen, on general acceptance for their validity. Justices Powell and O'Connor, with whom one may disagree on other matters—even the use of logistic itself—nonetheless have not deviated substantially from the logic of logistic. This logic or method of reasoning should be kept thinkable and credible by retaining the modern elements of causation set down by empiricist thinkers like Locke and Hume and not made obscure by importing distinctions against common sense and reason.[269]

As for the correct governmental unit to which to attribute discriminatory harm and the power to relieve it, the O'Connor constitutional point was that even a passive unit may take action if its ordinary functions have a sufficient relation to the discriminatory harm that would justify such action. This action was said to have a function to provide distributive justice as well as compensatory justice,[270] but this assessment is sheer speculation and need not be accepted to perceive the grounds of the compensatory justice so stoutly supported by Justice O'Connor in *J. A. Croson*. In this sense the University of Texas is much like the City of Richmond could have been if discrimination had been shown and linked to the fiscal functions of the city. Discrimination in Texas, if not at the Law School itself, *has* been shown, and it does perforce relate to the admissions functions of the Law School.

A law school with some of the most penetrating legal minds in Texas, with an uncommonly good vantage point on the problem of race and ethnicity in education, and which also suffers in its peculiar way from the effects of the discrimination, should be ceded the power to provide a proper legal remedy. Such a remedy would, among other things, prevent the use of public funds in furtherance of a pattern of discrimination that deprives minorities of a significant share in some of the state's most excellent educational facilities.[271] The use of such power would follow as a resolution to the Texas problem more closely *from the Supreme Court's appropriation of what I call logistic* than ever the Fifth Circuit might opine—this, by retaining the powerful concept of causation in the logistic sense, an integral part of our national thinking and adopted by justices of the Supreme Court, that there is necessity in the customary connection of antecedent and consequent, in the events that we perceive every day.

The judges of the Fifth Circuit have but to look out of their baroque courthouse in New Orleans at the mighty river partially encircling the city to see the effects of great causes hundreds or thousands of miles away. The animating principles of just such physical chains of causation, logistic projects into human affairs. The Law School should be seen as a passive, though highly pertinent, actor in this structure of causation.

CONCLUSION

Compensatory causation is the prevailing mode of affirmative action because its principles are wedded to the national character and perceived to be by private citizens and Supreme Court justices alike. Its paradigm of corrective justice is closely connected to the belief that actual wrongdoers should restore or redress intentional harm in a way that promotes equal treatment of individuals—an approach that avoids both "social engineering" and its adjustments for so-called societal discrimination.[272]

Justices Powell and O'Connor have been the leaders on the Court in fashioning a taut, yet in principle workable, conception of compensatory causation. Their main emphases have been on "color-blindness" and a concomitant rejection of the conception of "benign" discrimination, insistence on strict scrutiny as a standard of review and on hard evidence of prior discrimination as a standard of proof, firmness on exact and proportionate causation between harms and their effect and remedy, and rejection of mere quotas. At the same time, the Court—generally through Justices Powell or O'Connor, or both—have rejected more rigid arguments that would have snuffed out affirmative action. Thus the Court as a whole has never accepted the arguments propounded by the Reagan administration [273] and by Justice Scalia [274] that only those directly caused to suffer discrimination should be made whole—a position no different from individual disparate treatment in a Title VII case. Indeed, both Justice Powell and Justice O'Connor have accepted a limited conception of mediated causation— or a "causal chain"—in *Wygant* and *J. A. Croson.*

In the final analysis, and to return to a larger theme, logistic as a mode of thought is embodied in compensatory causation as nothing more than the causal connection of simples, whether merely individuals or constructed wholes, linked by causation in a way that establishes harm and the need for redress, from one directly to another. Our figures Nozick, Epstein, and (occasionally) Hume all use these elements or parts together with causation to construct wholes, whether that whole be an entire society or, as here, a system of justice that both defines and redresses wrong. But behind them all is John Locke

and the importance of the Lockean tradition in American political discourse. The idea of the ontological individual [the part], prior to society [an artificial construct], and the notion that a social contract refereeing self-interest was all that was necessary to produce justice [corrective, not distributive], led in the United States to the celebration of individual rights. . . . The land of opportunity was meritocratic; one deserved all that one could attain by talent and industry.[275]

Locke's thought has also led to the idea of a kind of bloodless, abstract individual whose moorings in epistemology, just as in social life, have been uncertain. For Locke the individual is simply another substance, stripped of all essential qualities (and thus of anything that could make him essentially a member of a group). "Thus we come to the idea[] of man . . . of [whose] substance[], whether any one has any other *clear* idea, further than of certain simple ideas co-existent together, I appeal to every one's own experience."[276] Thus the individual with whom Justice O'Connor must deal is a very abstract collection of accidental qualities inhering in an ethereal substance having no essential social characteristics. The individual, however, in our next type of affirmative action, social causation, is precisely the opposite: He is a product of society (and not society, of him).

NOTES

[1] City of Richmond v. J. A. Croson Co., supra Intro., note 33, 488 U.S. at 493, 498 (first internal quotation from plurality opinion of O'Connor, J.; second, from her opin-

ion for the Court) (quoting from, respectively, Shelly v. Kraemer, 334 U.S. 1, 22 [1948] and *Wygant*, 476 U.S. at 275).

[2] (1974).

[3] ROBERT NOZICK, ANARCHY, STATE, AND UTOPIA [hereinafter A, S, & U] 95 (1974) (emphasis supplied).

[4] Id. (emphasis in original).

[5] MCKEON, FREEDOM AND HISTORY, at 58, reprinted in MCKEON, FREEDOM AND HISTORY AND OTHER ESSAYS, at 209 (emphasis supplied).

[6] Id. at 53, reprinted in MCKEON, FREEDOM AND HISTORY AND OTHER ESSAYS at 209–10.

[7] David L. Norton, "Individualism and Productive Units," 87 Ethics 113, 115 (1977) (quoting from NOZICK, A, S, & U, at 33).

[8] NOZICK, A, S, & U, at 132–33. See also id. at 114–15 ("The moral objections of the individualist anarchist to the minimal state are overcome. It is not an unjust imposition of a monopoly; the *de facto* monopoly grows by an invisible-hand process and *by morally permissible means*, without anyone's rights being violated and without any claims being made to a special right that others do not possess.") (emphasis in original).

[9] Id. at 28–32.

[10] Id. at 32–33 (emphasis in original).

[11] Id. at 6.

[12] McKeon, "Philosophic Semantics and Philosophic Inquiry," supra Intro., note 40, at 7, reprinted in MCKEON, FREEDOM AND HISTORY AND OTHER ESSAYS, at 247.

[13] Id. at 249. *Cf.* DAVID HUME, A TREATISE OF HUMAN NATURE 469 (Selby-Bigge ed. 1968) ("[T]his *ought*, or *ought not*, expresses some new relation or affirmation . . . and at the same time . . . a reason should be given, for what seems altogether inconceivable, how this new relation can be a deduction from others, which are entirely different from it.") (emphasis in original).

[14] NOZICK, A, S, & U, at 33.

[15] Id. at 152.

[16] Id. at 150 (emphasis in original).

[17] Id. at 154–56. "Patterned" because they advance designs on property ownership generated through ahistorical end-state principles. "Time-slice" because they disdain the legitimacy of property rights acquired over the unbroken passage of time.

[18] Id. at 163.

[19] Id. at 151.

[20] Id. at 168.

[21] Id. at 172 *Cf. Wygant*, at 283 (opinion of Powell, J.) ("[L]ayoffs impos[ing] the entire burden of achieving racial equality on particular individuals [are] too intrusive [and] not sufficiently narrowly tailored [to protect] innocent persons.").

[22] B. J. Diggs, "Liberty without Fraternity," 87 Ethics 97, 105 (1977).

[23] NOZICK, A, S, & U, at 27, 153.

[24] Id. at 27 ("Returning stolen money or compensating for violations of rights [are subject to rectification]."); 173 ("[A] deviation from the first two principles of justice (in acquisition and transfer) will involve other persons' direct and aggressive intervention to violate rights, and moral constraints will not exclude defensive or retributive action in such cases.").

[25] Id. at 173 (emphasis supplied).

[26] *Cf.* text at Ch. 2, note 3, supra (right to rectification not supported by "the multitudinous actions of a long string of long-forgotten people").

[27] See text at Ch. 2, note 21, supra (quoting from id. at 172).

[28] Norton, "Individualism and Productive Justice," supra Ch. 2, note 7, at 124.

[29] (1992).

[30] RICHARD A. EPSTEIN, FORBIDDEN GROUNDS: THE CASE AGAINST EMPLOYMENT DISCRIMINATION LAWS [hereinafter FORBIDDEN GROUNDS] 21 (1992) (emphasis supplied). (Epstein's views follow on his reading of Locke as upholding "the traditional virtues of private property, individual liberty, and limited government." Id. at 99.)

[31] Id. at 21.

[32] Id. at 103.

[33] See id. at 413 ("Under a rigorous theory that regards all valuations as subjective, any private conception of merit will do as well as any other, but only to the extent that [a person] chooses to attach any weight to that conception." This is proposed as a standard for employee-employer relations.).

[34] See, *e.g.*, id. at 501 (The civil rights movement is at fault for having no "overall standard of social welfare that takes into account the preferences and desires of all persons within society."). See also RICHARD A. EPSTEIN, TAKINGS: PRIVATE PROPERTY AND THE POWER OF EMINENT DOMAIN 336 (1985) ("Nozick writes in an anti-utilitarian vein that places his historical theory in sharp opposition to a consequentialist one [associated by Epstein with utilitarianism]. Yet in one sense the intuitive base for much libertarian doctrine might be strengthened by a direct appeal to considerations of utility.").

[35] EPSTEIN, FORBIDDEN GROUNDS, at 164 ("With the subjective market system, the consent of the party is the sole test of merit.").

[36] Id. at 3.

[37] Id. at 412, 396.

[38] Id. at 42.

[39] Id. at 72.

[40] Id. at 28.

[41] *Cf.* LUCRETIUS, DE RERUM NATURA 173, 175, 181 (Loeb ed. 1966) ("But when the intelligence is more deeply moved by vehement fear, we see the whole spirit throughout the frame share in the feeling.").

[42] See, *e.g.*, St. Mary's Honor Center v. Hicks, 509 U.S. 501, 508 n.2, 513–15 & n.5 (1993) (Scalia, J.). See also notes and text at Ch. 2, notes 210–14, infra (more thorough discussion of Justice Scalia's views).

[43] Richard A. Epstein, "Nuisance Law: Corrective Justice and Its Utilitarian Constraints," 8 J. Legal Stud. 49, 49–50 (1979) (emphasis supplied; in earlier articles Epstein generally refers to "harms").

[44] Richard A. Epstein, "A Theory of Strict Liability," 2 J. Legal Stud. 151, 165 (1965).

[45] Id. at 160, 162 (citing and quoting H.L.A. HART AND TONY HONORÉ, CAUSATION IN THE LAW at 426 [1st ed. 1959]), 163, 184; Richard A. Epstein "Intentional Harms," 4 J. Legal Stud. 391, 399 (1975).

[46] Richard A. Epstein "Defenses and Subsequent Pleas in a System of Strict Liability," 3 J. Legal Stud. 165, 167–68 (1974).

[47] Paradoxically, Epstein opposes Title VII's version of strict liability, disparate impact, as exemplified in Griggs v. Duke Power Co., 401 U.S. 424 (1971). See EPSTEIN, FORBIDDEN GROUNDS, at 182 ff.

[48] See text at Ch. 2, note 40, supra. See also Richard A. Epstein, "Causation and Corrective Justice," 8 J. Legal Stud. 477, 489 (1979) ("Liberty is best understood as freedom from force and falsehood, not as a maximization of the things which are under one's disposition and control [a disparagement of law and economics].").

[49] See note and text at Ch. 2, note 42, supra.

[50] Epstein, "A Theory of Strict Liability," supra Ch. 2, note 44, at 166.

[51] Epstein, "Intentional Harms," supra Ch. 2, note 45, at 399 (emphasis supplied). See also Epstein, "A Theory of Strict Liability," supra Ch. 2, note 44, at 177ff.

[52] "The third paradigm [compulsion], A made B hit C . . . requires us to take into account the behavior of a third party." Epstein, "Defenses and Subsequent Pleas in a System of Strict Liability," supra Ch. 2, note 46, at 168.

[53] Epstein, "Intentional Harms," supra Ch. 2, note 45, at 399.

[54] Epstein, "Defenses and Subsequent Pleas in a System of Strict Liability," supra Ch. 2, note 46, at 168.

[55] See text at Ch. 2, note 53, supra.

[56] See text at Ch. 2, note 52, supra.

[57] Epstein, "A Theory of Strict Liability," supra Ch. 2, note 44, at 182 (A third party dislodges a boulder precariously placed by the defendant and harms the plaintiff. Interestingly enough, the third party's action is intentional, seemingly qualifying as a *novus actus interveniens.*).

[58] It should be borne in mind that Epstein's causal schema seeks to place liability on an initiator of a tortious act. The situation is somewhat different in affirmative action. The culpable employer, *etc.*, is, to be sure, assigned some type of liability, but the impetus of the tortious or discriminatory act is not so much used to trace liability to the employer through parties intermediary to a victim as that impetus is used to radiate entitlement to compensation to one or more layers of persons, many or most of whom are not immediate victims of the discrimination. Though the matter is one of degree and point of view, causation in affirmative action moves *outward* to determine which persons are entitled to corrective justice, while ordinary tort causation focuses more directly *inward* on the tortfeasor to determine his liability for the indirect effects of his act.

[59] Local 28, Sheet Metal Workers Int'l Ass'n v. EEOC, 478 U.S. 421 (1989) (hereinafter Sheet Metal Workers v. EEOC or *Sheet Metal Workers*).

[60] 42 U.S.C. § 2000e–5(g) (1994).

[61] *Sheet Metal Workers*, 478 U.S. at 462 (opinion of Brennan, J.) (emphasis supplied). Justice Brennan went on to explain:

The purpose of affirmative action [as court-ordered relief for a class] is not to make identified victims whole, but rather to dismantle prior patterns of employment discrimination and to prevent discrimination in the future. Such relief is provided to the class as a whole rather than to individual members; no individual is entitled to relief, and beneficiaries need not show that they are themselves victims of discrimination.

Id. at 474 (opinion of Brennan, J.).

In a similar remedial case involving a government employer, Justice Brennan found that "[a] party who has been guilty of repeated and persistent violations of the law bears the burden of demonstrating that the chancellor's efforts to fashion relief exceed the bounds of reasonableness." United States v. Paradise, 480 U.S. 149, 193 (1987) (opinion of Brennan, J.). This is precisely opposite of the burden of proof faced by the plaintiffs attacking voluntary affirmative action in a government agency when there are no proven violations of law. Id. See *Wygant*, 476 U.S. 277–78 (opinion of Powell, J.).

[62] *Sheet Metal Workers*, 478 U.S. at 444.

[63] EPSTEIN, FORBIDDEN GROUNDS, at 408 (emphases first in original, second, supplied).

[64] Id. at 166.

[65] Id. at 200.

[66] See text at Ch. 2, note 65, supra.

[67] See text at Ch. 2, notes 22–28, supra.

[68] Nongovernmental entities are addressed primarily through Title VII of the Civil Rights Act of 1964, which—for reasons to be explained later—does not employ logistic standards in affirmative action.

[69] ROSENFELD, AFFIRMATIVE ACTION AND JUSTICE, supra Ch. 1, note 284, at 166.

[70] Affirmative action, if based on corrective justice, must be initiated with a wrongful act. Thus Epstein's theory of strict liability and corrective justice, would miss the vital act of fault if fully applied in this context. See RICHARD POSNER, THE PROBLEMS OF JURISPRUDENCE 323–24 (1990) (Epstein's use of strict liability makes finding of wrongdoing required by classic corrective justice doubtful.).

[71] ARISTOTLE, ETHICS v, 3 1131a10–1131b25, in McKEON (ED.), THE BASIC WORKS OF ARISTOTLE, supra Ch. 1, note 100, at 1006–07. See also text of Ch. 1, note 101, supra.

[72] ARISTOTLE, ETHICS v, 4 1131b25–1132a20, in McKEON (ED.), THE BASIC WORKS OF ARISTOTLE, supra Ch. 1, note 100, at 1007–08; see text of Ch. 1, note 100, supra. See also notes and text at Ch. 1, notes 43–46, supra (Richard Epstein's definition of corrective justice).

[73] 438 U.S. at 269–311. These are pages chosen by me as the "first part" of the Powell opinion including general equal protection analysis, *before* the concept of diversity is taken up and discussed. See notes and text at Ch. 1, notes 163ff., supra, for the major portions of the "second part," dealing with diversity and the First Amendment.

[74] See text at Ch. 1, notes 153–62, supra, for the basic facts of the case.

[75] The theory of compensatory causation is entirely apart from the diversity theory of justification later found to be a compelling interest for equal protection *in general* but not with respect to the medical school, whose facts could not support constitutional diversity.

[76] *Bakke*, 438 U.S. at 288 (opinion of Powell, J.), quoting and referencing United States v. Carolene Products, Co., 304 U.S. 144, 152 n.4 (1938).

[77] *Bakke*, 438 U.S. at 290 (opinion of Powell, J.).

[78] Id. at 289–90.

[79] Id. at 291 (emphasis supplied).

[80] See *Carolene Products*, 304 U.S. at 152 n.4.

[81] *Bakke*, 438 U.S. at 356 (opinion of Powell, J.).

[82] Id. at 359.

[83] Id at 298.

[84] Id. at 294 n.34 ("*All*" emphasized in original; all other emphases supplied).

[85] Id. at 298.

[86] Id. at 302, 301.

[87] Id. at 305. This requirement was later dropped. See *Wygant*, 476 U.S. at 291 (O'Connor, J., concurring in part and concurring in the judgment) ("Where these employers . . . act on the basis of information which gives them sufficient basis for con-

cluding that remedial action is necessary, a contemporaneous finding requirement should not be necessary.").

[88] *Bakke*, 438 U.S. at 369 (opinion of Brennan, J.) (emphasis supplied).

[89] *Bakke*, 438 U.S. at 296 n.36 (opinion of Powell, J.).

[90] Id.

[91] See text at Ch. 1, note 66, supra.

[92] *Bakke*, 438 U.S. at 307 (opinion of Powell, J.).

[93] Id. at 300–301 (citing, *e.g.*, Dayton Bd. of Educ. v. Brinkman, 433 U.S. 406 [1977]).

[94] Id. at 304–05. Any requirement that there be an official finding has been dropped. See *Wygant*, 476 U.S. at 291 (O'Connor, J. concurring) and text of note 87, Ch. 2, supra.

[95] NOZICK, A, S, & U, at 95; see text at Ch. 2, notes 3–11, supra.

[96] See text at Ch. 2, note 45, supra.

[97] DAVID HUME, AN ENQUIRY CONCERNING HUMAN UNDERSTANDING 41 (Hackett ed. 1977).

[98] The medical school had advanced four grounds that would purportedly satisfy strict scrutiny by advancing a compelling state rationale for the program: "(i) 'reducing the historic deficit of traditionally disfavored minorities in medical schools and in the medical profession' [citation omitted]; (ii) countering the effects of societal discrimination; (iii) increasing the number of physicians who will practice in communities underserved; and (iv) obtaining the educational benefits that flow from an ethnically diverse student body." *Bakke*, 438 U.S. at 305–06 (opinion of Powell, J.). The first two fell to the compensatory requirements of identified, individual victims and wrongdoers and specific, limited causation. Id. at 307–10. The third failed for lack of sufficient evidence that affirmative action would serve the goal of directing medical professionals to underserved areas. Id. at 310–11. The fourth rationale—diversity—was, of course, found to provide the compelling interest needed, under certain conditions (not met by the medical school, see id. at 319–20), and in connection with free-speech interests. Id. at 311–15; see Chapter 1, text at notes 201–50, supra. A possible fifth compelling rationale—"fair appraisal of each individual's academic promise in the light of some cultural bias in testing or grading procedures"—was dismissed on the ground that to make such "corrections" to discover a person's authentic potential would not amount to a " 'preference' at all." Id. at 306 n.43. It is easy to see how Justice Powell could take this position: Such biased tests could be "based on a factor having no relationship to individual worth." Id. at 298. And revision of such biased scores would redress "distinctions [that] impinge upon personal rights, rather than the individual because of his membership in a particular group." Id. at 299. At any rate, however, Justice Powell noted that there was no evidence of the presence of such a guiding purpose, to allow for cultural bias, in the Davis program. Id. at 306 n.43.

[99] 448 U.S. 448 (1980).

[100] *Fullilove*, 448 U.S. at 491–92 (opinion of Burger, C. J., and two other justices).

[101] 42 U.S.C. §§ 6705(f)(2) (1976 ed., Supp. II).

[102] *Fullilove*, 448 U.S. at 453–54 (quoting section 103[f][2] of the 1977 Act) (opinion of Burger, C. J.).

[103] *Fullilove*, 448 U.S. at 481 (opinion of Burger, C. J.).

[104] Id. at 458.

[105] Representative Parren Mitchell, a black congressman from Baltimore and the provision's sponsor, relied on the administrative history of section 8(a) of the Small Business Act. Id. at 459–60.

The Court, in a rhetorical flourish, gave its authority and proof: "The legislative objectives of the MBE provision must be considered against the background of on-going efforts directed toward deliverance of the century-old promise of equality of opportunity." Id. at 463. "Congress, of course, may legislate without compiling the kind of 'record' appropriate with respect to judicial or administrative proceedings." Id. at 478.

[106] Id. at 475.

[107] Id. at 473 (emphasis supplied).

[108] See, *e.g.*, text at Ch. 2, notes 27–28, supra (Robert Nozick: "[D]istribution according to rectification [must be] measured by precise calculation of the causal linkage to the present objects of benefaction."); see also text at Ch. 2, notes 55–58, supra (views of Richard Epstein).

[109] See notes and text at Ch. 2, notes 21–23, 43, 62–63, supra.

[110] Chief Justice Burger and two others, including Justice Powell, upheld the statutory plan. *Fullilove*, 448 U.S. at 453ff. Justice Powell also concurred separately. Id. at 497ff. Justice Marshall and two others joined in the judgment. Id. at 517ff. Justice Stewart and one other dissented. Id. at 522ff. Justice Stevens dissented separately. Id. at 532ff.

[111] *Fullilove*, 448 U.S. at 501 (opinion of Powell, J.).

[112] Id. at 503.

[113] Id. at 508.

[114] See text of Ch. 2, note 98, supra.

[115] *Fullilove*, 448 U.S. at 513.

[116] Id. at 513–14 ("The choice of 10% set-aside thus falls halfway between the present percentage of minority contractors [4% nationwide] and the percentage of [all] [17%] minority group members in the Nation.").

[117] Id. at 514–15.

[118] 476 U.S. 267, 269–85 (opinion of Powell, J., in which Burger, C. J., Rehnquist, J., and O'Connor, J. [in part] joined).

[119] *Wygant*, 476 U.S. at 270–71 (opinion of Powell, J.).

[120] Id. at 272.

[121] Id.

[122] Id. at 273–74.

[123] Id. at 274–75.

[124] 433 U.S. 299 (1977) (Use of the word "treatment" signifies that the case was considered an intentional one, though statistics were used as the proof.).

[125] *Wygant*, 476 U.S. at 275 (opinion of Powell, J.).

[126] Id. at 275 (emphasis supplied); see also text at Ch. 2, note 90, supra.

[127] See text of Ch. 2, note 98, supra.

[128] *Wygant*, 476 U.S. at 276 (opinion of Powell, J.).

[129] Id. at 277–78 (Justice Powell's finding of causation in *Fullilove*).

[130] Yet Justice Powell suggested some slack in ends-means treatment may be appropriate. For example, he remarked that no year-by-year adjustments have generally been made by the federal courts once a public school has met its court-ordered duty to end a dual system. Id. at 276 (citing Swann v. Charlotte-Mecklenberg, 402 U.S. 1, 31–32 [1971]). He also stated that an employer show only "a strong basis in the evidence" to support its affirmative action. *Wygant*, 476 U.S. at 277 [opinion of Powell, J.]). This standard is later fleshed out in the opinions of Justice O'Connor. See notes and text at Ch. 2, notes 150–53, 200–202, infra.

[131] Id. at 277 (emphases supplied).

[132] Id. at 277.

[133] ROSENFELD, AFFIRMATIVE ACTION AND JUSTICE, supra Ch. 1, note 284, at 180 (emphasis supplied).

[134] See text at Ch. 1, notes 238–39, supra.

[135] See, *e.g.*, notes and text at Ch. 2, notes 56–57, supra.

[136] See notes and text at Ch. 2, notes 59–63, supra.

[137] *Wygant*, 476 U.S. at 281–83 (opinion of Powell, J.).

[138] Id. at 283–84.

[139] See notes and text at Ch. 1, notes 182–85, supra.

[140] *Wygant*, 476 U.S. at 280–81 (opinion of Powell, J.) ("[I]n order to remedy the effects of prior discrimination . . . it may be necessary . . . [for] innocent persons . . . to bear some of the burden of the remedy.").

[141] NOZICK, A, S & U, at 173.

[142] See text at Ch. 2, notes 17–21, supra.

[143] 467 U.S. 561 (1984).

[144] 42 U.S.C. § 2000e–2(h) (1994 ed.) (immunizing, under certain conditions, seniority issues from Title VII scrutiny).

[145] *Stotts*, 467 U.S. at 588 (O'Connor, J., concurring) (emphasis supplied).

[146] Id. at 588 (emphasis to show Justice O'Connor's insistence on proof of past, actionable discrimination as a predicate for affirmative relief). See also Local No. 93, Int'l Ass'n of Firefighters, AFL-CIO, CLC, v. City of Cleveland, 478 U.S. 501 (1986), a case also involving a consent decree. There the Court upheld the decree as not inconsistent with section 703(h) because it did not implicate seniority—and further held that direct causation was not necessary for relief because voluntary consent decrees "may include reasonable race-conscious relief that benefits individuals who were not actually victims of discrimination." *Firefighters Local No. 93*, 478 U.S. at 501 (Brennan, J., for the Court). It also held: "[T]he parties' consent animates the legal force of a consent decree." Id. No entanglement of section 703(h) was the further condition needed for affirmative relief. Id. at 527–28.

    Justice O'Connor joined the Court's opinion and briefly concurred separately. Her principal caveat was that the broad predicate, provided by the consent decree here, might not necessarily subsist if section 703(h) or the requirements posed by the Fourteenth Amendment were brought into play. Id. at 531 (O'Connor, J., concurring). Already she was aiming for precision.

[147] *Wygant*, 476 U.S. at 288 (opinion of O'Connor, J.).

[148] Id. at 290.

[149] Id. at 291.

[150] Id. at 292. (emphasis supplied). This benchmark arises prominently in the *J. A. Croson* case, when it is used to determine whether to use gross population figures, or the population of qualified minority contractors, as the standard by which to judge the propriety of the amount of set aside. See text at Ch. 2, note 177, infra, as well as text of that note.

[151] See *Wygant*, 476 U.S. at 277–78 (opinion of Powell, J.) ("The ultimate burden remains with the employees to demonstrate the unconstitutionality of an affirmative-action program."). See also Johnson v. Transp. Agency of Santa Clara Co., Calif., 480 U.S. at 626–27, for a succinct explanation of the allocation of the burdens of proof.

[152] *Wygant*, 476 U.S. at 292 (opinion of O'Connor, J.).

[153] Justice O'Connor, in *Sheet Metal Workers*, 478 U.S. at 489–99, concurred in part and dissented in part to Justice Brennan's opinion affirming broad remedies imposed by the district court under Title VII for egregious and persistent violations by the union in the case. See text and notes at Ch. 2, notes 59–61, supra. Her principal objection was that the relief imposed—including nonidentified victims as beneficiaries—constituted a "quota" in violation of section 703(j) of Title VII, 42 U.S.C. § 2000e-2(j). Consistently with her precision, she distinguished between a (legal) goal and an (illegal) quota:

> To be consistent with § 703(j), a racial hiring or membership goal must be intended to serve merely as a benchmark for measuring compliance with Title VII and *eliminating the effects of past discrimination*, rather than as a rigid numerical requirement that must unconditionally be met on pain of sanctions.

Sheet Metal Workers, 478 U.S. at 495 (emphasis supplied) (opinion of O'Connor, J.). Even in making this distinction, Justice O'Connor relied on the conception of causation that marks the logistic approach. In a similar case, United States v. Paradise, 480 U.S. 149 198 (1987) (opinion of O'Connor, J.), see note 61, Ch. 2, supra, Justice O'Connor again tilted against what she saw as a quota: "The one [black]-for-one [white] promotion quota used in this case far exceeded the percentage of blacks [in the employer's workforce], and there is no evidence that such an extreme quota was necessary to eradicate the effects of . . . delay."

[154] Kathleen M. Sullivan, "Sins of Discrimination: Last Term's Affirmative Action Cases," 100 Harv. L. Rev. 78 (1986) [hereinafter "Sins of Discrimination"].

[155] Id. at 80–81 (emphases supplied).

[156] See note and text at Ch. 2, note 61, supra (opinion of Brennan, J.); *Wygant* (see notes and text at Ch. 2, notes 131–34, supra [opinion of Powell, J.]); and *Firefighters Local No. 93* (see text of Ch. 2, note 146, supra).

[157] Sullivan, "Sins of Discrimination," at 94.

[158] Id. at 80.

[159] 2 PAUL TILLICH, SYSTEMATIC THEOLOGY 46–47 (1957). See text and note at Ch. 1, note 285, supra (setting forth Tillich's view of group dynamics).

[160] Sullivan, "Sins of Discrimination," at 91.

[161] Id. at 90.

[162] TILLICH, SYSTEMATIC THEOLOGY, supra Ch. 2, note 159, at 486.

[163] Sullivan, "Sins of Discrimination," at 96–97.

[164] Id. at 96. See also text at Ch. 2, note 155, supra.

[165] Id. at 97 (quoting from *Wygant*, 476 U.S. at 318 [Stevens, J., dissenting]) (emphasis supplied to show the concept of "benign" discrimination).

[166] IMMANUEL KANT, *RELIGION INNERHALB DER GRENZEN DER BLÖSEN VERNÜNFT* [RELIGION WITHIN THE LIMITS OF REASON ALONE] 24 (Green & Hudson trans. 1960) ("The disposition . . . [to adopt morality] . . . must have been adopted by free choice," 20; "The predisposition to *personality* is the capacity for respect for the moral law as *in itself a sufficient incentive of the will*," 22–23 [emphasis in original].).

[167] 1 REINHOLD NIEBUHR, THE NATURE AND DESTINY OF MAN: HUMAN NATURE 242 (1964) (emphasis supplied).

[168] KANT, RELIGION, supra Ch. 2, note 166, at 24.

[169] City of Richmond v. J. A. Croson Co., 488 U.S. 469, 510 (1989).

[170] 488 U.S. 469.

[171] 448 U.S. 448 (1980); see notes and text at Ch. 2, notes 101–07, supra.

[172] *J. A. Croson*, 488 U.S. at 479–80.

[173] Id. at 486–91 (opinion of O'Connor, J., joined by Rehnquist, C. J., and White, J.) (quoting *Fullilove*, 448 U.S. at 472 [opinion of Burger, C. J.], and 448 U.S. at 515–16) [citing Powell, J.]).

[174] But note her observation that because five of the nine seats on the city council were held by blacks, there was some danger of discrimination against whites. *J. A. Croson*, 488 at 495–96. See also EPSTEIN, FORBIDDEN GROUNDS, at 431–32 (Justice O'Connor quick to sense the very real danger of racial politics in forming affirmative action plans).

[175] Teamsters v. United States, 431 U.S. 324, 335 (1977). In *Teamsters* the disparities between the numbers of blacks and Hispanics in the workforces of the employer in different cities and the corresponding minority populations in the general populations in those cities were so egregious that the Court did not even feel the need to apply formal statistical techniques. It rather accepted the data as *ipso facto* compelling proof of illegal racial discrimination. 431 U.S. at 336, 337 & nn.17 & 18, 338 & n.18, 339–41, 342 & n.23 (The company's inability to rebut the inference of discrimination came not from the misuse of statistics [by the government] but from "the inexorable zero"— "the glaring absence of minority line drivers.").

[176] Hazelwood Sch. Dist. v. United States, 433 U.S. 299 (1977); see Justice Powell's treatment of *Hazelwood* as a standard of proof for past discrimination, note and text at Ch. 2, note 127, supra.

[177] *Hazelwood*, 433 U.S. at 308 n.13. ("In *Teamsters*, the comparison between the percentage of Negroes on the employer's workforce and the percentage in the general area-wide population was highly probative, because the job there involved—the ability to drive a truck—is one that many persons possess or can fairly readily acquire. *When special qualifications* [e.g., government subcontracting] *are required to fill particular jobs, comparisons to the general population (rather than to the smaller group who possess the necessary qualifications) have little probative value.*") (italicized part quoted by O'Connor, J., in *J. A. Croson*, 488 U.S. at 501).

[178] See text at Ch. 2, note 125, supra. See also Ch. 2, note 35, supra (Epstein's views).

[179] *J. A. Croson*, 488 U.S. at 501.

[180] Id. at 501–02.

[181] Id. at 502.

[182] Id. at 500 (emphasis in original) (quoting *Wygant*, 476 U.S. at 477 [opinion of Powell, J.]).

[183] Id. at 499 (quoting *Wygant*, 476 U.S. at 275 [opinion of Powell, J.]).

[184] *J. A. Croson*, 488 U.S. at 538 (opinion of Marshall, J., dissenting).

[185] *J. A. Croson*, 488 U.S. at 492 (opinion of O'Connor, J., joined by Rehnquist, C. J., and White, J.).

[186] See text at Ch. 2, note 184, supra; text at Ch. 3, note 99, infra.

[187] At least so in this case. But there seems no reason why Justice O'Connor might not begin at the other end of the causal chain in other cases.

[188] ROSENFELD, AFFIRMATIVE ACTION AND JUSTICE, supra Ch. 1, note 284, at 207.

[189] Id. at 208–09 ("[T]he ['passive'] interest now under consideration relates to a distributive rather than a compensatory use of affirmative action. Indeed, on the assumption that public authorities have had no hand in the institution and maintenance of private racially discriminatory practices in the construction industry, the government would

have no compensatory duty toward any of the victims of such private discrimination. . . . On the other hand, through implementation of the set-aside, the government would prevent the use of public funds in furtherance of a private scheme in the construction industry designed to prevent minorities from receiving any significant share of the available construction business.").

[190] See notes and text at Ch. 2, notes 131–34, supra.

[191] See text at Ch. 2, notes 6–7, 95–96, supra.

[192] HUME, AN ENQUIRY CONCERNING HUMAN UNDERSTANDING, supra Ch. 2, note 97, at 50–52 (emphasis in original).

[193] *Sheet Metal Workers*, 478 U.S. at 489 (O'Connor, J., concurring in part and dissenting in part).

[194] *J. A. Croson*, 488 U.S. at 492–93 (opinion of O'Connor, J., joined by Rehnquist, C. J., and White, J.) (quoting from Norwood v. Harrison, 413 U.S. 455, 465 [1973]).

[195] Mark Strasser, "The Invidiousness of Invidiousness: On the Supreme Court's Affirmative Action Jurisprudence," 21 Hastings L. Q. 323, 394 (1994).

[196] *J. A. Croson*, 488 U.S. at 493 (opinion of O'Connor, J., joined by Rehnquist, C. J., and White and Kennedy, JJ.) (quoting *Shelly v. Kraemer*, 334 U.S. 1 [1948]).

[197] Id. at 494.

[198] Id. at 493 (citing *Bakke*, 438 U.S. at 298 [opinion of Powell, J.]).

[199] See notes and text at Ch. 2, notes 150–51, supra.

[200] See text and notes at Ch. 2, notes 151–52, supra.

[201] *J. A. Croson*, 488 U.S. at 725 (emphasis supplied and original emphasis deleted); Justice O'Connor chose this same standard of *prima facie case* in Johnson v. Transp. Agency, 480 U.S. at 649 (opinion of O'Connor, J., concurring in the judgment).

[202] See text and notes at Ch. 2, notes 150–53, supra.

[203] See dissenting opinion of Thomas, J., in Adarand Constructors v. Pena, 515 U.S. 200, 241 (1995) ("[R]acial paternalism and its unintended consequences can be as poisonous and pernicious as any other form of discrimination.").

[204] See note and text at Ch. 2, note 198, supra.

[205] *J. A. Croson*, 488 U.S. at 493 (opinion of O'Connor, joined by Rehnquist, C. J., and White and Kennedy, JJ.) (Note that because one other justice—Justice Scalia, whose views favored imposing strict scrutiny, *J. A. Croson*, 488 U.S. at 520 [opinion of Scalia, J., concurring in the judgment]—had joined the plurality on this point, the standard of strict scrutiny [at least for states and their subdivisions] was finally established by a majority of the Court.).

[206] *J. A. Croson*, 488 U.S. at 509 (opinion of O'Connor, joined by Rehnquist, C. J., and White and Kennedy, JJ.).

[207] Id. at 509. *Cf. Sheet Metal Workers*, 478 U.S. at 490 ("Even assuming that some forms of race-conscious affirmative relief . . . are permissible as remedies for egregious and pervasive violations . . . the remedies in [Sheet Metal Workers] were impermissible because they operate not as goals but as social quotas.") (opinion of O'Connor, J.).

[208] *J. A. Croson*, 488 U.S. at 509 (opinion of O'Connor, joined by Rehnquist, C. J., and White and Kennedy, JJ.) (Race-neutral devices to increase accessibility to bidders of all races could be used in place of affirmative action when no discrimination was proved.).

[209] Id. at 510.

[210] *J. A. Croson*, 488 U.S. at 521 (Scalia, J., concurring in the judgment).

[211] Id. at 524.

[212] *Cf.* Ronald Dworkin, "Is Affirmative Action Doomed?" N.Y. REVIEW OF BOOKS 56, 58–59 (Nov. 5, 1998) (distinguishing between Justice Scalia's "overriding necessity" mode of interpreting strict scrutiny and Justice O'Connor's more lenient "rebuttal" approach).

[213] *Adarand*, 515 U.S. at 239 (Scalia, J., concurring in part and concurring in the judgment).

[214] Johnson v. Transp. Agency, 480 U.S. at 664 (Scalia, J., dissenting).

[215] 509 U.S. 502 (1993).

[216] Id. at 508 n.2 (dubious that blacks would racially discriminate against other blacks), 513–14 & n.5 (flimsy and uncorroborated evidence of racial discrimination).

[217] See notes and text at Ch. 2, notes 40 & 48, supra.

[218] Kathleen Sullivan, "*City of Richmond v. J. A. Croson Co.*: The Backlash against Affirmative Action," 64 Tul. L. Rev. 1609, 1609 (1990).

[219] Id. at 1612.

[220] See *Fullilove*, 448 U.S. 448 (see note and text at Ch. 2 note 100, supra), which indicated that such a congressional program need not be subjected to strict scrutiny, 448 U.S. at 492 (opinion of Burger, C. J.); see also *Metro Broadcasting*, 497 U.S. 547, in which a majority of the Court held that an affirmative action program, based on a diversity rationale and administered by the FCC according to statute, need only withstand intermediate scrutiny. Id. at 211–12; see text in Ch. 1, at notes 268–69, supra.

[221] See explanation of *Metro Broadcasting* in id.

[222] *J. A. Croson*, 488 U.S. at 490–91 (opinion of O'Connor, J., joined by Rehnquist, C. J., and White, J.). Note that also, up to that time and extending through *J. A. Croson*, there was no majority support on the Court even for applying strict scrutiny to states and their subdivisions. See text of note Ch. 2, 205, supra.

[223] 515 U.S. 200 (1995).

[224] Id. at 206 (citing and quoting from the Small Business Act, section 8[d][1], 15 U.S.C. § 644 [g][1]). The italicized portions of the Act, to the extent that they are race neutral, are—according to the Court—subject to the "most relaxed judicial scrutiny." Id. at 213.

[225] Id. at 2102.

[226] Id.

[227] Id. 2112 (quoting from *J. A. Croson*, 448 U.S. at 493 [opinion of O'Connor, J., joined by Rehnquist, C. J., and White and Kennedy, JJ.]); in his dissenting opinion, 515 U.S. 242–64, Justice Stevens makes the reality of this distinction—benign versus invidious discrimination—the crux of an argument for equality imposed by the majority on itself. This argument will be fully explored in Chapter 4.

[228] *Adarand*, 515 U.S. at 227 (emphases in original) (citation omitted). The Court went on to hold univocally that the strict scrutiny standard of judicial review thenceforth would be applied to racial classifications imposed by the federal government as well as by state and local governments. Id. at 226. Curiously, however, Justice O'Connor had already asserted that the Court had, *e.g.*, "agreed" in *J. A. Croson* that strict scrutiny applies to the states, *Adarand*, 515 U.S. at 222–23, and that the Court had so "concluded," id. at 226.

[229] Id. at 237. For confirmation of Justice O'Connor's statement here and at Ch. 2, note 230, infra, see, *e.g.*, McNamara v. City of Chicago, 138 F.3d 1219, 1222, 1224 (7th Cir.) (Posner, J.) ("[favored racial or ethnic] treatment [is] justified [under] 'strict

scrutiny' [which is met by] the City's discrimination against blacks and Hispanics in the past.") (citing *Adarand*), *cert. denied*, 525 U.S. 981 (1998).

[230] See text at Ch. 2, note 133, supra.

[231] This case style will be used to refer to two closely interconnected opinions, *Podberesky I*, 956 F.2d 52 (4th Cir. 1992) and *Podberesky II*, 38 F.3d 147 (4th Cir. 1994), *cert. denied*, 514 U.S. 1128 (1995).

[232] *Podberesky I*, 956 F.2d at 55.

[233] Id. at 55–56.

[234] Id. at 55 (quoting *J. A. Croson*, 488 U.S. at 500).

[235] *Podberesky II*, 38 F.3d at 154 ("The effects must themselves be examined to see whether they were caused by the past discrimination and whether they are of a type that justifies the program.").

[236] Id. at 154.

[237] Id. at 156 (*cf.* notes and text at Ch. 2, notes 175–81).

[238] Id. at 157 & n.8.

[239] Id. at 158.

[240] 42 U.S.C. § 2000d *et seq.*

[241] *Podberesky I*, 956 F.2d at 54.

[242] "[T]he President of [the university] testified that with regard to admission and financial aid, [the university] had not discriminated against blacks for many years." Id. at 56–57.

[243] *Podberesky II*, 38 F.3d at 158.

[244] 78 F.3d 932 (15th Cir.), *cert. denied*, 518 U.S. 1033 (1996).

[245] A parallel rejection of the Law School's diversity defense is reviewed at notes and text at Ch. 1, notes 182–88, supra.

[246] Hopwood v. Texas, 861 F. Supp. 551, 555–57 (W.D. Tex. 1994), *rev'd and remanded*, 78 F.3d 932 (5th Cir.), *cert. denied*, 518 U.S. 1033 (1996), *on remand*, 999 F. Supp. 872 (W.D. Tex. 1998), *appeal perfected*, April 17, 1998. See text of Intro., note 4, supra.

[247] *Hopwood*, 78 F.3d at 939.

[248] *Hopwood*, 78 F.3d at 937.

[249] Id. at 939 (citing lower court, 861 F. Supp. at 572).

[250] *On remand*, 999 F. Supp. 872, the district court found grounds to add injunctive relief to the decree—an element missing and unreviewed originally by the court of appeals. An appeal to this modified decree has now been perfected.

[251] *Hopwood*, 78 F.3d at 949 (quoting from *Wygant*, 476 U.S. at 274 [opinion of Powell, J.]).

[252] Id. at 950 (quoting from *Wygant*, 476 U.S. at 275 [opinion of Powell, J.]).

[253] *Hopwood*, 78 F.3d at 954.

[254] 411 U.S. 1 (1973).

[255] 457 U.S. 202 (1982).

[256] See, *e.g.*, Edgewood ISD v. Kirby, 777 S. W.2d 391 (Tex. 1989) (*Edgewood I*). Several years later the legislature amended the state's education code to provide that the top ten ranking graduates of every high school in the state could matriculate at the public university or college of his or her choice. Tex. Educ. Code § 51.803 (1999) (Acts of 1997, 75th Legis., ch. 155, 1, eff. Sept. 1, 1997). Many saw this as a functional substitute for affirmative action; since the school districts cover such a wide disparity of wealth and are highly segregated by race and ethnicity, Hispanics and

blacks—and the poor generally—would be guaranteed seats in the entering class of the University of Texas and other state schools. See also Danielle Holley and Delia Spencer, "The Texas Ten Percent Plan," 34 Harv. C. R.–C. L. L. Rev. 245 (1999).

[257] *Hopwood*, 78 F.2d at 952 (quoting *Podberesky II*, 38 F.3d at 153).

[258] HUME, A TREATISE OF HUMAN NATURE, supra Ch. 2, note 13, at 173.

[259] See note and text at Ch. 2 note 5–7 and the text of note 13 (Hume's invoking distinction between factual causes and moral causes).

[260] *Hopwood*, 78 F.3d at 952–55.

[261] HUME, AN ENQUIRY CONCERNING HUMAN UNDERSTANDING, supra Ch. 2, note 97, at 52 (first emphasis in original and second, added).

[262] See notes and text at Ch. 2, notes 27–28.

[263] See notes and text at Ch 2, notes 52–54, supra.

[264] 478 U.S. 421 (1989).

[265] See notes and text at Ch. 2, notes 59–61. Epstein found this treatment to be too causally broad. See notes and text at Ch. 2, notes 62–63, supra.

[266] *Wygant*, 476 U.S. at 277 (opinion of Powell, J.).

[267] *J. A. Croson*, 488 U.S. at 942 (opinion of O'Connor, joined by Rehnquist, C. J., and White, J.). See also notes and text at Ch. 2 notes 185, 194. See also ROSENFELD, AFFIRMATIVE ACTION AND JUSTICE, supra Ch. 1, note 284, at 207–08 (showing the types of multiple causation advanced by Justices Powell and O'Connor).

[268] *Compare* Carter v. Carter Coal Co., 298 U.S. 238 (1936) ("Whether the effect of a given activity . . . is direct or indirect is not always easy to determine. The word 'direct' implies that the activity . . . invoked or blamed shall operate proximately—not mediately, remotely, or collaterally—to produce the effect. It connotes the absence of an efficient intervening agency.") *with* NLRB v. Jones & Laughlin Steel Corp., 301 U.S. 1 (1937) ("Although activities may be intrastate in character when separately considered, if they have such a close and substantial relation to interstate commerce that their control is essential or appropriate to protect that commerce from burdens and obstructions, Congress cannot be denied this power to exercise that control.").

[269] The First Circuit has repeated some of these same errors in holding that there was no causal linkage between vestiges of past discrimination in the Boston Public School System and patterns of racial and ethnic disparity in admissions to one of its most prestigious components, the Boston Latin School (BLS). Wessmann v. Gittens, 160 F.3d 790 (1st Cir. 1998). See Ch. 1, notes and text at 270–78, 280, supra (showing the court's rejection of a diversity rationale for the School Committee's affirmative action program.). The School Committee justified its remedial affirmative action program in admission to BLS by reference to an "achievement gap" between applicants of white and Asian race, on the one hand, and Hispanic and African American race and ethnicity, on the other. Id. at 802–04. The achievement gap, in turn, was purportedly caused by "low teacher expectations" among lower-grade teachers of Hispanics and African American students. Id. at 804.

The court attacked the links in this causal chain. "[T]he raw achievement gap statistics presented in this case do not by themselves isolate any locus of discrimination for measurement [but may simply reveal] societal discrimination." Id. at 803. As for the causal origin of the achievement gap in low teacher expectations, the court found that the committee's expert witness had relied too much on his study of the phenomenon in another city without adequate attention to Boston, so that "with no methodological support, he could not produce a meaningful analysis of causation." Id. at 805.

The conclusion: "[T]he [admissions] [p]olicy indicates that it was not designed to assuage past harms, but that it was simply a way of assuring racial/ethnic balance, howsoever defined, in each [BLS] class." Id. at 808.

The dissenter answered these parts of the court's argument point by point. Id. at 814ff. (Lipez, J., dissenting). A causal link could be established between the achievement gap in applicants to BLS and prior *de jure* segregation in Boston schools. The link could be inferred from the weight of the committee's burden of production in a hypothetical minority suit against the committee, arising from "an identifiable barrier to entry that could be challenged by minority applicants in the event the race-conscious aspects of the Boston Latin admissions were elided." Id. at 818 (Lipez, J., dissenting). There was evidence that African Americans' and Hispanics' composite admission scores were not properly validated to future performance. Thus, under Title VI, 42 U.S.C. § 2000d (1994) (which the dissent stated could be the basis of a disparate impact theory), the committee could have had *prima facie* liability to minority applicants because "the mere act of selection exposes the school system to challenge from minorities based on the disparate impact of the selection criteria used." Id. at 819 (Lipez, J., dissenting). As for low teacher expectations during the past, the dissenter found that such expectations, "grounded in the long history of segregation in the Boston school system, were a substantial causal factor in the undeniable achievement gap found in the Boston school system." Id. at 827 (Lipez, J., dissenting).

Finally the dissenter concluded that

[b]y asserting that the district court erred in crediting the extensive observational testimony of experienced, well trained administrators, and by requiring quantifiable data to establish a causal link between past discrimination and present outcomes, *the majority would reduce strict scrutiny to a standard that is indeed "fatal in fact."*

Id. at 828 (Lipez, J., dissenting) (emphasis supplied) (citing Adarand Constructors v. Pena, 515 U.S. 200, 237 [1995]) (alluding to statement of Justice O'Connor that "we wish to dispel the notion that strict scrutiny is 'strict in theory but fatal in fact.' ") (footnote omitted). See note and text at Ch. 2, note 229, supra.

[270] See text of note and text at Ch. 2, note 189, supra.

[271] See id.

[272] See ROSENFELD, AFFIRMATIVE ACTION AND JUSTICE, supra Ch. 1, note 284, at 166.

[273] KAHLENBERG, THE REMEDY: CLASS, RACE AND AFFIRMATIVE ACTION, supra Ch. 1, note 283, at 19.

[274] See notes and text at Ch. 2, notes 213–14, supra.

[275] SKRENTNY, THE IRONIES OF AFFIRMATIVE ACTION, supra Intro., note 24, at 27.

[276] JOHN LOCKE, AN ESSAY CONCERNING HUMAN UNDERSTANDING ch. xxiii, §§ 2 & 3, reprinted in Great Books of the Western World, vol. 35, 204 (Robert Maynard Hutchins ed. 1952) (emphasis in original).

3

Problematic and Social Causation

THE NATURE OF PROBLEMATIC

In dissenting from the majority's decision in *J. A. Croson*, Justice Marshall had occasion to distinguish what I have called compensatory causation and logistic from what I now denominate social causation, the embodiment of the problematic mode of thought.

The majority takes the disingenuous approach of disaggregating Richmond's local evidence, attacking it piecemeal, and thereby concluding that no *single* piece of evidence adduced by the city, "standing alone" . . . suffices to prove past discrimination. But items of evidence do not, of course, "stan[d] alone" or exist in alien juxtaposition; they necessarily work together, reinforcing or contradicting each other.[1]

Justice Marshall's concluding clause reflects the congruence of his thinking with the problematic mode of thought. Adherents of this mode understand reality to be composed of a plurality of subject matters, each constituted by its own specific principles that define that subject and that cannot be disaggregated into simpler, reductionist causes. These principles function to identify and to explain subject matters that are different in kind—separate subject matters that must be understood holistically through their own separate principles if they are to be understood at all. Thus ethics and politics, the practical sciences of human conduct, are different in kind from the theoretic sciences, like physics or zoology, because the former are concerned with action, whereas the latter are concerned with scientific knowledge and truth. This mode of thought accordingly differs both from dialectic, which collapses all distinctions, including the one between action and knowledge, into a single comprehensive whole found in unity with all things, thoughts, words, and deeds; and from logistic, which subjects human action to the strictures of scientific proofs based on the causal linkages of simples—proofs not different in kind from those inherent in the construction of machines, the exploration of the cosmos, or the advancement of technical science.

As Justice Marshall indicated, the logistic approach of compensatory causation is disaggregative and reductionist—it seeks simple or single causes for social phenomena such as racial discrimination, causes that differ only in the degrees of force that they exert. Social causation, functioning through problematic, demarcates the boundaries of social institutions perceived through observation (and not postulation) and apprehends the role of unique principles animating each institution as a whole.

For problematic, action is *sui generis*. It is both empirical and "natural" in the sense that all men (and women) do in fact engage in action with fellow human beings in order to attain meaning and purpose in their lives. Though this process is not a quest for dialectical freedom in a unity of knowledge or of all humanity, neither is it merely the construction of a minimal, artificial state to protect property and freedom conceived as unlimited movement, as we saw in logistic. Rather, problematic seeks freedom in the democratic exchange of ideas, and in such discussions it finds politics as the meaningful art of ruling and being ruled in turn by one's equals, in a constitutional state, under the rule of law.

For the study of affirmative action problematic offers perhaps the most practical approach—if by "practical" we refer to knowledge gained *a posteriori* from the outcomes of social action. This knowledge can then become one or more premises of a kind of practical syllogism,[2] whose origin and structure enable citizens and rulers alike to reason out or deliberate about the means to achieve justice and the good. The principles that define racial disparities and their resolution are, of course, found neither in abstractions about the nature of man nor in his conjectured transcendental qualities but in his social and political nature as lived out in America for over 200 years under the Constitution and for 150 years earlier in colonial times. History here becomes the study of a specific problem—how racial discrimination has arisen and how it might be resolved in its unique context of American historical development.

Justices Brennan and Marshall have used this approach, one of social causation in service to justice under the Constitution, with both the Fourteenth Amendment and Title VII, with much more success in achieving affirmative action under the latter than the former. John Dewey, though, leads my discussion with a powerful philosophy illustrating problematic—a pragmatic philosophy urging *social* solutions for *social* problems; and then I turn to his modern disciple Cass R. Sunstein for a contemporary application of the mode of thought to the very problem presented in this inquiry.

JOHN DEWEY AND HIS PUBLIC

John Dewey is known as a pragmatic philosopher of democracy, and it is in his books *The Public and Its Problems*[3] and *Democracy and Education*[4] that we will find that part of his thought that is most relevant to this inquiry. The nub of Dewey's thought is the inseparability in origin and purpose of knowledge *and* social organization. Pragmatism means that knowledge emerges from human action and is necessarily *a posteriori* in its origin, since human interactions and institutions are its source (and its consequents). "[M]an acts from crudely intelligized emotion and from habit rather than from [solitary] rational consideration."[5] The association of individuals is a basic fact (or principle) to be accepted as a given without need for or possibility of proof. (Indeed this fundamental yet unprovable grounding of human association is an example of how problematic separates the social and the political from other subject matters, through such a starting point or principle rooted in human nature.) Accordingly, "knowledge [of the 'distinctly human'] is a function of association and communication . . . not [a] function[] of . . . mind or [pure] consciousness which originate[s] in individuals by means of isolated contact with objects [as in the thought of Locke, Hume, and Kant]."[6] This knowledge necessarily depends on the observation of human actions.[7] And practical knowledge reflects "the perfecting of the means and ways of communication of meanings so that genuinely shared interest in the consequences of interdependent activities may inform *desire* and thereby direct action."[8]

Given that individuals' association is a basic fact, Dewey's largest problem is how to shape and influence that association so that the aberrations in man's social functioning are identified and best corrected. In this undertaking he sets out a basic distinction:

[The consequences of human acts upon others] are of two kinds, those which affect the persons directly engaged in a transaction, and *those which affect others beyond those immediately concerned.* In this distinction we find the germ of the distinction between the *private* and the *public. When indirect consequences are recognized and there is an effort to regulate them, something [i.e., a public] having the traits of a state comes into being.* When the consequences of an action are confined . . . mainly to the person directly engaged in it, the transaction is a private one.[9]

Thus not only does Dewey avoid the kind of reductionism of all actions to simples in a private realm—a reductionism approached by Locke, Nozick, and Epstein—but he creates a distinctive public realm in which the actions and speech of individuals, given adequate root in the social milieu, become empowered to resolve the problems of that public.

Furthermore, while the public must identify its problems in a texture of indirect consequences in which causation is not always sharply focused, the public first must identify *itself*, for in a democracy the *real* public—the collection of persons that ought to recognize the authentic issues that concern them commonly—remains largely inchoate. This potential public remains inchoate either because its members are distracted either by the necessity of making a living or by sensationalistic and trivial amusements and so-called news[10] or are betrayed by the basic failure of institutions such as the schools and the media to provide the knowledge and information needed for the public to form itself.[11] In this respect Dewey's views substantially overlap Habermas's, for the latter depends upon uncoerced dialogue and discourse to resolve basic issues of the public. But whereas Habermas proceeds through the processes of the mind or intellect alone without a major role for emotion, and through such processes in which particulars are folded into unities, Dewey remains concerned with perception of "the consequences of the behavior of *individuals* joined in groups"[12] and with the role of "human habits . . . not wholly informed by reasoned purpose and deliberate choice [yet] amenable to them."[13] Dewey also seems to be concerned with the role of the emotions and desire as a beginning point of action, in a way that Habermas is not.[14] Yet for both Dewey and Habermas, "*the* problem of the public . . . [is] [t]he essential need . . . [for] the improvement of the methods and conditions of debate, discussion and persuasion."[15]

Under Dewey private individuals certainly do not disappear, but their relation to social institutions changes to reflect their inherently social nature. Thus, under the rule of law, legal precepts "are [not] commands only [as they would be in logistic]" but are mainly "structures which canalize action," thereby enabling persons to cooperate with one another and "make their arrangements."[16]

Liberty is that secure release and fulfillment of personal potentialities which take place only in rich and manifold association with others. . . . Equality denotes the unhampered share which each individual member of the community has in the consequences of associated action. It is equitable because it is measured only by need and capacity to utilize, not by extraneous factors which deprive one in order that another may take and have.[17]

It is in this context that we must ask what light Dewey's thought might throw on the public and its problem of racial inequality to which affirmative action is proposed as a resolution. The answer is necessarily bound up with access to socially generated information taken from concrete situations.

A democracy is more than a form of government; it is primarily a mode of associated living, of conjoint communicated experience. The extension in space of the number of individuals who participate in an interest so that each has to refer his own action to that of others, and to consider the action of others to give point and direction to his own, is equivalent to the breaking down of those barriers of class, race, and national territory which [have] kept men from perceiving the full import of their activity.[18]

[I]f democracy has a moral and ideal meaning, it is that social return be demanded from all and that opportunity for development of distinctive capacities be afforded to all.[19]

From these selections we may infer that a major role of law is to shape, "to canalize," those institutions that can break down barriers of class and race by making the public aware of the unique social causes that have these barriers as their consequences and by making the public aware of the fact that race discrimination is a harm to society as well as to the individual. Groups are the bearers of inequality and require adjustment in their positions in society to equalize opportunity for human realization. At the same time the powers of oligarchic groups to escape their social obligations to the genuine public must be trimmed. This is primarily, then, an approach of distributive justice. It fits the assessment of our next, contemporary author, who examines the role of law in race relations and finds that the place of race in our social organization thwarts the ideals of democratic society found in Dewey's thought.

CASS SUNSTEIN'S PRAGMATISM AND THE ANTICASTE PRINCIPLE

In his description of and prescriptions for legal reasoning,[20] Cass R. Sunstein allies himself with what I call the problematic method, which he would apply to resolve, among other things, the affirmative action controversy. Eschewing any attempt to secure agreement on general principles of universal application,[21] he urges "agreement on particulars."[22] " '[T]here are some things about which it is not possible to pronounce rightly in general terms: therefore in cases where it is necessary to make a general pronouncement, the law takes account of the majority of cases. . . . This is the essential nature of equity; it is a rectification of law in so far as law is defective on account of its generality.' "[23] "Thus we often have in law an *incompletely theorized agreement*"—frequently meaning agreement on particulars, including low-level principles, without agreement on high abstractions.[24]

Understanding this point is the key to understanding the proper relation of reasoning to effective social and political reform. " '[T]he sanctification of ready-made antecedent universal principles as methods of thinking is the chief obstacle to the kind of thinking which is the indispensable prerequisite of steady, secure and intelligent social reforms.' "[25] Sunstein accordingly appears to adopt Dewey's emphasis on deriving social knowledge from observations of individuals' particular (though socially related) actions.[26]

Therefore, an inquiry into the justification of affirmative action will depend on "practical [problematic] reason rather than on deduction [logistic]" and thus will not depend upon putative "neutral or natural . . . mechanisms—usually the market—thought[, largely by proponents of logistic and reductionist postulation,] to be free from distortion by racial discrimination."[27] It will depend, instead, on a nondeductive assessment of the current position of blacks as the particular "product of past and present social choices."[28] The first point to which this practical/pragmatic/problematic reasoning is to be applied is to the meaning of the Equal Protection Clause itself—which as interpreted logistically in *J. A.*

Croson, Adarand, and *Wygant* has greatly, in Sunstein's view, narrowed the permissible scope of affirmative action.

The Equal Protection Clause provides that no state shall "deny any person the equal protection of the laws." The majority of the Supreme Court, says Sunstein, have treated the term "any person"—because phrased as applying to the individual and not to groups—in a way that depicts *any* choices made by the government according to a racial criterion as *a priori* suspect, thus making little or no allowance for affirmative action.[29] Little allowance is left because the extemely useful (pragmatic) idea of benign discrimination—a product of group understanding—is virtually eliminated. But this interpretation "is a product of undisclosed substantive judgments"—presuppositions—which are "a dishonorable species of formalism" in light of the particular history and social purposes behind the Fourteenth Amendment's emergence.[30]

The constitutional proponent of logistic understands "any person" as Locke's pale, solitary, and abstract individual. The Deweyan analysis of the matter, however, treats this "any person" both as part of a group and as shaped by the particular social consequences of his time. This perspective leads to Sunstein's thesis that "[o]riginally the Fourteenth Amendment [including the words 'any person'] was understood as an effort to eliminate racial caste—emphatically not as a ban on distinctions on the basis of race [*simpliciter*]."[31] This understanding of the original purpose is obviously more conducive to affirmative action, as it actually may permit racial distinctions as needed to address social reality, not virtually prohibit them in the name of abstract individualism.

This problematic methodology leads to Sunstein's major ground of support for affirmative action: *the anticaste principle.* Caste, normally associated with socially frozen groups on the Indian subcontinent, exists in the United States in the form of racially defined groups systematically denied the most rudimentary advantages ordinarily associated with citizenship and, indeed, with humanity. "A systematic disadvantage [imposed on a caste] might include [deprivation] of education, freedom from private and public violence, income and wealth, political representation [and] influence, longevity, [and] health."[32] As a consequence, "[t]he anticaste principle, if taken seriously, calls for significant restructuring of social practices"[33]—in short, distributive justice based on a different form of equality from that held by the authors of the prevailing Supreme Court view of affirmative action.

In his book V on the causes of revolution, in the *Politics*, Aristotle notes that citizens' different ideas about equality stir up constant strife and controversy. "[T]herefore, both parties [democrats and oligarchs], whenever their share in the government does not accord with their perceived ideas, stir up revolution[—][a] change[] in the government[]"[34] Sunstein follows this Aristotelian view of the social origins of norms of equality, not the logistic view that locates its meaning in pristine definitions. Thus "the competing conceptions of equality that underlie different views about affirmative action programs [are not decided or delimited by] the constitutional words *equal protection.'* "[35] "The word *equal* [alone] cannot resolve the question, for there are plausible but different conceptions of equality, arguing for or against affirmative action."[36] Behind the dictionary definitions of equality are in fact the diverse substantive judgments of the disputants, and despite efforts to link our judgments about equality to the individual only, the term, and the value, is also inextricably linked to group membership. "In this sense, claims of unconstitutional discrimination are always group-based claims, even if they are made by 'any person.' "[37] Perhaps the factor in equality most susceptible to change in social causation is the ascertainment of the norm or "baseline" of the distribution of benefits (often claimed by supporters of logistic to be the "market"), a deviation from which is thought to constitute inequality. Sunstein builds on this point.

"The existing distribution [of benefits between blacks and whites] is not natural [or preordained] and does not provide a neutral baseline; it [has] resulted in part from government decisions, notable among them slavery and segregation itself[, which are examples of social causes]."[38] Because the "baseline" or status quo of distribution is conditioned by social causes, the claims of blacks and other victims of discrimination cannot be "connected in any *simple* way with past discrimination, and certainly not [merely] with acts of discrimination that can be tightly connected with their particular complaint[s], [as proponents of logistic require]. Nor [can their claims be restricted to] the status quo and existing entitlements."[39] Accordingly the concept of corrective justice is poorly designed to be an engine of liberation from the bondage of caste. Corrective justice is primarily designed to redress injuries among individual wrongdoers and victims,[40] apart from the group dynamics of society as a whole. The attack on caste must be turned away from this corrective paradigm of justice and, in a "dramatic softening of the traditional ideas of causation,"[41] pointed toward an analysis of societal discrimination, not individual discrimination.[42] Caste is a problem of the public, and it requires a resolution suited for the public sphere— not one designed for disputes among private parties, as corrective justice traditionally has been.

Sunstein is well settled in this mode of thinking. He is well known as a member of the "republican" movement, which seeks to reconstruct public life through debate, discussion, and reverence of distinctly public values.[43] In this respect he and Dewey are like Habermas.[44] "[L]iberal republicanism" holds that "political outcomes should not be a reflection of the self-interest of well-organized private groups."[45] Thus he rejects the logistic notion that parts precede the whole and that the construction of such parts—interest groups as well as individuals—into an artifice somehow transforms their collective character into a "public" whole. The public realm, from whose perspective the problem of caste must be judged, is different in kind, not just in degree or size, from collections of private entities; it is for this reason that affirmative action must be understood and implemented as a remedy for a social ill that is the outgrowth of society in its entirety.[46]

To achieve equality, affirmative action must move to delete "discriminatory purposes and effects connected to the maintenance of the caste system."[47] To combat the *effects* of societal discrimination, we may have to move toward the statutory disparate impact model of Title VII[48] in order to eradicate the broad "socially conditioned phenomena" causing discrimination, but without proof of intention demanded by the logistic model of affirmative action.[49] Guilt and innocence, sin and atonement, lose their narrow meaning (even metaphorically) in this context, because there need be no identified wrongdoer, nor is there "harm to innocent victims."[50] "Because it represents a conspicuous rejection of the status quo as non-neutral and unjust, those who accept the anticaste principle are not bothered if some people are made worse off by the results for which it calls."[51] "For example, affirmative action does not appear an impermissible taking of any real entitlement held by whites and men."[52] This reasoning dovetails with my criticism of the sin and atonement metaphor by Dean Sullivan, together with my suggestion of expiation as the appropriate religious metaphor. The need for expiation means that there is no individualization to be made of guilt—it belongs to all of society.

This feature of society-wide responsibility is also accompanied, in Sunstein's view, by "a dramatic softening . . . of causation;"[53] and causes become the principles that explain societal discrimination from the only perspective from which it can be explained—from the whole. The consequences of these causes in turn become the grounds from which to address this discrimination—holistically.

Though the apprehension or intuition (not the deduction) of these causal principles is from particulars, a familiar maxim of general application applies: "[One conception] of equality requires the similarly situated to be treated the same; a less familiar but also important understanding requires the differently situated to be treated differently, also in the interest of equality."[54] Proponents of logistic tend to follow the first branch of the maxim exclusively, to emphasize the basic or near equality of all individuals in material possessions or in the potentiality to acquire them, and find a need for restitution only in the event of narrowly based deviations from such equality. Sunstein appears to say that we must go beyond this understanding of equality and accept that some differences, both material and intangible, among individuals and especially among groups are so profound and so pervasive that reparations of a redistributive nature are *ipso facto* indicated. The anticaste principle permits—requires—this kind of distributive justice through affirmative action because it permits racial distinctions (benign discrimination) "as an effort to eliminate racial caste."[55] Thus the second branch of the maxim of equality would be satisfied: The differently situated would be treated differently, also in the name of equality.

Sunstein's approach from the direction of problematic is exhibited in two kinds of judicial cases, those arising from the Constitution *and* those bottomed on Title VII. I begin with the former.

SOCIAL CAUSATION AND EQUAL PROTECTION

Problematic criteria for affirmative action have already been displayed in the debate between Justice Powell and Justice Brennan in their respective opinions in *Bakke*, particularly regarding the contrasting logistic and problematic views toward the distinction between "invidious" and "benign" discrimination[56] and toward the element of causation.[57] These issues and others separating logistic from problematic have also been discussed and the problematic perspective refuted by Justice O'Connor, from the logistic perspective, in *J. A. Croson.*[58] The distinctions argued and debated in these opinions deal at bottom with the efficacy of "societal discrimination" as an ample ground for affirmative action, though proponents of problematic do not always accept that characterizing terminology to describe this key element of their justification.[59]

Justice Marshall

To take up the issue of causation first, Justice Marshall, dissenting in the constitutional case of *J. A. Croson,*[60] found the causal link necessary for "a remedial and *prophylactic* governmental response"[61] in the relation between the history of "past exclusionary practices" and "a pitifully small presence of minorities" in desired positions, here in contractor positions in the construction industry in Richmond, Virginia.[62] The necessary causation could also be inferred from "the *continuing exclusion* of minorities [from the city's force of contractors] . . . [shown in] a contrast between [the much larger proportion of minorities in the general, undifferentiated] population and [the corresponding minuscule proportion found in the targeted] work force."[63] Accordingly, "[t]he fact that just 0.67% of public construction expenditures over the past five years had gone to minority-owned prime contractors," despite the city's fifty percent minority population, constituted an "enormous disparity" leading to the damning conclusion of the " 'the inexorable zero.' "[64] The conclusion posed in these words pointed to the stark absence, for all intents and purposes, of blacks from the contracting force.

Of course, Justice O'Connor in *J. A. Croson* rejected a comparison of the workforce or the composition of the contracting industry with the gross, undifferentiated population of the city or other arguably appropriate geographic area and, following the *Hazelwood* case, required that the comparison be made with the racial composition of the predictably much smaller proportion of *skilled* or otherwise qualified persons in the whole geographic pool.[65] This is precisely where the decisive break between Justices Marshall and O'Connor, between problematic and logistic, is made.

In a rhetorical jab, Justice Marshall used quotations from Justice O'Connor herself when he argued that "when it is alleged that discrimination has *prevented* blacks from 'obtaining th[e] experience' needed to qualify for a position, the 'relevant comparison' is not to the percentage of blacks in the pool of qualified candidates but to 'the total percentage of blacks in the labor force.' "[66] But what the two Justices meant by "prevented"—having caused an applicant not to be qualified—are worlds apart. In her *Johnson v. Transportation Agency* concurrence, Justice O'Connor left no doubt that prevention of minorities from obtaining skills must, if such prevention is to count as a legally cognizable cause of discrimination, be traced to the by-now-familiar logistic causal basis in specificity and particularity.[67] Later in *J. A. Croson* she further stated that generalized assertions of past discrimination could not account for lack of qualification.[68]

According to Justice Marshall, however, a *group* can be " 'saddled with such disabilities, or subjected to such a history of purposeful unequal treatment, or relegated to such a position of political powerlessness' " that it may be retarded in its advancement in skills and qualifications.[69] This circumstance indeed satisfies Sunstein's definition of "caste."[70] In such a situation a general population comparison is justified, just as the anticaste principle requires "significant restructuring of [general] social practices."[71] Social "causes" or explanations supply an extra layer of causation that logistic does not have. The proponent of the logistic approach wants to know only *that* these persons in the general population are skilled or unskilled, but the practical and problematic jurist goes beyond that level in his inquiry and wants to know *why* (or why not).[72] The Richmond City Council, said Justice Marshall, knew the *why*, having "witness[ed] multifarious acts of discrimination, including, but not limited to, the deliberate diminution of black residents' voting rights, resistance to school desegregation, and publicly sanctioned housing discrimination,"[73] as well as the discriminatory history of the construction industry in Richmond itself. "[T]he continuing impact of [city] government acceptance or use of private institutions or structures[, structures that have perpetuated a caste system in contracting and were indeed] once wrought by [official or Jim Crow] discrimination . . . [t]hus [justified the city and justifies this] Court to eschew rigid tests which require the provision of particular species of evidence, statistical or otherwise."[74] This situation, in Sunstein's words, called instead for "softening . . . the traditional [logistic] ideas of causation."[75]

The impact of past and present institutions of racial caste, to continue with Cass Sustein's terminology, justified the city's thirty percent MBE affirmative program because redressing that residual racial impact of Jim Crow would have satisfied an "important governmental objective[],"[76] an essential component of the *intermediate* level of constitutional review. Strict scrutiny would not be appropriate in such a *remedial* use of racial classifications.[77] By the same token, the requirement that the city be able to adduce a *prima facie* case of racial discrimination against itself, in order to meet its rebuttal burden to a charge of racial discrimination brought by hypothetical white plaintiffs attacking its affirmative action plan, became a procedural requirement reduced significantly in its stringency because of "this constitutional history and social reality."[78] The upshot is that the social nature of causation, as reflected by Justice Marshall's dissent in *J. A. Croson*, recognizes a more powerful and a more flexible rationale for affirmative action. So also for Justice Brennan.

Justice Brennan

Justice Brennan seemed in his *Bakke* opinion to be challenging the equal protection requirement of intentionality for securing constitutional relief[79] when he argued that affirmative action is constitutionally allowable "to remove *the disparate racial impact* [that is] the product of past discrimination."[80]

[W]ithout [any requirement of] . . . individual[] . . . findings of intentional racial discrimination . . . [the] States . . . may adopt race-conscious programs designed to overcome substantial, chronic minority underrepresentation where there is reason to believe that the evil addressed is a *product* of past racial discrimination.[81]

Such relief does not require as a predicate proof that recipients of preferential advancement have been *individually* discriminated against; *it is enough that each recipient is within a general class of persons likely to have been the victims of discrimination.*[82]

This approach is not centered on intent as a means to trace narrow causes to specific individuals (whether victims or wrongdoers) but, rather, is turned to "the consequences of the behavior of individuals *joined in groups*"[83] so that shared interests in these consequences "may inform desire and thereby direct action."[84]

The causes of a condition of racial injustice to be redressed by affirmative action are broad social phenomena, not the highly particularized factors applied by logistic to individuals in order to determine causation,[85] as emphasized by Justices Powell and O'Connor and by Richard Epstein. These social causes— in contrast—can be traced back to the "open compromise[] [of the] principle of equality with its antithesis: slavery. The consequences of this compromise are well known and have aptly been called our 'American Dilemma.' "[86] Under this approach presented in social causation, "the presence or absence of past discrimination by universities or employers is largely irrelevant to resolving [a white challenger's] constitutional claims . . . [because if] the effects of past discrimination [kept minority applicants from attaining the disputed position], then there is a reasonable likelihood that, but for pervasive racial discrimination, [the white challenger—here, Bakke] would have failed even in the absence of [the affirmative action program.]"[87]

Thus it is clear that Justice Brennan's approach to causation, at least in *Bakke*, might well have been a model for Cass Sustein's abandonment of corrective justice in favor of causes that cannot be "connected in any simple way with past discrimination, and certainly not with acts of discrimination that can be tightly connected with their particular complaint[s]."[88]

One major inference to be drawn from the Marshall/Brennan approach to causation is that it lays a basis for distributive justice. Although individuals certainly do not disappear from these justices' thought, the shift to broad social causation means that society itself is now being re-formed to eliminate the gross racial barriers having their roots in decades and centuries of racial discrimination. The proponent of problematic is concerned more with the whole outcome, not simply with the individual effects of affirmative action. Society as a whole is being reshaped toward equality through a process resting on the ideal of egalitarianism—making unequal distributions to those who are unequal.

Individuals are also being restored to material and moral dignity in a deontological sense—and in a way that could not happen otherwise. It could not be otherwise because redistribution goes beyond corrective justice to address a victim's need to gain his dignity against the cumulative impact of *many* injuries, not simply his need to regain an arbitrary status quo determined by the scope and origin of a *single* injury. For as Sunstein informs us, distributive justice establishes its own baselines and looks at the distribution of jobs, and of those other things that we value in our society, in a fresh way unwedded to the status quo. The fact that this kind of potential effect on society can be contemplated at all depends most heavily on the unique experience of black Americans. This structure of social and racial inequality enabled Justices Marshall and Brennan to reject the "color-blind" theory of antidiscrimination and rather to embrace the contrary theory of "benign" discrimination—a social theory directly derivable from the social fact of blacks' existence as a caste.

"BENIGN" DISCRIMINATION

The so-called "color-blind" theory of discrimination stands for the proposition that discrimination against *anyone* because of race is equal in severity and illegality to discrimination against anyone *else* because of race—*even if one such person is white and the other is black.* Logistic holds this position. The proponent of the problematic view, while conceding that sometimes this maxim holds true, argues that it need not apply to a properly constructed affirmative action program. "The apparent symmetry between the plight of racially discriminated blacks and innocent whites disadvantaged by affirmative action . . . is purely abstract and superficial. Remedial affirmative action plans, such as those [approved] in various Supreme Court decisions . . . cannot seriously be considered the product of racist animus against whites."[89]

Proponents of the problematic view therefore believe that *asymmetrical* discrimination is both actually possible and morally necessary in establishing affirmative action programs. As Justice Brennan argued in *Bakke*, "[R]acial classifications are not *per se* invalid under the Fourteenth Amendment."[90] Blacks and other minorities bear the burden of stigma—a social phenomenon that creates "the presumption that one race is inferior to another" and that generates "racial hatred and [a belief in racial] separatism."[91] "[W]hites as a class [do not] have any of the 'traditional indicia of [stigmatization]: the class is not saddled with such disabilities, or subjected to such a history of purposeful unequal treatment, or relegated to such a position of political powerlessness as to command extraordinary protection' [under strict scrutiny]."[92]

Thus affirmative action programs that assign preferences to blacks and other minorities and that necessarily discriminate against whites are *benign*—they are not based on racial hatred, stigma, or beliefs in racial inferiority but rather on the need to achieve racial justice. The judicial standard of review is not, however, rational-basis review, because such a standard would provide a virtual "automatic shield" blocking the inquiry into the purpose of the program. Intermediate scrutiny, which requires proof of an important governmental purpose (satisfied by virtually any bona fide affirmative action plan) and a substantial relation to serving that purpose (assuring both that whites are not gratuitously harmed and that blacks are benefited), is the proper measure of the constitutional validity of an affirmative action plan.[93]

It must be noted that, in problematic, the ground for establishing the crucial concept of benign discrimination (against whites) is *empirical*—it is based on actual observations about the history of the races in America. This reliance on empiricism is so to the extent that I have used Dewey's (and Sunstein's) undoubted empiricism, as they are informed by *a posteriori* particularized perceptions of social phenomena.[94] Thus Justice Brennan began with this empirical basis for his argument for social causation as the ground of affirmative action.

From the inception of our national life, Negroes have been subjected to unique legal disabilities impairing access to equal education opportunity. Under slavery, penal sanctions were imposed upon anyone attempting to educate Negroes. [Even after enactment of the Fourteenth Amendment, and well into this century,] the States continued to deny Negroes equal educational opportunity [and] denied them intercourse in the mainstream of professional life necessary to advancement.[95]

When I reach my discussion of the operational mode of thought and its conception of justified affirmation action, the notion of benign discrimination becomes *a priori* and turns on distinctions of the mind to reach a similar conclusion to that of problematic.

Logistic, never denying the concept of stigmatization, indeed denies that it can ever be absent from racial discrimination of *any* sort, especially so-called benign discrimination.[96] Logistic, with its "color-blind" theory, cannot accept the asymmetry of benign discrimination because it cannot accept that individuals suffer an ontological or fundamental alteration in their existences as human beings through the experiences of their social and group histories.[97] Racial discrimination against one individual is essentially the same as discrimination against any other, regardless of race.

Stigmatization means caste, in Sunstein's usage of the term, and in this vein, Justice Marshall added to the argument that benign discrimination is both justified by the stigma of caste and necessary to overcome it. "By contrast [to racial classifications laid down on notions of racial inferiority or racial hatred], racial classifications drawn for the purpose of *remedying* the effects of discrimination that itself was race based [in caste] have a highly pertinent basis: the tragic and indelible fact that discrimination against blacks and other racial minorities in this Nation has *pervaded* our Nation's history and continues to scar our society."[98] In Richmond, Virginia, alone, the city officials "spent long years witnessing multifarious acts of discrimination, including, but not limited to, the deliberate diminution of black residents' voting rights, resistance to school desegregation, and publicly sanctioned housing discrimination."[99] Justice O'Connor had, of course, rejected the notion of two morally distinct types of racial preference, because her reliance on logistic notions of the individual and the "color-blind" constitution did not permit her to recognize the existence of castelike conditions that affect only minorities and not the majority.[100]

It cannot be emphasized enough that without the concept of benign discrimination and the social source of its emergence in a caste-pervaded society, the problematic mode would not be able to justify its bold approach to remediation of pervasive discrimination on so broad a front. In comparison, it would be most limited, like the logistic approach, which seems able only to proceed in a distinctly deductive fashion.[101] Indeed, Justice Marshall called this narrower approach one "of disaggregating [the] evidence [and] attacking it piecemeal."[102] Nowhere are the splits in their respective views of social reality more prominent than in the contrast between problematic and logistic on this issue of the dual or uniform impact of discrimination, empirically or more abstractly and deductively, under the Equal Protection Clause. The problematic view, however, has fared considerably better under Title VII, where, among other things, its standards of review and of proof have prevailed, signaling a relaxation of causation from the constitutional side.

SOCIAL CAUSATION AND TITLE VII OF THE CIVIL RIGHTS ACT OF 1964

The issue in *United Steelworkers of America v. Weber*[103] was largely whether a plausible construction of key provisions of Title VII would permit the institution by a private employer of an affirmative action plan having the characteristics of a "quota," or a specific percentage or number of minorities—a concept that had been derided by Justice Powell in *Bakke.*[104] The joint plan by the employer and the union set up a special crafts training program whose positions were to be filled with fifty percent black trainees until the racial composition of the employer's skilled workforce (filled from the training program) "approximated the percentage of blacks in the local labor force."[105] Theretofore blacks from the local labor pool in the New Orleans/Baton Rouge area of Louisiana had been virtually excluded from craft union membership, the chief route of entry into skilled positions with the employer.[106]

Opponents of the plan (represented by plaintiff Brian Weber, an unsuccessful white applicant to the training program) argued that it plainly violated several key provisions of the Civil Rights Act of 1964, *viz.*, sections 703(a) and 703(d),[107] which forbid employers and unions to discriminate on the basis of race, and section 703(j)[108]—the famous antiquota provision that provides that the government or courts are not to be interpreted under the Act to have power to "*require* any employer . . . to grant preferential treatment . . . on account of an imbalance which may exist with respect to the total number or percentage of persons of any race . . . in comparison with the total number or percentage of such persons of such race . . . in any community."[109]

Justice Brennan, writing for the Court, relied heavily on the legislative history of Title VII to refute these arguments. As to the strictures of sections 703(a) and 703(d) on racial discrimination, he argued and wrote for the Court that these provisions were designed to prohibit discrimination against individuals and groups, as these acts of discrimination arose; but that they did not entirely reflect the systematic purpose of the Act to sweep away the very social structures of pervasive discrimination. "[I]t was clear to Congress that '[t]he crux of the problem [was] to open employment opportunities for Negroes in occupations which have been traditionally closed to them.' "[110] Justice Brennan chose to read the Act *as a whole* to address a hitherto intractable problem—the destruction of caste barriers—not to read the Act as limited to resolution of individualized disputes. This is the heart of the problematic approach. He read the language in section 703(j) as prohibiting the government from "requir[ing]" a putative "quota" but carrying a distinct meaning *favorable* to affirmative action—the *favorable* negative implication of allowing the government and the courts to "permit" a *voluntary* plan.[111] Thus the plan in question was validated under Title VII, though this decision evoked great criticism.[112]

The standard of proof in the case was the existence of "manifest racial imbalances in traditionally segregated job categories."[113] The comparison made under this standard closely resembled the comparison in *Teamsters,*[114] where the proportion of minorities in an unskilled workforce was compared with the general proportion of minorities in the surrounding population. Here in *Weber,* to be sure, the minority individuals were not literally refused employment; but because the training requisite for the job was completely denied them, they were functionally denied employment so effectively that the "inexorable zero"[115] could aptly apply to the employer's workforce. Justice Brennan did not even discuss whether there was prior intention by the employer and union to discriminate unlawfully. Quite plausibly the case is an analogue to *Griggs,*[116] because the *Weber* case involved employment practice skills, arguably neutral in the *Griggs* sense, that produced a "manifest . . . imbalance" in race.[117] Moreover, this was not a constitutional case expressly requiring intent. Arguably, then, the employer and union might have been defensively using a voluntary affirmative action plan to avert a *Griggs*-style disparate impact lawsuit against themselves by blacks and other minority citizens in the surrounding labor pool.

The standard of proof is here relaxed: There is no need for express statistical proof, as in *Hazelwood*,[118] no express need to prove prior intent to discriminate unlawfully, and there is a standard for respecting the rights of "innocent" whites that is not exceptionally demanding and is here met.[119] In problematic's constitutional terms (from Justice Brennan in *Bakke* and which, of course, are not at issue here), no more than the standard of intermediate scrutiny would be required to be met, with no required strong, direct proof of discrimination. Therefore, that arguably less demanding constitutional standard is met because redressing the manifest imbalance serves an important government interest, and the action taken serves that interest without unduly prejudicing the rights of third parties ("innocent" whites).

The tension between *Teamsters* and *Hazelwood School District*, on the nature of the required statistical proof of "manifest imbalance," came up again in *Johnson v. Transportation Agency*.[120] The voluntary plan adopted there included the agency's *skilled* workers, but the undifferentiated general population formed the comparison group. Because "the agency stated that its long-term goal was to attain a workforce whose composition reflected the proportion of minorities and women in area labor force,"[121] the plan can be said to have been based on "societal discrimination."

The case, which concerned gender as a factor in determining *Weberian* justification for an affirmative action plan, focused on the legality under Title VII of a local government employer's having passed over a veteran male employee for promotion in favor of a female employee, slightly less objectively qualified. The "manifest imbalance" "for the job classification" was that "none of the 238 Skilled Craft Worker positions [with the employer] was held by a woman."[122] Added to this was the employer's long-term goal of a proportionate workforce of minorities and women from the surrounding labor pool. "Thus . . . the Agency's aspiration was that eventually about 36% of the jobs [skilled or unskilled] would be occupied by women."[123]

Justice Brennan defended *Weber*'s "manifest imbalance" standard and, in the process, distinguished its standard of proof from the strong standard of proof in *Hazelwood*. While nominally preserving the distinction between *Teamster* comparisons to the entire labor pool and *Hazelwood* comparisons only to skilled workers available from the population (when the job or jobs called for are skilled),[124] in a footnote he seemed to have moved toward a collapse of the distinction. He pointed out that in *Weber* a comparison along the lines of *Hazelwood* would have been inapt, because the unions provided no training to blacks, and for this reason there *were* no skilled black workers in the general population.[125] But in the problematic scheme of things, there are *always* reasons why blacks, other minorities, and women are untrained and unprepared for certain jobs.[126] Thus the theory behind "societal discrimination" seems to control all of these cases; this theory finds reasons and causes for discrimination under most or all circumstances (shaped, of course, by the concept of societal discrimination itself) *and* for its remediation where a logistically driven approach finds none.[127]

Furthermore, Justice Brennan argued that the burden of proof for constitutional cases like *Wygant* and for Title VII cases should be different, with a Title VII defendant's not being required to demonstrate a *prima facie* case of unlawful discrimination against itself in order to carry its burden of production against white or male plaintiffs attacking its voluntary affirmative action plan. "Application of the 'prima facie' standard in Title VII cases would be inconsistent with *Weber*'s focus on [broad] statistical imbalance, and could inappropriately create a significant disincentive for employers to adopt an affirmative action plan."[128] Indeed, in comparison with constitutional standards of causation, the burden of proof in Title VII cases seems relaxed, with the employer's having to adduce neither the quality (*e.g.*, specific, intentional acts of discrimination) nor quantity (weight of evidence needed to defend a plan) that one does in Fourteenth Amendment cases, especially in comparison with *Wygant* or *J. A. Croson*.[129] This assessment also fits in with the previously asserted constitutional standard of review of intermediate scrutiny, applicable implicitly in *Weber*[130] and *Johnson*.

Justice O'Connor, entirely displeased with the Court's rationale but finding herself unable to dissent because of the "inexorable zero"—revealed by the total absence of female skilled employees in the workforce—concurred in the judgment in *Johnson*. First she argued (as she later wrote for the court in *J. A. Croson*) that a *prima facie* case, "no different from that required by the Equal Protection Clause," is required for an employer to sustain a viable affirmative action plan.[131] Ordinarily she would have rigidly followed *Hazelwood*.[132] The *Hazelwood* method of comparison screens out societal discrimination as a factor in the putative illegal discrimination and thus retains a strong focus on intent as a necessary element.[133] But because here there were *no women* in the employer's skilled workforce (but five percent of the relevant labor pool were skilled women workers),[134] there was a sufficient statistical disparity to sustain the plan under Title VII.[135] More important, though, was the "inexorable zero," no women employees in a *unit* of 238. Thus only at the most extreme point in the discrimination spectrum—where it is impossible to conjecture about the employer's hiring purposes or practices—can the two sides of problematic and logistic coincide. This is the one point where the *Teamsters* scheme of statistical proof converges with the stricter, more intent-oriented standards of *Hazelwood*. But Justice O'Connor made it plain in her separate *Johnson* opinion that such convergence will be rare.

CONCLUSION

The crux of the problematic approach to and justification of affirmative action can be quickly revealed in an aphorism of John Dewey:

When we look in the wrong place we naturally do not find what we are looking for. The worst of it is, however, that looking in the wrong place, to causal forces instead of consequences, the outcome of the looking becomes arbitrary. . . . For, as we have previously remarked, the main facts of political action, while the phenomena vary immensely with diversity of time and place, are not hidden even when they are complex. They are facts of human behavior accessible to human observation. [Other views] spring from the root of [a] shared error: the taking of causal agency instead of consequences as the heart of the problem.[136]

The problem of social causation, which I have associated with the problematic or practical rationale for affirmative action, is a social, political, and historical one—the residual *effect* of hundreds of years of brutal slavery, of over a century of Jim Crow, of educational and employment deprivation, and of dignity-robbing practices upon African Americans and other demeaned groups. Proponents of the problematic approach to affirmative action view the station of racially and ethnically deprived groups as forming a castelike stratum in American society, requiring broad understanding to perceive the nature of their status and broad changes in society to grant them justice. These broad changes are concerned more with distributive justice than with compensatory justice attuned to individually measured injustices.

Justices Brennan and Marshall have been the main proponents of the problematic approach on the Supreme Court. In the constitutional cases of *Bakke* and *J. A. Croson* they reviewed the history of the race problem in this country and then set out steps needed to resolve this problem—steps that far outstrip, from the point of view of problematic, the resolutions proposed by logistic. Causation is not simply the universal and customary relation of a single antecedent to a single consequent but, rather, takes the form of explanation of group behavior in several dimensions—including the dimension of social institutions, both those that foster race hatred and those that must endure and resist it. Discrimination in this view is asymmetrical, trained with ferocity on blacks but not on whites—a fact learned from social observation that entitles officials and employers to exercise preferential treatment toward blacks without maligning whites.

The Title VII cases preserve and extend these principles and practices. *Weber* and *Johnson* establish that demonstration of a "manifest imbalance" between the percentage of blacks and other groups traditionally suffering discrimination in the employer's workforce and their percentage in the *general* population can provide the evidence needed to defend an affirmative action program, without causally rigorous proof that the employer had previously discriminated unlawfully.

What the social causation rationale does essentially is to liberate employers, lawyers, and jurists from narrow deductive chains of quantitative causation tied to individual persons, employers, schools, or agencies—considered abstractly and uniformly without controlling attention to social experience. In terms of its reliance on equality and on justice as a systematic social equality available to all, Michel Rosenfeld has called the problematic approach "the most justified position on the scope of the constitutional legitimacy of affirmative action thus far expressed on the Supreme Court."[137]

By focusing on broad social causes and their consequences for the public and its problem of racial injustice, proponents have little need to identify this great problem, either literally or metaphorically, with the concept of sin and the assignment of repercussions of discrimination to any particular wrongdoers or to assign associated guilt to any person or institution. There is no need to make such an identification or assignment before imposing the legal duty to reform on a malefactor or to defend him when he affirmatively undertakes reform. But yet there is a sense in which the concepts of sin and guilt do pervade the entire society—far beyond their assignment to individuals. The problematic perspective, if anything, teaches that a kind of secular sin ("the wickedness of human nature")[138] and its mark of injustice do pervade the entire society, here in the form of castelike structures. The expiation of guilt associated with "societal discrimination" may then represent a very meaningful and powerful metaphor or a vivid symbol resting on these broad social causes. Expiation may also be linked to the paradoxical discrimination against the discriminators, if not the *actual* discriminators, then against the dominant group. It is part of this paradox that the discrimination designed to pull down caste is, in this view, weaker and more nearly harmless than the discrimination used to create caste.

In Chapter 4, *social equality* becomes a rival to *social causation*, not because of insistence on equality as such but because it associates equality with autonomy rather than with participation in the polity. But it, too, presents a paradox by offering discrimination against the discriminators to achieve this equality.

NOTES

[1] *J. A. Croson*, 488 U.S. at 541 (Marshall, J., dissenting) (emphasis in original; citation omitted).

[2] ARISTOTLE, ETHICS vi, 12, 13, 1144a30–37, 1146b35–1147a5, 1147b66–17, in McKEON (ED.), THE BASIC WORKS OF ARISTOTLE, supra Ch. 1, note 100, at 1035, 1040 & 1042. It is especially important to grasp the nature of the particulars of action in the use of the practical syllogism. Id. at 1146b35–1147a8, BASIC WORKS, at 1040.

[3] (1927; 1954).

[4] (1916; 1944; Free Press ed.) (subtitled: AN INTRODUCTION TO THE PHILOSOPHY OF EDUCATION).

[5] JOHN DEWEY, THE PUBLIC AND ITS PROBLEMS 158 (1927; 1954) [hereinafter THE PUBLIC AND ITS PROBLEMS].

[6] Id. (internal quotation at id. at 11).

[7] Id. at 12.

[8] Id. at 155 (emphasis supplied).

[9] Id. at 12–13 (emphasis supplied).

[10] Id. at 138–39, 142, 179–80.

[11] *Cf.* id. at 31.

[12] Id. at 32 (emphasis supplied).

[13] Id. at 6.

[14] Id. at 155. *Cf.* ARISTOTLE, ETHICS vi, 2, 1139a27–b5, in MCKEON, THE BASIC WORKS OF ARISTOTLE, supra Ch. 1, note 100, at 1024. ("The origin of action—its efficient, not final cause—is choice, and that of choice is *desire* and reasoning with a view to an end. . . . Intellect itself . . . moves nothing . . . for good action is an end, and *desire* aims at this. Hence choice is either desiderative reason or ratiocinative desire, and such an origin of action is a man.") (emphasis supplied).

[15] DEWEY, THE PUBLIC AND ITS PROBLEMS, at 208 (emphasis in original).

[16] Id. at 54.

[17] Id. at 150.

[18] DEWEY, DEMOCRACY AND EDUCATION, supra Ch. 3, note 4, at 87.

[19] Id. at 122.

[20] CASS R. SUNSTEIN, LEGAL REASONING AND POLITICAL CONFLICT [hereinafter LEGAL REASONING] (1996).

[21] Thus he rejects John Rawls's reliance on reflective equilibrium, which, he says, is an attempt to adjust a general theory "to what we think [are] our considered views about particulars." Id. at 17 (referring to JOHN RAWLS, A THEORY OF JUSTICE 20, 48–51 [1971]).

[22] SUNSTEIN, LEGAL REASONING, at 49.

[23] Id. at 131 n.11 (quoting from ARISTOTLE, ETHICS [v, 10 1137b5–33], reprinted in THE ETHICS OF ARISTOTLE 200 (J.A.K. Thomson, trans. 1976).

[24] SUNSTEIN, LEGAL REASONING, at 35 (emphasis in original), 37, 49. *Cf.* ARISTOTLE, PRIOR ANALYTICS ii, 24, 68b37–69a19, in MCKEON, THE BASIC WORKS OF ARISTOTLE, supra Ch. 1, note 100, at 103. ("Clearly then to argue by example is neither like reasoning from part to whole, not like reasoning from whole to part, but rather reasoning from part to part.")

[25] SUNSTEIN, LEGAL REASONING, at 131 n.11, quoting John Dewey, "Logical Method and Law," 10 Cornell L. Q. 17 (1924).

[26] See note and text at Ch. 3, note 12, supra (same view attributed to Dewey).

[27] CASS R. SUNSTEIN, THE PARTIAL CONSTITUTION 11, 77–78 (1993) [hereinafter THE PARTIAL CONSTITUTION]. *Cf.* O'Connor, J., in *J. A. Croson*, 488 U.S. at 501–02 (reliance on a relevant labor market to provide a neutral norm in statistically gauging racial discrimination); see also note and text at Ch. 2, note 178, supra.

[28] Id. at 78.

[29] SUNSTEIN, LEGAL REASONING, at 25.

[30] Id.

[31] Cass R. Sunstein, "The Anticaste Principle," 92 Mich. L. Rev. 2410, 2439 (1994).

[32] Id. at 2429. The first Justice Harlan, dissenting in *Plessy v. Ferguson*, supra Ch. 1, note 141, 163 U.S. at 559, used the term "caste" to emphasize his normative belief that social or racial classes should not exist (but by negative inference his descriptive belief was that "caste" did exist). Justice Stevens in our day has used the term "caste" to describe the system at which eradication of "racial subordination" is and should be aimed. *Adarand*, 515 U.S. at 243. So Sunstein's use of the term "caste" in the legal context is not novel.

[33] Sunstein, "The Anticaste Principle," supra Ch. 3, note 3, at 2440.

[34] ARISTOTLE, POLITICS, v, 1, 1301a36–37; 1301b6, in MCKEON, THE BASIC WORKS OF ARISTOTLE, supra Ch. 1 note 100, at 1233.

[35] SUNSTEIN, THE PARTIAL CONSTITUTION, at 102 (emphasis in original).

[36] Id. at 157 (emphasis in original).

[37] Cass R. Sunstein, "Public Deliberation, Affirmative Action, and the Supreme Court," 84 Calif. L. Rev. 1179, 1188 (1996).

[38] SUNSTEIN, THE PARTIAL CONSTITUTION, at 76.

[39] Id. at 321 (emphasis supplied).

[40] See notes and text at Ch. 2, notes 33, 43, & 72, supra (Aristotle, Nozick, & Epstein).

[41] SUNSTEIN, THE PARTIAL CONSTITUTION, at 322.

[42] Id. at 7.

[43] Cf. id. at 133–41.

[44] See note and text at Ch. 3, note 612, supra.

[45] SUNSTEIN, THE PARTIAL CONSTITUTION, at 134.

[46] Cf. Daniel A. Farber and Philip B. Frickey, "Is *Carolene Products* Dead? Reflections on Affirmative Action and the Dynamics of Civil Rights Legislation," 79 Calif. L. Rev. 685, 726 n.222 (1991) ("The republican argument for affirmative action is based on the importance of civic community. Because participation in the community is for republicans a basic element of human thriving, exile or marginalization is a grave injury to individuals.").

[47] SUNSTEIN, THE PARTIAL CONSTITUTION, at 79.

[48] See notes and text at Intro., note 29 & Ch. 2, note 64 supra.

[49] SUNSTEIN, THE PARTIAL CONSTITUTION, at 329, 164 (quotation is mine, from DEWEY, THE PUBLIC AND ITS PROBLEMS, 3, at 104). Cf. Washington v. Davis, 426 U.S. 229 (1976) (requiring proof of intent to discriminate to state a cause of action under the Equal Protection Clause).

[50] SUNSTEIN, THE PARTIAL CONSTITUTION, at 331.

[51] Id. at 343.

[52] Id.

[53] Id. at 322.

[54] SUNSTEIN, LEGAL REASONING at 132. Cf. H.L.A. HART, THE CONCEPT OF LAW 155 (1961) ("[The] leading precept of [justice] is often formulated 'Treat like cases alike'; though we need to add to the latter 'and treat different cases differently.' ").

[55] SUSTEIN, THE PARTIAL CONSTITUTION, at 340.

[56] See notes and text at Ch. 2, notes 80–83, supra.

[57] See notes and text at Ch. 2, notes 86–92, supra.

[58] See, *e.g.*, notes and text at Ch. 2, notes 92–95, 123, 127–29, 147 (societal discrimination); 176–82, 195–98, supra.

[59] Cf. J. A. Croson, 488 U.S. at 541 (Marshall, J., dissenting) (Richmond's reliance on "localized, industry-specific findings is a far cry from the reliance on generalized 'societal discrimination' which the majority decries as a basis for remedial action.").

[60] Id. at 528–61 (Marshall, J., dissenting).

[61] Id. at 540 (emphasis supplied) (the term "prophylactic" indicates a role for distributive justice).

[62] Id. at 540.

[63] Id. at 540, 542 (emphasis in original).

[64] Id at 540, 542 (citing the term "the inexorable zero" to Teamsters v. United States, 431 U.S. 324, 342, n.23 (1977) (the term's meaning " 'the glaring absence of minority [contractors]' "); *Johnson v. Transp. Agency*, 480 U.S. at 656–57 (opinion of O'Connor, J., concurring) (quoting *Teamsters*).

[65] See notes and text at Ch. 2, notes 174–82, supra.

[66] *J. A. Croson*, 488 U.S. at 542 (opinion of Marshall, J., dissenting) (quoting from Justice O'Connor's concurring opinion in *Johnson v. Transp. Agency*, 480 U.S. at 651) (emphasis supplied).

[67] *Johnson v. Transp. Agency*, 480 U.S. at 651 (opinion of O'Connor, J., concurring) (explaining that *unskilled* workers in the population could be counted in comparison with the employer's workforce in United Steelworkers v. Weber, 443 U.S. 193 (1979), because blacks were specifically excluded from union training programs. Thus in *Weber* there *was* a specific reason for the lack of skilled workers in the general population.).

[68] See note and text at Ch. 2, note 183, supra.

[69] *J. A. Croson*, 488 U.S. at 533 (Marshall, J., dissenting) (quoting from San Antonio Ind. Sch. Dist. v. Rodriguez, 411 U.S. 1, 28 [1973]).

[70] See note and text at Ch. 3, note 32, supra.

[71] See note and text at Ch. 3, note 33, supra.

[72] See ARISTOTLE, POSTERIOR ANALYTICS, ii, 1, 89b23–30, 174–75 (Loeb ed. 1966) ("These are four kinds of questions that we ask . . . the question of fact ['that'], the question of reason or cause ['why'], the question of existence [whether a thing is], and the question of essence [what a thing is]." In general logistic is interested only in the first and third questions.).

[73] *J. A. Croson*, 488 U.S. at 544 (opinion of Marshall, J., dissenting).

[74] Id. at 538–39.

[75] See note and text at Ch. 3, note 41, supra.

[76] *J. A. Croson Co.*, 488 U.S. at 535 (Marshall, J., dissenting).

[77] Id. at 551–52.

[78] Id. at 558.

[79] See Washington v. Davis, 426 U.S. 229 (1976) (disallowing disproportionate impact as a ground for unconstitutionality of governmental action).

[80] *Bakke*, 438 U.S. at 369 (opinion of Brennan, J.) (emphasis supplied); see also notes and text at Ch. 2, notes 89–92, supra) (attack by Justice Powell on disparate impact as not giving rise to intent and thus not to causation itself).

[81] Id. at 366 (emphasis supplied to indicate concern with the end state or effect).

[82] Id. at 363 (emphasis supplied).

[83] DEWEY, THE PUBLIC AND ITS PROBLEMS, at 32 (emphasis supplied).

[84] Id. at 12.

[85] See, *e.g.*, the views of Powell, J., in *Bakke*, 438 U.S. at 289–90, 298; notes and text at Ch. 2, note 43, 195–96.

[86] *Bakke*, 438 U.S. at 326 (opinion of Brennan, J.) (quoted reference is to GUNNAR MYRDAL, AN AMERICAN DILEMMA, supra Intro., note 8, supra.)

[87] Id. at 365–66.

[88] SUNSTEIN, THE PARTIAL CONSTITUTION; see notes and text at Ch. 3, notes 47–53, supra.

[89] ROSENFELD, AFFIRMATIVE ACTION AND JUSTICE, supra Ch. 1, note 284, at 306.

[90] *Bakke*, 438 U.S. at 356 (opinion of Brennan, J.).

[91] Id. at 357–58.

[92] Id. at 357 (citing United States v. Carolene Products Co., 304 U.S. 144, 152 n.4 [1938]).

[93] Id. at 358–59.

[94] See notes and text at Ch. 3, notes 4, 12, 21–24, supra.

[95] *Bakke*, 438 U.S. at 371 (footnotes and citations omitted).

[96] *Bakke*, 438 U.S. at 294 & n.34 (opinion of Powell, J.); see note and text at Ch. 2, note 12, supra.

[97] See notes and text at Ch. 2, notes 275–76, supra (arguing that Lockean individuals are stripped of all properties except their bare, abstract selves as substances).

[98] *J. A. Croson*, 488 U.S. at 552 (opinion of Marshall, J., dissenting) (emphasis supplied).

[99] Id. at 544.

[100] See notes and text at Ch. 2, notes 195–98, 203–06, supra. See also notes and text at Ch. 2, notes 146–47, supra.

[101] See note and text at Ch. 2, note 183, supra ("[S]ome form of narrowly tailored racial preference . . . necessary to break down patterns of deliberate exclusion [might have been possible in Richmond].") (*J. A. Croson*, 488 U.S. at 509 [opinion of O'Connor, J., joined by Rehnquist, C. J., and White and Kennedy, JJ.]).

[102] *J. A. Croson*, 488 U.S. at 541 (Marshall, J., dissenting).

[103] 443 U.S. 193 (1979).

[104] 438 U.S. at 307 ("[P]urpose . . . to assure . . . [inclusion of] some specified percentage of a particular group merely because of its race or ethnic origin . . . must be rejected as . . . facially invalid. . . . This the Constitution forbids.") (citations omitted) (opinion of Powell, J.).

[105] *Weber*, 443 U.S. at 198–99.

[106] Thus at the time of the institution of the plan only 1.83 percent (or 5 out of 373) of the employer's skilled workers were black, whereas the workforce in the relevant geographic area was 39 percent black.

[107] 42 U.S.C. §§ 2000e–2(a) and (d).

[108] 42 U.S.C. § 2000e–2(j).

[109] Id. (emphasis supplied).

[110] *Weber*, 443 U.S. at 204 (quoting from 10 Cong. Rec. 6548 [1964] [remarks of Senator Humphrey]).

[111] *Weber*, 443 U.S. at 204–06.

[112] See, *e.g.*, Meltzer, "The *Weber* Case: The Judicial Abrogation of the Antidiscrimination Standard in Employment," supra Intro., note 22, supra.

[113] *Weber*, 443 U.S. at 197.

[114] See note and its text at Ch. 2, note 177, supra.

[115] See Ch. 3, note 106, supra, showing the extreme disparities involved, and note 64, showing the origin of the term "inexorable zero."

[116] See note and text at Intro., note 29, supra.

[117] *Cf.* notes and text at Ch. 3, notes 105–06, supra.

[118] See notes and text at Ch. 2, notes 124 & 174–77, supra.

[119] From *Weber*, 443 U.S. at 208–09:

> [T]he plan does not require the discharge of white workers and their replacement with new black hires. [citation omitted] Nor does the plan create an absolute bar to the advancement of white workers. . . . [It is] a temporary measure . . . not intended to maintain racial balance . . . but simply to eliminate a manifest racial imbalance. Preferential selection of craft trainees at the Gramercy plant will end as soon as the percentage of black skilled craft workers in the Gramercy plant approximate the percentage of blacks in the local labor force.

[120] 480 U.S. 616 (1987).

[121] Id. at 621–22.

[122] Id. at 621.

[123] Id. at 621–22. This plan also had certain "short-range" goals related to specifically qualified persons in the local area. Id. at 622.

[124] Id. at 632.

[125] Id. 633 n.10.

[126] See notes and text at Ch. 3, notes 66–69, supra.

[127] Justice O'Connor, in her concurring opinion in *Johnson, did* find that a general labor pool comparison was apt in *Weber*, because "discrimination . . . at entry level into the craft union[s] . . . [which] provided the sole ground for obtaining this [training] . . . was powerful evidence of prior race discrimination." 480 U.S. at 651.

[128] *Johnson*, 480 U.S. at 632–33.

[129] See notes and text at ch. 2, notes 199–202, supra (Justice O'Connor's adoption of the *prima facie* standard in *J. A. Croson*). See also David Benjamin Oppenheimer, "Understanding Affirmative Action," 23 Hastings L. Q. 921, 933 & nn.32, 33 (1996) (Title VII has "relative moderate standard," whereas the constitution has an "extremely strict standard.").

[130] See notes and text at Ch. 3, notes 118–19, supra.

[131] *Johnson*, 480 U.S. at 649 (opinion of O'Connor, J., concurring in the judgment).

[132] Id. at 652. ("A statistical imbalance between the percentage of women in the work force generally and the percentage of women in the particular specialized job classification, therefore, does not suggest past discrimination for purposes of proving a Title VII prima facie case." [citing *Hazelwood*, 433 U.S. at 308 & n.13]).

[133] *Johnson*, 480 U.S. at 653 (opinion of O'Connor, J., concurring in the judgment).

[134] She was aided in this finding, and in making her subsequent comparison, by the plan's "short-term" goals, which focused on workforce comparisons with the proportion of identified, qualified persons in the local labor pool. This allowed her to make an *initial Hazelwood*-type comparison before going on to recognize "the inexorable zero." Id. at 654 (O'Connor, J., concurring in the judgment).

[135] Id. at 656–57 (citing *Teamsters*, 431 U.S. at 342 n.23).

[136] DEWEY, THE PUBLIC AND ITS PROBLEMS, at 19–20.

[137] ROSENFELD AFFIRMATIVE ACTION AND JUSTICE, supra Ch. 1, note 284, at 328.

[138] ARISTOTLE, POLITICS ii, 5, 1263b23, in MCKEON, THE BASIC WORKS OF ARISTOTLE, supra Ch. 1, note 100, at 1152.

4

Operational and Social Equality

THE NATURE OF OPERATIONAL

In my exploration of understanding and justifying affirmative action through the operational mode of thought, I complete my initial aim to analyze affirmative action from four fundamental viewpoints, as elucidated by McKeon, that are "formally exhaustive of [all] possibilities."[1] Accordingly the first three modes—dialectic, logistic, and problematic—have been organized formally by the relation of whole to part: Dialectic selects the whole for priority and makes it englobing of all otherwise differentiated parts; logistic takes the opposite approach by defining parts, or simples, as constitutive of the nature of any whole; and problematic occupies the middle region between the two by positing a reality composed of a plurality of wholes, a reality neither determined by a single overarching comprehensive principle nor constructed of least parts.

The operational mode takes the logically remaining position: abandonment of the whole/part relation altogether for the assumption that all distinctions (as applied to the external world) are initially arbitrary. In this position, operational completes the mutually exclusive and exhaustive schema for all possible modes of thought. Meaning is given to these operational distinctions through the power of the mind itself, by means of concepts that organize and give purpose to an external world whose existence is postulated but never ceded the status of ultimate ground of truth and action. Thus the knower or speaker appeals through speech to a reality constructed in the mental faculties of himself and his audience, not to a reality shown through proof of eternal ideas, external things, or objective natures. The operational method follows the maxim of Protagoras that "man is the measure of all things"[2]—or in Kantian terms, the perspective of a

Copernican revolution in which "objects must conform to our knowledge,"[3] and not our knowledge, to objects.

The operational mode and its method proceed by discrimination and distinction and is the method of debate. Unlike dialectic, in which the interlocutors seek to assimilate conflicting views to a greater whole, in operational the interlocutors engage in discrimination among the different senses that apparently conflicting ideas and opinions may have, and distinction from, rather than refutation of, the opposition's ideas is the main approach.

Operational's greatest writers, such as Kant and Cicero in ancient times, have employed the clash of opinions and arguments in the law courts (Kant, figuratively; Cicero, more literally) as the paradigm of obtaining and fashioning truth and standards of conduct. Kant thus entitles his method "the *skeptical method* ... [and says that it] aims at certainty. It seeks to discover the point of misunderstanding in the case of disputes which are sincerely and competently conducted by both sides."[4] "By its means we can deliver ourselves ... from a great body of sterile dogmatism, and set in its place a sober *critique* [of the powers of reason itself]."[5] The knower becomes active in *making* knowledge from given materials of the external world. As a moral agent acting in a practical sense, the knower formulates for himself, completely apart from the necessities of the external world, the moral law, which assumes the form of the categorical imperative, requiring him to recognize the inherent humanity of all persons.[6] The free person is thus one who can exercise his faculties spontaneously—that is, without external hindrance—and arrive at valid grounds of truth and action. Freedom is found in law imposed upon oneself, whether in judging a debate between others or—what is more likely—in the special kind of debate for truth and morality internalized within oneself. History is the record of men and women who have left a legacy of their words and deeds that illumine the appearance of freedom within the world.

The place of operational as the method of debate and of the law courts is not, paradoxically, prominently reflected in the opinions of the Supreme Court concerned with affirmative action. Its influence *is* felt, though, in approaching the problem that affirmative action seeks to address, from operational's *a priori* perspective—one that sets out a constitutional policy that redresses racial injustice by recognizing the inherent humanity in victims of discrimination and by addressing their stigmatized condition, when contrary to the unstigmatized condition of the majority. In this distinction, between the deep prejudice to minorities and the unthreatened equality of the majority, lies the key to reordering society to recognize *a priori* the humanity of *all*, with only secondary attention to the consequential effects of this policy. Equality, closely associated with freedom, is both the engine and the aim of this approach, which begins in the active powers of the mind and finds its achievement in the validation of self-determination through subjection to valid norms universally and equally applicable to all. Since these norms are *a priori* universally applicable to all, they can remove the stigma of race prejudice (and thus grant freedom and equality) without diminishing the freedom and equality of the majority.

Of all the justices on the Court, only Justice Stevens seems to have taken such an approach grounded in autonomy and directed to self-determination, together with a form of reasoning not bound to external phenomena. This view is primarily found in his dissenting opinions in *Wygant* and in *Adarand*. The principal systematic proponent is Ronald Dworkin, in both his general work and in items specifically addressing affirmative action. Dworkin, in turn, receives support from John Rawls's version of liberal justice, and it is with him that I begin.

JOHN RAWLS AND THE LIBERAL JUSTICE OF SOCIAL EQUALITY

Justice as Fairness and the Original Position

For John Rawls the premier subject of justice is "the basic structure of society,"[7] "or more exactly, the way in which the major social institutions *distribute* fundamental rights and duties and determine the advantages from social cooperation."[8] The conception of justice that emerges from his careful and discriminating analysis is called "justice as fairness," which—though modeled after the "theory of social contract found in . . . Locke, Rousseau, and Kant"[9]—is an operational, not a logistic, theory. Rather than based on the assemblage of individuals into a composite whole, his contractarian theory is founded on a shared, *a priori* conception of justice, animated by "principles that free and rational persons concerned to further their own interests would accept in an initial [hypothetical] position of equality."[10]

The justification of these principles is operational in nature because they are the product of the shared mental faculties of the participants in the assumed "initial situation," where special uniform conditions imposed on these participants make them interlocutors in purely rational, disinterested discourse and debate. The descent of a "veil of ignorance"[11] deprives the participants of any knowledge of their exploitable contingent interests (social class, natural endowments, race and sex, etc.) in the actual world—interests of the sort that Kant would call "pathological conditions, *i.e.*, conditions only contingently [and not categorically] related to the will."[12] Under these formal and hypothetical constraints, denominated the "original position," the participants, universally equalized in their "state of nature," agree to principles that are entirely right and just to impose on themselves upon their emergence as citizens in actual political society. They are just because each participant in the original position, not knowing his own real position in society, is reasonably and rationally compelled to take all possible positions into account in making his agreement to the principles—because some or all of them may turn out to affect him specifically when the veil is lifted. The principles gain additional legitimacy by being subject to verification—in a process called reflective equilibrium—to determine whether they bear a close correspondence to the moral conditions and their correlative principles that "we do in fact accept."[13]

For Rawls in the philosophy of political liberalism, "the objective [universally valid] point of view is always understood as that of certain reasonable and rational persons suitably specified. In Kant's doctrine, it is the point of view of such persons as members of a realm of ends. . . . Similarly, in justice as fairness it is the point of view of free and equal citizens as properly represented."[14] So the original position—set up so as to generate such properly represented free and equal citizens by definition—is a formal explanatory or legitimating device that draws out principles of justice already found in the human capacity to be a free moral agent—illustrating superbly the essence of the operational mode that places man at the center of his world of knowledge and action.

"Overlapping Consensus"

In his first major book, *A Theory of Justice*,[15] Rawls develops his theory of justice as fairness to provide principles for development of the basic structure of society. In a second major book addressing this subject, *Political Liberalism*,[16] Rawls has developed the idea of "an overlapping consensus" as necessary for the stable implementation of justice as fairness.[17] In the second book Rawls recognizes that complete uniformity of belief developed by representatives in the original position cannot be directly extended to actual society because of the fundamentally divergent and comprehensive views of religion, morals, and society existing there.[18] Justice as fairness will require a modified framework to sustain and stabilize its application to political society. This necessitates viewing justice as fairness as a purely political conception so that it can become the focus of an "overlapping consensus," a species of convergence. "In such a consensus, the [divergent] reasonable [and comprehensive] doctrines endorse the political conception [justice as fairness] each from its own point of view."[19]

The necessity, however, of an overlapping consensus for the stability of justice as fairness need not interfere with the principles for the basic structure,[20] which, extending beyond Rawls's own explicit thought, are relevant to affirmative action. "Their content is not affected in any way by the particular comprehensive doctrines that may exist in society. This is because, at the first stage [the original position], justice as fairness abstracts from the knowledge of citizens' determinate conceptions of the good and proceeds from shared political conceptions of society and person."[21]

Later I shall decisively distinguish overlapping consensus from dialectic.[22] Unlike dialectic, overlapping consensus does not attempt to transform views. "Rather, justice as fairness is not reasonable in the first place unless in a suitable way it can win its support by addressing each citizen's reason, as explained within its own framework."[23] This structure of belief is indeed characteristic of operational, for it depends on the powers of the mind to adapt themselves to any reasonable position, much as a lawyer must be prepared to assume and become an advocate for any position in a controversy.

The Difference Principle and the Primary Good of Self-Respect

Returning now to the basic structure and the formulation of principles of justice as fairness, the projected discourse and debate in the original position and behind the veil of ignorance yield a social contract regulated by two basic principles:

- "First: each person is to have an equal right to the most extensive basic liberty compatible with a similar liberty for others."[24]
- "[Second:] [s]ocial and economic inequalities are to be arranged so that they are both (a) to the greatest benefit of the least advantaged [the 'difference principle'] and (b) attached to offices and positions open to all under conditions of fair equality of opportunity ['fair equality of opportunity']."[25]

Here I will be especially concerned with the second principle and in particular with its part (a), called the difference principle.

The difference principle concerns a partial or modified form of equalization of the primary goods[26] of income and wealth. It is accordingly a form of economic distribution. Another primary good—intangible and the most important of all such goods—is self-respect.[27] Though the distribution of the two is related (as I shall later show), the distribution of this latter primary good demands absolute equality and is thus unqualified.[28] It accordingly becomes the real driving force behind operational-style affirmative action. It supports the notion of benign discrimination by making it possible to distinguish between discrimination (based on stigmatization) that destroys self-esteem and nonstigmatizing discrimination that, though based on race, need not destroy persons' capacity for belief in their self-worth.

The "least advantaged group" for whose benefit the difference principle is designed is not composed of any particular group but is rather a pragmatic, hypothetical device through which the operation of justice as fairness in the distribution of wealth and income can be explained.[29] Here it is entirely plausible to feature minorities and women, the normal beneficiaries of affirmative action, as composing the least advantaged groups or group. It could certainly envelop the concept of "caste." Rawls makes plain, though, that the term "least advantaged group" has no fixed reference and can be pragmatically assigned to any group that approximates the condition.[30] The difference principle, when joined to the principle of fair equality of opportunity, forms what Rawls calls the condition of democratic equality. "The difference principle . . . requires that the higher expectations of the more advantaged contribute to the prospects of the least advantaged[—or that] social and economic inequalities must be in the best interests of the representative men in *all* social positions."[31]

Thus the difference principle has a marked tendency toward equality and self-respect: It benefits the least advantaged group by providing them with an economic floor beneath which self-respect would hardly be possible. It also benefits society as a whole through "chain-connected[ness]" that results in economic gains to all other groups in society with inequalities in expectation, gains from a ripple effect started initially from having "maximiz[ed] the expectations of those *most* disadvantaged."[32] Yet the difference principle retains a basis for some inequality when "the greater expectations allowed to entrepreneurs encourage[] them to do things which raise the long-term prospects of the laboring class."[33] Those with greater wealth and income also benefit "from a scheme of social cooperation without which no one could have a satisfactory life."[34] Fair equality of opportunity, the other component of democratic equality, adds the meaningful chance to "experienc[e] the realization of self which comes from a skillful and devoted exercise of social duties."[35]

Taken together the difference principle and fair equality of opportunity set out a schema of distributive justice. Groups (through the device of their representative men) are allocated primary goods on the basis of *a priori* principles of fair social cooperation derived from the original position and validated by reflective equilibrium. These principles do not set forth a theory of retributive or compensatory justice designed simply to remove private injustices among individuals.[36] Rather,

[w]e see then that the difference principle represents . . . an agreement to regard the distribution of natural talents as a common asset and to share in the benefits of the distribution whatever it turns out to be. Those who have been favored by nature [and by the absence of social, sexual, or racial stigmatization], whoever they are, may gain from their good fortune only on terms that improve the situation of those who have lost out.[37]

Pure procedural justice, whose value is assured by the maintenance of fair equality of opportunity, is a system whereby this form of just distribution can be carried out without encountering all the problems associated with a detailed allocation of goods. Once the proper social and political institutions are set in place, and are operated impartially according to pure procedural justice, "distributive justice [will] take care of itself."[38]

Although the distribution of economic goods is permitted on an *unequal* basis by the difference principle, the primary good of self-respect is associated with the *equal* distribution of basic liberties mandated by the first principle, agreed to in the original position—the principle of equal liberties. These basic liberties have lexical or ordered priority over "material means that are relegated to a subordinate place."[39] Nonetheless, the tendency to economic equalization, promoted by the difference principle for maintenance of self-esteem, is vital to justice as fairness—at least until the basic liberties can establish a much firmer basis for this critical view of the self.[40] Self-respect is also obviously closely related to fair equality of opportunity, which allows for basic self-realization.

Indeed, "[s]elf-respect is rooted in our self-confidence as a fully cooperating member of society capable of pursuing a worthwhile conception of the good over a complete life. . . . [S]elf-respect depends upon and is encouraged by certain public features of basic social institutions, how they work together and how people who accept these arrangements are expected to treat one another."[41]

Race, sex, and other traits of their type based on "fixed natural characteristics" can lead to unequal treatment for the purpose of applying the difference principle,[42] and these traits surely apply to the vital concept of self-respect as well, its absence being the basis for erosion of self-esteem. Rawls makes plain, though, that it is not simply race alone that creates injustice and loss of self-respect. It is the stigma and animus of racism that creates those conditions. "[T]he principles of explicit racist doctrine are not only unjust. They are irrational . . . we could say they are not moral conceptions at all, but . . . simply means of suppression. They have no place on a reasonable list of traditional conceptions of justice."[43] "Without self-respect nothing may seem worth doing, and if some things have value for us, we lack the will to pursue them."[44] "Therefore the parties in the original position would wish to avoid at almost any cost the social conditions that undermine self-respect."[45] Racism, and its concomitant stigmatization, is one of those social conditions.

Affirmative Action

Now having sketched the grounds for the difference principle and the social bases of self-respect, I can indicate in my own right how justice as fairness could hypothetically support affirmative action and what form such a program of affirmative action might take in the actual world. First, it must be reiterated that despite the origins of the system in an *a priori* explanatory device, the original position, justice as fairness "understands itself as the defense of the [real] possibility of a just constitutional regime."[46] It *can* be implemented. Its implementation depends, however, neither on the existence of a specific injury to be redressed nor on a "causal process" to make good certain "reasons of right and justice."[47] The difference principle, applied to groups deemed least advantaged, would justify restructuring industry- and career-related educational opportunities to include more minorities and women, yet not insist on absolute equalization or "quotas."

The required social bases of self-respect could play an even larger justifying role for affirmative action by supporting the concept of benign discrimination. A representative person of the majority race who is negatively affected by affirmative action still need not have suffered a blow to his self-esteem, the most vital of his primary goods, though he may have experienced some loss in wealth and income. He is not of a group marked by traits associated with stigmatization. But groups that are stigmatized can gain that *élan vital* in personal esteem and in economic incentive necessary to achieving authentic humanity, while the flexible operation of the difference principle—through, *e.g.*, "chain-connectedness" and a residual place for some merited inequalities of higher income and wealth—can provide adjustments needed to avoid major economic injustice to the majority race.

These applications reflect the Rawlsian imperative that the conditions of justice as fairness be available to all through the equalizing distribution of certain primary goods—basic liberties, income and wealth, and self-respect. Such a distribution would lead to the capacity to work, to realize oneself, and to share equitably in the tangible and intangible proceeds of the system. Above all, the principles of justice as fairness should be followed because they are those principles "that [minorities *and* the majority alike] would . . . autonomously . . . consent to as free and equal rational beings . . . were [they] to take up together the appropriate general point of view . . . define[d] [by] [t]he original position."[48]

RONALD DWORKIN, THE RIGHT TO EQUAL RESPECT AND CONCERN, AND THE POLICY GROUNDS OF AFFIRMATIVE ACTION

In his article "Justice and Rights,"[49] legal theorist and jurisprudent Ronald Dworkin admiringly analyzes John Rawls's *A Theory of Justice* in order to determine the underlying basis for the original position and how it makes possible Rawls's deontological, rights-based theory. Implicit in the inquiry is how Rawls's basis for a rights-based theory can also support Dworkin's own deontological theory of first law itself and then the law of affirmative action. Dworkin concludes that "[t]he original position is well designed to enforce the abstract right to *equal concern and respect*, which must be understood to be the fundamental concept of Rawls's deep theory."[50] Dworkin essentially accepts this principle of equality in his own prescriptions for liberal politics and jurisprudence when he asks,

What does it mean for the government to treat its citizens as equals: That is, I think, the same question as the question of what it means for the government to treat all its citizens as free, or as independent, or with equal dignity . . . that is, as entitled to its equal concern and respect.[51]

In yet another place Dworkin has put the idea of equality in this way: "[T]he equal protection clause [supports] a principle of quite breathtaking scope that government must treat everyone as of equal status and with equal concern."[52] This principle is an *a priori* conception of the broader but more indefinite concept of equality laid down by the authors of the Fourteenth Amendment.[53] The derivation is *a priori*, and thus typically operational, because it relies on no detection of original intent or similar contemporaneous device of *a posteriori* origin to produce the meaning taken up—yet it does not strain or violate the original *wording* of the amendment. The *wording* provides a *concept* from which a *conception* narrowed in meaning, but fitting in application to the issues of our times, can be derived.[54] Thus construed from the constitutional language and its

broad concept of equality, the conception of equality as equal concern and respect underlies Dworkin's defense of affirmative action by providing the
grounds for the distinctions that ultimately support "reverse discrimination."[55]
By expressly taking his principle of equality in this direction, Dworkin expands
his rights-based position to new ground, never directly explored by Rawls except
in the implications attributed to his thought.

Before, however, unveiling his express arguments for affirmative action, I
must introduce some rudiments of Dworkin's distinctive jurisprudence by which
he distinguishes positivism, or a *rules*-based justification for law, from his own
self-described *rights*-based justification. In his legal world the main sources of
law are policies and principles. "Arguments of policy justify a political decision
by showing that the decision advances or protects some collective goal of the
community seen as a whole. . . . Arguments of principle justify a political decision by showing that the decision respects or secures some individual or group
right."[56] Of the two, principles are more important in, and usually have superior
rank for, resolution of cases by the judiciary,[57] whereas policy is typically of
legislative origin and expresses some balance of collective interests or preferences.[58] "[W]e make a case for a principle . . . by appealing to an amalgam of
practice and other principles in which the implications of legislative and judicial
history figure along with appeals to community practices and understandings."[59]

Policies may be utilitarian and reflect the weight of preferences, or they may
reflect a societal ideal regardless of empirical preferences.[60] The enactment of
policy may even be constitutive of principles and rights.[61] The method of arriv-
ing at principles (and, subsidiarily, at policies that may embody principles)—
"by appealing to an amalgam of practice"—is both operational in a larger sense,
because of its critical focus on human faculties and their creation of legal facts
and norms, and also Rawlsian, because a principle "can be shown by the overall
success over time of the shared practice of practical reasoning by those who are
reasonable and rational."[62] Although for Dworkin there may remain substantial
disagreement among reasonable legal minds about the correctness of principles
and their derivative rights,[63] the centeredness of that debate on legal *practices*
(and not on rigid rules or other inflexible legal devices), together with the concomitant skepticism to resist dogmatism, stamps Dworkin firmly as an operationalist.

As I indicated before, principles and their derivative rights normally outrank
policy, especially in the courts. "[E]ach [right] acts as a trump over the balance
of pure gains and losses that forms an ordinary utilitarian calculation."[64] "These
rights will function as trump cards held by individuals. . . . The ultimate justification for these rights is that they are necessary to protect equal concern and
respect."[65] "It follows[, accordingly,] from the definition of a right [as a 'trump']
that it cannot be outweighed by *all* social goals [embodied in policies]."[66] A
right, however, need not always trump a policy for the sake of individual equality if there is no inconsistency between the two or if the policy embodies the
principled basis of the right. Or a right will not trump a policy if the policy is

so weighty—so important for the collective good—that it resists the power of the right to trump, even if individual equality is involved. It is with these distinctions among principle and right, and policy, and their possible relations, that Dworkin defends affirmative action.

In *Law's Empire* Dworkin distinguishes three theories of racial equality in a discussion or internalized debate that leads to his defense of affirmative action.[67] In the first theory, "suspect classifications," the government views as equal the rights of all groups to protection against discrimination, except where history or circumstances show that some groups are entitled to a presumption of discrimination because of maltreatment. Even then the presumption can be rebutted by proof that community preferences have been distributed neutrally or equally. If the presumption remains unrebutted, the group's members will receive no more than fair average benefits to assuage the inequality, and these by *majority* standards, which may retain prejudice (*e.g.*, "separate but equal" schools).[68] In the second, "banned categories," the government decrees that no classifications based on race, ethnicity, and perhaps gender may be used to distinguish groups in the distribution of preferences or benefits, even if such a distribution would erase a preexisting inequality. This is the familiar "color-blind" theory, used primarily in cases like *Wygant* and *J. A. Croson* of the logistic mode.

Finally, there is the "banned sources" theory—the most complex. Its operation would turn on Dworkin's distinction between *personal* preferences and *external* preferences in the formulation of utilitarian-type policy. While the calculation of amassed personal preferences (*i.e.*, those held by persons for their own enjoyment) generally leads to an egalitarian policy, the admission of external preferences (persons' preferences for distribution to others) to the policy process can lead to inequalities and disadvantages for others in society—in short, to prejudice, including racial prejudice.[69] The source of policy that Dworkin would ban is prejudice. Put succinctly, the government in the formulation of policies would ban certain kinds of citizens' preferences from consideration, namely, those "rooted in some form of prejudice."[70] To enforce this ban the government and its courts would have to devise a presumption, with a sophisticated rebuttal to substitute for actual (but virtually unobtainable) knowledge of persons' preferences; this presumption would have to go further than that of the first theory, "suspect classifications," here being rebuttable only by proofs of the absence of prejudice altogether.[71] This third theory, of "banned sources," differs from the first by transcending a merely neutral standard of distribution among the races, one that can bend to majority prejudice. More important, it differs from the second theory, of "banned categories."

The two come apart in confronting legislation whose purpose and effect is to benefit people who have historically been the victims of prejudice, not [legislation meant] to harm them. The banned sources theory would distinguish between affirmative action programs designed to help blacks and Jim Crow laws designed to keep them in a state of economic and social subjugation. The banned categories theory would treat both in the same way.[72]

The banned sources theory then is open to support a *policy* of affirmative action, because it allows the creator of such a program of redistribution to rebut an initial presumption of illegal discrimination and show that its plan "did not reflect covert prejudice against some other [largely majority white] group."[73]

"Banned sources," although presented here as related more to a utilitarian policy from which external preferences must be excluded, might also be based on a policy derived from an ideal. An "ideal argument[] do[es] not rely upon preferences at all, but on an independent argument that a more equal society is a better society even if its citizens prefer inequality. That argument does not deny anyone's right to be treated as an equal himself."[74]

In leaning toward policy as the way of resolving the issue of affirmative action, and the problem of racial inequality out of which it arises, Dworkin seems to abandon his normal paradigm that rights trump policies. In writing of the *Bakke* case, he states, "Affirmative action programs use racially explicit criteria because their immediate goal is to increase the number of members of certain races in their professions. But their long-term goal is to *reduce* the degree to which American society is overall a racially conscious society."[75] Minority individuals, though, are not entitled by right to a place in the university or to a job. "That is a plain mistake: the programs are not based on the idea that those who are aided are entitled to aid [by right], but only on the strategic hypothesis that helping them is now an effective way of attacking a national problem."[76] And in Dworkin's view, neither did Alan Bakke have an authentic constitutional right to trump the affirmative action plan at Davis.

The only principle conceivably at issue in *Bakke* was "the principle that no one should suffer from the prejudice or contempt of others. . . . [And] the idea that the *Bakke* case presents a conflict between a desirable social [policy] and important individual rights is a piece of intellectual confusion."[77] Bakke was "excluded not by [racial] prejudice but because of a rational calculation about the socially beneficial use of limited resources."[78] He was not excluded for any malign reason, least of all because "he is a member of a group thought less worthy, as a group, than other groups."[79] No right of his was offended by the policy. In Dworkin's view "the principle that affirmative action of the sort used [here]—a race-conscious policy aimed at improving racial equality and not subjecting anyone to disadvantage because his or her race is disfavored"[80]—did not offend Bakke's civil rights.

Thus Dworkin establishes by appeal to his own ground of equality that a policy can be devised to promote equality in the field of race relations through affirmative action. He proceeds by a method of discrimination that distinguishes critically between such terms as *concept* and *conception, principle* and *policy.* But what about the principle of and the right to equality? Can these ever come into conflict with policy so that the trumping power of the right must be invoked against the policy, even if the policy is one of affirmative action? (This situation evidently did not occur in *Bakke,* where there was no threshold conflict between right and policy.)

His general reply to this query is to distinguish two sorts of rights to equality—first, "the right to *equal treatment*, which is the right to an equal distribution of some opportunity or resource of burden." Then there is the second: "the right to *treatment as an equal*, which is the right, not to receive the same distribution of some burden or benefit, but to be treated with *the same respect and concern* as anyone else."[81] In the first instance, since no one has a right to a university or professional education or career,[82] the formulation presented, the right to treatment as an equal, does not come into play at all for higher education and most employment, as it does for such services as public education.[83] All that an applicant to a professional school is entitled to is consideration for admission with the same respect and concern accorded to all other applicants. That means admission or its denial without sexual or racial *bias*—not that race or sex *simpliciter* must not be considered. Because "American society is currently a racially conscious society[—]the inevitable and evident consequence of a history of slavery, repression, and prejudice"[84]—a black citizen treated according to race is normally not treated with equal concern and respect, because racism is frequently an element in that treatment; but a white citizen, such as Bakke or DeFunis (another affirmative action plaintiff)[85] is treated with equal respect and concern, even if race is a factor, because in that instance there is no mark of stigmatization to injure his basis for self-respect. In affirmative action the treatment of blacks becomes beneficial, but the character of the treatment of the majority remains the same, because consideration of their race is benign, without prejudice.

Thus there should not be a conflict between the right to equal respect and concern and the operation of a properly constructed affirmative action program, that is, one designed only to meet the goal of racial justice and not to perpetuate the long reign of prejudice. Even if there is a conflict, "[a]n individual's right to be treated as an equal means that his potential loss must be treated as a matter of concern, but that [his] loss may nevertheless by outweighed by the gain to the community as a whole."[86]

Thus Dworkin's justification of affirmative action may seem to pit a principle of, and a right to, equality against a policy of equality. This apparent antinomy disappears, though, when he both removes the element of prejudice or stigma from the making of an otherwise altogether beneficial racial policy and distinguishes two senses of the right to equality, the second being the conception of that right as equal respect and concern for all. That is his bedrock, answering the call of Rawls through preservation of the primary good of self-respect, without which all efforts in life are debased and worthless. His arrangement of policy also concretely answers the call of another Rawlsian demand for justice: the difference principle (and equal opportunity). Thus affirmative action, a policy with no *entitlements* to wealth, income, and position, nonetheless establishes a redistributive scheme to improve the condition of minorities materially by admitting them to the professions and other sources of wealth and income sequestered by racism. So buttressed economically, and intrinsically, self-respect soars.

The approach supported by Dworkin is not a scheme of redress or corrective justice, looking backward for its justification and for fine measurements to limit its scope. It is a program of distributive justice, forward looking, seeking social equality on a broad scale equal to the scale of life that it aims to change. The law has not been quick to adopt this rationale for and version of affirmative action, but there is considerable evidence that something substantial of this operational thought lies behind the separate opinions of Justice John Paul Stevens.

JUSTICE JOHN PAUL STEVENS AND THE OPERATIONAL VISION OF AFFIRMATIVE ACTION

General Views

Justice John Paul Stevens's record in the Supreme Court's affirmative action cases may stand as something of a paradox, for he has opposed legislatively created compensatory plans in two leading cases, *Fullilove v. Klutznick*[87] and *City of Richmond v. J. A. Croson Co.*,[88] but favored broad measures for distribution of benefits racially in two cases where the Court decisively restricted remedial relief, *Wygant v. Jackson Board of Education*[89] and again in *Adarand Constructors, Inc. v. Pena*.[90] The paradox vanishes, however, when Justice Stevens's preference for "the legitimacy of race-based decisions that may produce tangible and fully justified benefits"[91] is compared with his rejection of *legislative* plans that typically have trouble "identif[ying] both the particular victims and the particular perpetrators of *past* discrimination [without] a *remedial* [purely retrospective] justification for race-based legislation [that] will almost certainly sweep too broadly."[92] His rejection of the typical remedial or compensatory approach, like the City of Richmond's legislative approach for contractors, freed him to advocate a type of approach unknown to logistic or even to problematic: *future-oriented* affirmative action plans of distributive aim, carried out with care to avoid racially maligning either the disadvantaged majority (if disadvantaged they be) or the benefited minority. His judicial writings show that he would use (deliberately or implicitly) a number of the devices of Rawls and Dworkin to achieve social equality.

Remedial action can actually cause prejudice to the beneficiary class because "a [loosely drafted] statute of [the] kind in *Fullilove*[93] inevitably is perceived by many as resting on an assumption that those who are granted this special preference are less qualified in some respect that is identified purely by their race."[94] This stigmatization occurs "unless Congress clearly articulates the need and basis for a racial classification . . . and tailors the classification to the justification."[95] Legislative policies may also unfairly or unlawfully "use . . . the political process to punish or characterize past conduct of private citizens,"[96] whose alleged treatment of minorities may be used to justify "a remedy for *sins* that were committed in the past."[97] "It is the judicial system, rather than the legislative process, that is best equipped to identify past wrongdoers."[98]

Justice Stevens's Support of Affirmative Action

Now I turn to the policies that Justice Stevens *would* fashion—and their sources. Writing in the *Johnson* case under Title VII, Justice Stevens remarked:

As construed in *Weber* . . . [Title VII] does not absolutely prohibit preferential hiring in favor of minorities; it was merely intended to protect historically disadvantaged groups *against* discrimination and not to hamper managerial efforts to benefit members of disadvantaged groups. . . .

Given th[is] interpretation of the statute . . . I see no reason why the employer has any duty, prior to granting a preference to a qualified minority employee, to determine whether his past conduct might constitute an arguable violation of Title VII. Indeed . . . the employer may find it more helpful *to focus on the future* [and] to consider other legitimate reasons to give preferences to under-represented groups.[99]

This stance reflects an outlook operational at its core. It is accordingly nonremedial. Causal relations from the past do not dictate the direction of the law. The agent who designs and implements an affirmative action plan ideally acts autonomously, free from causes of the past. While narrow redress for specific injuries in the past is possible and desirable in some circumstances, it should be reposed in the courts, because redress from wrongdoers is controlled by the past, and adjudication of past events is the speciality of the courts. This preference suggests that, like Dworkin, Justice Stevens favors policymaking for affirmative action by nonjudicial bodies, such as legislatures or even private entities like unions—all of which are more suited to making policy to promote equality *in the future*. Forward-looking law must also be based on distinctions that avoid stigmatization, and thus dehumanization, of anyone. Some distinctions must allow for growth in social equality and must be as powerful and as clear as "the difference between a 'No Trespassing' sign and a welcome mat."[100] This orientation is confirmed by looking at some of Justice Stevens's similarities to Rawls and Dworkin.

In the *Wygant* case, nonminority teachers resisted in the federal courts a layoff provision, requiring a partial switch in priority for avoiding layoff, between tenured and nontenured positions—a switch that ultimately caused some white teachers, who would otherwise have been protected by their seniority, to be laid off. A provision created under a collective bargaining agreement was designed to retain at least some minority teachers, even if untenured, in the event of layoffs. Minority teachers without tenure were subsequently being retained on the theory that they served as "role models" needed for minority schoolchildren.[101] In a plurality opinion, Justice Powell declared this practice to be in violation of the Equal Protection Clause, because it did not establish a causal relation to past discriminatory harm.[102] Justice Stevens dissented and, in arguing that the role model theory *does* serve a constitutional and salutary purpose, made this peroration: "I am persuaded that the decision to include more minority teachers served *a valid public purpose* . . . that it *transcends the harm to the petitioners* [majority white teachers], and that it is a step toward *that ultimate goal* of eliminating entirely from governmental decisionmaking such factors as a human being's race."[103]

Likewise, in *Adarand*, where the issue was whether to retain intermediate scrutiny in federal affirmative action programs,[104] he again argued that benign discrimination against the majority to benefit the minority "is, in some circumstances, entirely consistent with *the ideal of equality*."[105] Thus Justice Stevens, like Rawls, is disposed to reject utilitarianism in favor of a deontological ground or a collective ideal for social justice and affirmative action. Rejected, in Rawlsian terms, is "the greatest sum of satisfaction of the rational desires of individuals"[106] in favor of "justice as fairness . . . [that] does not take men's propensities and inclinations as given, whatever they are, and then seek the best way to fulfill them . . . but [instead] defines the scope within which [men] must develop their aims."[107] Justice Stevens's preference for *policy* to implement affirmative action ("a valid public purpose") also seems to correspond to Dworkin's same preference[108] and to Dworkin's assertion that individuals' preferences or rights do not always and probably will not "trump" properly constructed affirmative action plans.[109] Such a plan in Justice Stevens's view "transcends the harm to the [individual members of the disfavored group]."[110] Finally, Justice Stevens also eschews utilitarianism as a source for affirmative action policy on Dworkin's, as well as on Rawls's grounds, in urging that plans be based on an ideal ("th[e] ultimate goal"; "the ideal of equality")[111] rather than on preferences.[112]

Comparison to Rawls

In looking strictly at Justice Stevens's similarities to Rawls and justice as fairness, it is noteworthy that in *Wygant* Justice Stevens argued that "the race-conscious layoff policy here [in the collective bargaining agreement] was adopted with the full participation of the [later] disadvantaged individuals with a narrowly circumscribed berth for the policy's operation."[113] Thus the legitimization of the layoff policy is found in a device and a process—debate and discussion among presumably rational and reasonable citizens (teachers) within their union and with their school management—that is like the Rawlsian initial position of equality or the original position.[114] Racial justice is thus produced, not as in logistic by carefully tracing causal linkages into the past but by discussion and debate among the affected persons themselves. Moreover, procedures were strictly adhered to in determining the layoffs. "[N]ot a shred of evidence in the record suggests *any* procedural unfairness in the adoption of the [collective] bargaining agreement[, a kind of social contract] . . . in striking contrast to the procedural inadequacy and unjustified race-based [legislative] classification in *Fullilove*."[115] This passage suggests a worldly, nonhypothetical

operation of the trade union system of worker representation as a kind of Rawlsian "pure procedural justice" in which the outcome among the participants is a
version of distributive justice—clearly not retributive or compensatory because
the tenure-related provision for layoffs was not meant to redress injuries,[116] but
instead another salutary social ideal.

Finally, Justice Stevens justifies the role model theory in *Wygant* on the
grounds that it would shore up and promote self-esteem.

[O]ne of the most important lessons that the American public schools teach is that the
diverse ethnic, cultural, and national backgrounds . . . do not [embody] essential differences among the human beings that inhabit our land. It is one thing for a white child to
be taught by a white teacher that color, like beauty, is only "skin deep"; it is far more
convincing to experience that truth during the routine, ongoing learning process [through]
"multi-ethnic representation on the teaching faculty."[117]

This statement has an obvious relation to the diversity rationale and especially
to the *Piscataway* case[118] where teacher (and worker) diversity was at issue. But
it bears noting that this statement is really operational, not dialectical, in nature.
Truth is gained in this instance through authentic encounters with others—encounters that may involve dialogue, to be sure, but that are essentially concerned
with subjective experience that can be gained, as Justice Stevens pointed out,
only when these encounters are concrete and placed in familiar context. This
kind of situation, which points beyond the merely cognitive (the white teacher
teaching the white child about color) toward how the human mind is redirected
(through the children's encounters with persons of other races) to accept a different worldview of race, presents a clear instance of the operational mode of
thought. Here knowledge depends on the personal perspective as influenced by
both elements of cognition and of feeling, not strictly on objective sources removed from experience. It should also be noted that the worldview of race that
is promoted benefits both the majority race and the minority race. The example
given is of a white child's gaining from a multiracial experience, but black
children would benefit in self-esteem from an integrated faculty as well.[119]

Comparison to Dworkin

I begin my comparison of Justice Stevens's ideas and arguments on affirmative action to Ronald Dworkin's with the latter's theories of racial equality
in *Law's Empire*.[120] Under Dworkin's "suspect classifications"[121] may be placed
Justice Stevens's criticism of the Japanese-American exclusion cases of World
War II,[122] in which strict constitutional scrutiny did not restrain invidious discrimination.[123] Under "banned categories"[124] Justice Stevens made it plain in his
Adarand dissent that he did not agree with Justice O'Connor's maxim of "consistency" that " 'the standard of review under the Equal Protection Clause is not
dependent on the race of those burdened or benefitted by a particular classification.' "[125] His response:

The Court's concept of "consistency" assumes that there is no significant difference between a decision of the majority to provide a benefit to certain members of a minority race and a decision by the majority to provide a benefit to certain members of that minority notwithstanding its incidental burden on some members of the majority.[126]

And again, when he was discussing Title VII: "Neither the 'same standards' language in *McDonald*,[127] nor the 'color blind' rhetoric used by the Senators and Congressmen who enacted the bill is now controlling."[128] Thus when one turns to Dworkin's favored conception of "banned sources,"[129] it is doubly plain that Justice Stevens rejects the color-blind approach and is willing to accept race *simpliciter* as a ground of policy.[130] He plainly and squarely accepts Dworkin's distinction, in the "banned sources" theory of racial equality, between Jim Crow laws and laws designed to help minorities:[131] "There is no moral or constitutional equivalent between a policy that is designed to perpetuate a *caste* system and one that seeks to eradicate racial subordination. Invidious discrimination is an engine of oppression. . . . Remedial based preferences [benign discrimination] reflect the opposite impulse: a desire to foster equality in society."[132] Justice O'Connor's maxim of consistency, which denies this crucial distinction between invidious and benign discrimination, in effect "disregard[s] the difference between a 'No Trespassing' sign and a welcome mat. . . . [T]he term 'affirmative action' is common and well understood. Its presence in everyday parlance shows that people understand the difference between good intentions and bad."[133] Thus by drawing critical distinctions and appealing to commonly understood yet powerful words, Justice Stevens took a position highly congruent with Dworkin's preferred theory, "banned sources."

Beyond Dworkin's three theories of racial equality, I want finally to take up his treatment of the very concept of equality and the operative distinctions that he uses to expound it for comparison to Justice Stevens's. Dworkin begins with the premise "that the government [is required to] treat all those in its charge *as equals*, that is, as entitled to equal concern and respect."[134] "Equal concern and respect" is in fact the surviving limb of a distinction that Dworkin makes between "equal treatment" and "treatment as an equal," that is, treatment with "equal concern and respect."[135] As already noted, this distinction enables Dworkin to deny benefits to the majority without subjecting them to demeaning prejudice and the destruction of self-worth.[136] Justice Stevens takes the same route to realize equality. First he notes that "[n]o sensible conception of the Government's constitutional obligation to 'govern impartially' . . . should ignore this distinction [between invidious and benign discrimination]."[137] He goes on to state that while

a decision by representatives of the majority to discriminate against . . . a minority race is . . . virtually always repugnant to . . . a free and democratic society . . . [,] those same representatives' decision to impose incidental costs on the majority . . . in order to provide a benefit to a disadvantaged minority . . . is, in some circumstances, entirely consistent with the ideal of equality.[138]

This description of how a proper policy of equalization of benefits, through affirmative action, can prevail over any rights that the majority *may* have is a further illustration of how Justice Stevens's and Dworkin's views on this matter are congruent. But more important, it shows how Justice Stevens, like Dworkin, preserves the self-respect of all concerned. This is the deontological element encapsulated in their respective policies. The placement of "incidental costs" on the majority, whose burden is assigned them only after they are treated with equal respect and concern and not with animus or invidiousness, though remaining an imposition of costs, is nonetheless outweighed by the policy of affirmative action.[139] Lest there be any doubt that the majority need not be stigmatized in the implementation of an affirmative action plan, and that its members' self-respect can be preserved, Justice Stevens's statement in *Wygant* about the reasons for the projected layoffs of senior teachers powerfully allays such doubt:

Finally, we must consider the harm to petitioners [the senior teachers]. Every layoff, like every refusal to employ a qualified applicant, is a grave loss to the affected individual. However, the undisputed facts in this case demonstrate that this serious consequence is not based on any lack of respect for their race, or on a blind habit or stereotype. . . . [As explained through two hypothetical examples] the harm [was] . . . generated by the combination of economic conditions and the special contractual protection given a different group of teachers—a protection that . . . was justified by a valid and extremely strong public interest.[140]

Professor Dworkin himself could hardly have expressed more directly and forcefully how an affirmative action plan can work to address minority inequality while protecting the self-respect of all through their common treatment with equal concern and respect.

CONCLUSION: OPERATIONAL—A METHOD OF DISTINCTIONS

Operational and dialectic, the mode closest to it in structure and ground of argumentation, both depend on a universal reason in all persons to which they make their appeal. (Logistic and problematic, it will be recalled, begin their reasoning with simples and particulars, and the appeal of their arguments depends on the special circumstances or breadth of experience of the audience.) Unlike dialectic, however, which depends on rational dialogue among interlocutors to assimilate parts into a comprehensive whole, the operational method uses debate in which a proponent of a position attacks or rebuts opposing ideas through discrimination, in the general sense of distinguishing one aspect of a matter from another. While the dialectical method depends on the origination of truth and morals in a dialogical process that grasps the mind (just as Socrates was like the torpedo fish, stunning the mind with his discourse), the operational proponent proceeds on the assumption that knowledge and moral right originate in the powers of the mind itself.[141] From the dialectical point of view, operational is seen as reductive, distinguishing aspects of a subject to the point that nothing distinctive is left—only the subjective viewpoint of the speaker or knower. This view reflects the dialectical emphasis on comprehensive *knowledge* and its role in leading, in general, to wise action in a rational society, promoted specifically by affirmative action drawing together *diverse* citizens whose dialogue leads to comprehensive truth.

Operational sees the social and political world in a different way. Instead of dialogue, it employs persuasion. Operational finds a world of essentially rational persons whose tastes and preferences do not always coincide. If purposive, moral action is to be initiated, these persons must be persuaded by the power of speech—rhetoric—upon the faculties of their minds that all hold in common. Especially, when action is required, this power of persuasion must be brought to bear upon the faculty of the *Will*. In this process, operational relies on initially "arbitrary [distinctions] . . . in the formulation and interpretation of the real and in the advancement of . . . [the] public good;"[142] but these distinctions ultimately become acceptable and persuasive when they are given meaning through argument. In this light the operational mode of viewing affirmative action can be seen through the force of a number of critical distinctions that appeal to the minds of the audience—distinctions derived neither from external causality nor from dialogue but from the receptiveness of and the appeal to the minds of the audience through words, words that though powerful nonetheless are respectful of the audience's autonomy.

In John Rawls's work, no distinction is more critical for justice as fairness than the one that creates his hypothetical original position—a device that he uses to explain and to justify the difference principle and the conception of the primary good of self-respect, as well as other aspects of his two basic principles of justice. The device of a veil of ignorance is used to distinguish the actual world, where self-interest tends to prevail, from the hypothetical original position, and makes possible the creation of the latter. The conjectured yet reasonably grounded outcome of the process of debate and discussion in the original position yields basic principles of justice that we already accept through reason in the actual world—a fact that is shown through the use of reflective equilibrium to reconcile our normal, considered conceptions of justice with those from the original position, where disinterested reason prevails.[143] But it is the rhetorical power drawn from an initial position of equality, or original position, that forces the principles of justice as fairness upon the mind. The concept of an "overlapping consensus" adds another dimension to the actual implementation of affirmative action.

Dworkin argues by discrimination. His distinction of the concept of equality into the right to equal treatment as opposed to the right to treatment as an equal—*i.e.*, the right to be treated by the government with equal concern and respect[144]—splits the affirmative action atom insofar as equality had been thought to be an absolute quality, identically applicable to each individual without thought for social context or degrees of preexisting injustice. His general distinction between principle and policy[145] leads to the paradigm of advancing the affirmative action program as a *policy* of equalization (though not as a policy of entitlement for anyone benefited by the program)—a policy that either does not come into conflict with, or if it does, outweighs, the individual, *principled* rights of the seemingly disfavored majority.[146] By applying such distinctions it would be possible to avoid racially stigmatizing either the favored minority or, as a result of the relinquishment of benefits under a form of distributive justice, the disfavored majority.[147]

As previously noted, Justice Stevens has utilized, at least tacitly, many of Rawls's and Dworkin's distinctions, none more important than his distinction between invidious and benign (or unstigmatized) discrimination.[148] His emphatic remark to skeptics—that their refusal to recognize this distinction "disregard[s] the difference between a 'No Trespassing' sign and a welcome mat"[149]—employs one of the oldest of rhetorical techniques, placing reliance on "the force . . . of words" and "bend[ing] everything to the advantage of his case . . . by telling his own side of the story carefully and clearly."[150] Though he uses a conception of benign discrimination, it lacks the same empirical or historical origin as the problematic conception.[151] His usage of the term tends more toward reliance on commonly accepted social facts—a kind of *a priori* common sense or "*public sense*, *i.e.*, a critical faculty which in its reflective act takes account (*a priori*) of the mode of representation of every one else, in order, *as it were*, to weigh its judgment with the collective reason of mankind."[152] This, of course, is very much unlike the causal support used and taken from history by problematic.[153]

Justice Stevens's contributions to the law of affirmative action, though not found in an opinion for a majority of the Court in any case, have been recognized as both innovative and insightful, primarily because of his refusal to be bound to remedial plans with their inevitable reliance on causal linkages to the past. His operational frame of reference has no doubt helped to give him the independence of mind to pursue this style of jurisprudence. Kathleen Sullivan, after *Wygant*, praised him in these terms:

Trapped in the paradigm of sin,[154] the Court shrinks . . . from declaring that the benefits of building a racially integrated society for the future can be justification enough [for affirmative action]. Justice Stevens stood alone in even suggesting as much last Term, writing in *Wygant* that public school boards are entitled to conclude that taking affirmative steps to get and keep black teachers on their faculties will provide "obvious" educational benefits that "an all white . . . faculty could not provide."[155]

The Department of Justice has mirrored this assessment in a post-*Adarand* review of affirmative action law:

Since *Bakke*, Justice Stevens has been the most forceful advocate on the Court for non-remedial affirmative action measures. He has consistently argued that affirmative action makes just as much sense when it promotes an interest in creating a more inclusive and diverse society for today and the future, as when it serves an interest in remedying past wrongs.[156]

Aside from the character of the man who made and asserted them, these accomplishments and the positions that they embody have emerged because of a method of discrimination and distinction grounded in "[t]he concept of freedom . . . the keystone of the whole architecture of the system of pure reason."[157]

NOTES

[1] McKeon, "Philosophic Semantics and Philosophic Inquiry," supra Intro., note 40, at 4, reprinted in MCKEON, FREEDOM AND HISTORY AND OTHER ESSAYS, at 245.

[2] PLATO, CRATYLUS 386a, reprinted in THE COLLECTED DIALOGUES OF PLATO, supra at Ch. 1, note 87, at 421, 424.

[3] IMMANUEL KANT, *KRITIK DER REINEN VERNÜFT* [CRITIQUE OF PURE REASON] Ak. B xvii, at 22 (Norman Kemp Smith trans. 1929).

[4] Id. Ak. B451–52, at 394 (emphasis in original).

[5] Id. at Ak. B14, at 436 (emphasis supplied).

[6] IMMANUEL KANT, *GRUNDLEGUNG ZUR METAPHYSIC DER SITTEN* [FOUNDATIONS OF THE METAPHYSICS OF MORALS] Ak. 428–29, at 46–47 (Lewis White Beck trans. 1959).

[7] RAWLS, A THEORY OF JUSTICE, 3 (1971) [hereinafter A THEORY OF JUSTICE].

[8] Id. at 7 (emphasis supplied, to indicate that distributive justice is at work here).

[9] Id. at 11.

[10] Id.

[11] Id. at 12, 136.

[12] IMMANUEL KANT, *KRITIK DER PRAKTISCHEN VERNÜFT* [CRITIQUE OF PRACTICAL REASON], Ak. 20, at 18 (Lewis White Beck trans. 1956).

[13] RAWLS, A THEORY OF JUSTICE, at 20, 21.

[14] RAWLS, POLITICAL LIBERALISM, 115–16 (1993) [hereinafter POLITICAL LIBERALISM].

[15] Supra, Ch. 4, note 7.

[16] Supra Ch. 4, note 14.

[17] As Rawls explains:

> Justice as Fairness is best presented in two stages. In the first stage it is worked out as a free-standing political (but of course moral) conception for the basic structure of society. . . . We take up, in the second stage, the problem [of] whether justice as fairness is sufficiently stable . . . [whether it] can be the focus of an overlapping consensus . . . [in which] reasonable doctrines endorse the political conception [justice as fairness], each from its own point of view.

RAWLS, POLITICAL LIBERALISM, at 140–41, 134. Because the difference principle and another major factor in my discussion, the primary good of self-respect, are mainly discussed under the topic of the basic structure, I look mainly to A THEORY OF JUSTICE.

[18] RAWLS, POLITICAL LIBERALISM, at 134, 143.

[19] Id. at 134.

[20] Id. at 141.

[21] Id.

[22] See notes and text at Concl., notes 60–67, infra.

[23] RAWLS, POLITICAL LIBERALISM, at 143.

[24] RAWLS, A THEORY OF JUSTICE, at 60.

[25] Id. at 83. See also RAWLS, POLITICAL LIBERALISM, at 271.

[26] RAWLS, A THEORY OF JUSTICE, at 62, 92–93.

[27] Id. at 440.

[28] Id. at 546 ("Thus the best solution [to the problem of envy] is to support the primary good of self-respect as far as possible by the assignment of basic liberties that can indeed be made equal, defining the same status for all.").

[29] Id. at 96–98.

[30] Id. at 96–99.

[31] Id. at 95–96 (emphasis supplied).

[32] Id. at 80 (emphasis supplied).

[33] Id. at 78.

[34] Id. at 103.

[35] Id. at 84.

[36] Id. at 101 (redress not the aim of the difference principle); RAWLS, POLITICAL LIBERALISM, at xxvii.

[37] RAWLS, A THEORY OF JUSTICE, at 101.

[38] Id. at 86–88.

[39] Id. at 546–43.

[40] Cf. id. at 545, 535 (prevention of envy).

[41] RAWLS, POLITICAL LIBERALISM, at 318–19.

[42] RAWLS, A THEORY OF JUSTICE, at 99.

[43] Id. at 149–50.

[44] RAWLS, POLITICAL LIBERALISM, at 318; see also RAWLS, A THEORY OF JUSTICE, at 440.

[45] RAWLS, A THEORY OF JUSTICE, at 440.

[46] RAWLS, POLITICAL LIBERALISM, at 101.

[47] Id. at 119.

[48] RAWLS, A THEORY OF JUSTICE, at 516.

[49] Ronald Dworkin, "Justice and Rights," reprinted in RONALD DWORKIN, TAKING RIGHTS SERIOUSLY [hereinafter TAKING RIGHTS SERIOUSLY] 150, 83 (1978).

[50] Id. at 181 (emphasis supplied) (Here "equal concern and respect" is understood to underlie Rawls's entire schema, essentially including the basic liberties, the right to self-respect, and the difference principle.).

[51] Ronald Dworkin, "Liberalism," in RONALD DWORKIN, A MATTER OF PRINCIPLE [hereinafter A MATTER OF PRINCIPLE] 181, 191, 190 (1985).

[52] Ronald Dworkin, "How to Read the Constitution," 43 N.Y. REVIEW OF BOOKS 48 (Mar. 21, 1996), reprinted in RONALD DWORKIN, FREEDOM'S LAW: THE MORAL READING OF THE AMERICAN CONSTITUTION 10 (1996).

[53] Id.

[54] Ronald Dworkin, "Hard Cases," in DWORKIN, TAKING RIGHTS SERIOUSLY, at 93 (distinction between abstract rights and concrete rights) & 103 (distinction between concept and conception); "Constitutional Cases," id. at 134 (distinction between concept

and conception); "The Forum of Principle," in A MATTER OF PRINCIPLE, at 49–55 (principles of interpretation for concept and conception).

[55] Ronald Dworkin, "Reverse Discrimination," in DWORKIN, TAKING RIGHTS SERIOUSLY, at 223.

[56] Ronald Dworkin, "Hard Cases," in DWORKIN, TAKING RIGHTS SERIOUSLY, at 81, 82.

[57] Id. at 84.

[58] Id. at 83, 85.

[59] Ronald Dworkin, "The Model of Rules I," in DWORKIN, TAKING RIGHTS SERIOUSLY, at 14.

[60] "Reverse Discrimination," supra Ch. 4, note 55, at 232.

[61] "Hard Cases," supra Ch. 4, note 54, at 83 ("[U]noriginal judicial decisions that merely enforce the clear terms of some plainly valid statute are always justified on arguments of principle, even if the statute itself was generated by policy.").

[62] RAWLS, POLITICAL LIBERALISM, at 119.

[63] "Hard Cases," supra Ch. 4, note 54, at 81.

[64] Ronald Dworkin, "Principle, Policy, Procedure," reprinted in DWORKIN, A MATTER OF PRINCIPLE, at 72, 89.

[65] "Liberalism," supra Ch. 4, note 51, at 198.

[66] "Hard Cases," supra Ch. 4, note 54, at 92.

[67] RONALD DWORKIN, LAW'S EMPIRE [hereinafter LAW'S EMPIRE] 381–82 (1986).

[68] Id. at 383, 385.

[69] "Reverse Discrimination," supra Ch. 4, note 55, at 234–35. See also "Liberalism," supra Ch. 4, note 51, at 197.

[70] DWORKIN, LAW'S EMPIRE, at 384.

[71] Id. at 386.

[72] Id. at 386–87. For a critique of Dworkin's use of these distinctions in addressing affirmative action, see Jerry Kang, "Negative Action against Asian Americans: The Internal Instability of Dworkin's Defense of Affirmative Action," 31 Harv. C. R.– C. L. L. Rev. 1 (1996).

[73] DWORKIN, LAW'S EMPIRE, at 394.

[74] "Reverse Discrimination," supra Ch. 4, note 55, at 239.

[75] Ronald Dworkin, "Bakke's Case: Are Quotas Unfair?" in DWORKIN, A MATTER OF PRINCIPLE, at 293, 295.

[76] Id. at 297.

[77] Id. at 298.

[78] Id. at 301–02.

[79] Id. at 302.

[80] Ronald Dworkin, "How to Read the Civil Rights Act," in DWORKIN, A MATTER OF PRINCIPLE, at 316, 331 (quotation refers to the respondent in Steelworkers v. Weber, 443 U.S. 265).

[81] "Reverse Discrimination," supra Ch. 4, note 55, at 227 (first two emphases in original; third, supplied).

[82] Id. at 223; see also "Bakke's Case: Are Quotas Unfair?" supra Ch. 4, note 75, at 297.

[83] See, e.g., Plyer v. Doe, 457 U.S. 202 (resident alien children entitled to admission to public schools, regardless of parents' illegal status).

[84] "Bakke's Case: Are Quotas Unfair?" supra Ch. 4, note 75, at 294.

[85] See Defunis v. Odegaard, 416 U.S. 312 (1974) (dismissed as moot).

[86] "Reverse Discrimination," supra Ch. 4, note 55, at 227.

[87] 448 U.S. at 532 (Stevens, J., dissenting from approval of a broad remedial plan enacted by Congress).

[88] 488 U.S. at 511 (Stevens, J., concurring in part and concurring in the judgment against a broad remedial plan enacted by the Richmond City Council); in *Regents of the Univ. of Calif. v. Bakke*, 438 U.S. at 408 (opinion of Stevens, J.), he authored an opinion against Davis Medical School's remedial plan, but on narrow statutory grounds that excluded constitutional reasoning under the Equal Protection Clause. Although in the opinion Justice Stevens did discuss whether lack of stigmatization can justify exclusion of the majority (and rejected the idea), id. at 414, I choose not to include *Bakke* in my discussion because the Stevens opinion is not based on constitutional grounds.

[89] 476 U.S. at 313 (Stevens, J., dissenting from Court's refusal to sanction a racial role model justification for affirmative action).

[90] 515 U.S. at 242–64 (Stevens, J., joined by Ginsburg, J., dissenting from Court's refusal to find intermediate scrutiny as the correct equal protection standard for federal affirmative action programs).

[91] *J. A. Croson*, 488 U.S. at 511 n.1 (Stevens, J., concurring in part and concurring in the judgment).

[92] Id. (first emphasis in original; second, supplied).

[93] See note and text at Ch. 2, note 102, supra.

[94] *Fullilove*, 448 U.S. at 546 (Stevens, J. dissenting).

[95] Id. See also id. at 553 (legislative classification may imply that preferred classes are "less able to compete in the future"). Note the apparent similarity of this position to Justice Thomas's: "So-called 'benign discrimination' . . . provoke[s] resentment . . . and stamp[s] minorities with a badge of inferiority." *Adarand*, 515 U.S. at 241 (Thomas, J., concurring in part and concurring in the judgment). *But cf.* id. at 247 n.5 (Stevens, J., dissenting) ("I would not find Justice Thomas' extreme position—that there is a moral and constitutional equivalence between an attempt to subjugate and an attempt to redress the effects of a *caste* system—at all persuasive.") (emphasis supplied; citation deleted).

[96] *J. A. Croson*, 488 U.S. at 513 (Stevens, J., concurring in part and concurring in the judgment) (footnote omitted).

[97] *Wygant*, 476 U.S. at 313 (Stevens, J., dissenting) (emphasis supplied).

[98] *J. A. Croson*, 488 U.S. at 513–14 (Stevens, J., concurring in part and concurring in the judgment) (emphasis supplied).

[99] *Johnson*, 480 U.S. at 646 (Stevens, J., concurring) (emphasis supplied); followed by an excerpt, 480 U.S. at 647, from Sullivan, "Sins of Discrimination," supra Ch. 2, n.154 at 78, 96 (1986) ("[E]mployers might advance different forward looking reasons for affirmative action . . . aspir[ing] to a racially integrated future.").

[100] *Adarand*, 515 U.S. at 245 (Stevens, J., dissenting) (reflecting the difference between invidious discrimination and benign discrimination).

[101] See note and text at Ch. 2, note 121, supra.

[102] See, *e.g.*, note and text at Ch. 2, note 128, supra.

[103] *Wygant*, 476 U.S. at 320 (Stevens, J., dissenting) (emphases supplied to identify terms used in later text and argument).

[104] See notes and text at Ch. 2, notes 222 & 228, supra.

[105] *Adarand*, 515 U.S. at 248 (emphasis supplied).

[106] RAWLS, A THEORY OF JUSTICE, at 25–26.

[107] Id. at 31.

[108] See notes and text at Ch. 4, notes 64–65, 66–69, 75, supra.

[109] See note and text at Ch. 4, note 76, supra.

[110] *Wygant*, 476 U.S. at 320 (Stevens, J., dissenting).

[111] See notes and text at Ch. 4, notes 103 & 105, supra.

[112] See notes and text at Ch. 4, notes 58–59, supra.

[113] *Wygant*, 476 U.S. at 318 (Stevens, J., dissenting).

[114] See notes and text at Ch. 4, notes 9–11, supra.

[115] *Wygant*, 476 U.S. at 318 (Stevens, J., dissenting); see also note and text at Ch. 2, note 120, supra.

[116] *Wygant*, 476 U.S. at 270–71 (plurality opinion of Powell, J.).

[117] Id. at 315 (Stevens, J., dissenting) (second internal quotation from the collective bargaining agreement).

[118] See notes and text at Ch. 1, notes 250–54, supra.

[119] *Wygant*, 476 U.S. at 315 (Stevens, J., dissenting).

[120] See note and text at Ch. 4, note 67, supra.

[121] See note and text at Ch. 4, note 68, supra.

[122] Korematsu v. United States, 323 U.S. 214 (1944) and Hirabayashi v. United States, 320 U.S. 81 (1943).

[123] *Adarand*, 515 U.S. at 244 (Stevens, J., dissenting). Justice Stevens went on to point out, however, that the invidious discrimination imposed on these citizens would not give rise to invidious discrimination against the majority if Japanese-American veterans were rewarded for their valor in combat with an extraordinary civil service preference. In fact, Congress in 1984 did provide reparations for those involved in the evacuation. Pub. L. No. 100–338; 102 Stat. 903 (1984).

[124] See note and text at Ch. 4, note 69, supra.

[125] *Adarand*, 515 U.S. at 224 (quoting from *J. A. Croson*, 488 U.S. at 494 [plurality opinion of O'Connor, J.]).

[126] *Adarand*, 515 U.S. at 242 (Stevens, J., dissenting). See also Bush v. Vera, 517 U.S. 952, 1010 (1996) (Stevens, J., dissenting in a redistricting case brought under the Equal Protection Clause) ("In certain circumstances . . . when the state action . . . uses race as a classification because race is 'relevant' to the benign goal of the classification, we need not view the action with the typically fatal skepticism.").

[127] *McDonald v. Santa Fe Trail Transp. Co.*, supra Intro., note 22, 427 U.S. 273 (a case frequently cited for the "color-blind" maxim).

[128] *Johnson*, 480 U.S. at 644 (Stevens, J., dissenting).

[129] See notes and text at Ch. 4, notes 69–73, supra.

[130] *Wygant*, 476 U.S. at 314 (Stevens, J., dissenting) ("Nevertheless, in our present society, race is not always irrelevant to sound governmental decisionmaking."); *J. A. Croson*, 488 U.S. at 512 (Stevens, J., concurring in part and concurring in the judgment) ("[E]ven if we completely disregard our history of racial injustice, race is not always irrelevant to sound governmental decisionmaking." [citing and quoting *Wygant* at length, 488 U.S. at 512 n.2]).

[131] See note and text at Ch. 4, note 72, supra.

[132] *Adarand*, 515 U.S. at 243 (Stevens, J., dissenting) (emphasis supplied).

[133] Id. at 245 (Stevens, J., dissenting).

[134] "Liberalism," supra Ch. 4, note 51, at 190.

[135] See notes and text at Ch. 4, notes 81–83, 86, supra.

[136] See notes and text at Ch. 4, notes 84–86, supra.

[137] *Adarand*, 515 U.S. at 243 (Stevens, J., dissenting) (citing Hampton v. Mow Sun Wong, 426 U.S. 88 [1976]).

[138] *Adarand*, 515 U.S. at 247–48 (Stevens, J., dissenting).

[139] See note and text at Ch. 4, note 86, supra.

[140] *Wygant*, 476 U.S. at 318–19 (Stevens, J., dissenting).

[141] See generally, McKeon, "Philosophic Semantics and Philosophic Inquiry," supra Intro., note 40, at 4, in MCKEON, FREEDOM AND HISTORY AND OTHER ESSAYS, at 245.

[142] Id. at 10, reprinted in MCKEON, FREEDOM AND HISTORY AND OTHER ESSAYS, at 249.

[143] See notes and text at Ch. 4, notes at 13ff., supra.

[144] See note and text at Ch. 4, note 81, supra.

[145] See note and text at Ch. 4, note 56, supra.

[146] See notes and text at Ch. 4, notes 75–86, supra.

[147] Id.

[148] See notes and text at Ch. 4, notes 100, 103, 106, 137–38, supra.

[149] See notes and text at Ch. 4, note 133, supra.

[150] CICERO, DE INVENTIONE 23, 63 (Loeb ed. 1968).

[151] See notes and text at Ch. 4, notes 126–33, 137–38, supra.

[152] IMMANUEL KANT, *KRITIK DER ÜRTEILSKRAFT* [CRITIQUE OF JUDGEMENT] § 40, at 151 (Creed Meredith trans. 1952; 1969) (emphasis in original).

[153] See notes and text at Ch. 3, notes 88–93, supra.

[154] Strict, logistic compensatory rationales. See notes and text at Ch. 2, notes 160–62, supra.

[155] Sullivan, "Sins of Discrimination," at 98 (quoting *Wygant*, 476 U.S. at 315 [Stevens, J., dissenting]).

[156] U.S. Department of Justice, Office of Legal Counsel, "Justice Department Memorandum on [the] Supreme Court's *Adarand* Decision," 11 (June 29, 1995), reprinted in BNA Daily Labor Report, 1995 DLR 125 d33.

[157] KANT, *KRITIK DER PRAKTISCHEN VERNÜNFT* [CRITIQUE OF PRACTICAL REASON], supra Ch. 4, note 12 Ak. 4, at 3 ("Der Begriff der Freiheit . . . den Schlusstein von dem ganzen Gebäude eines Systems der reinen . . . Vernünft.").

Conclusion

The four modes of thought—dialectical, logistic, problematic, and operational—generate four possible justifications for affirmative action: diversity, compensatory causation, social causation, and social equality. All of these modes of thought and their corresponding justifications apply, however, to only one world and one reality, the world of race relations in the United States, descriptively but especially prescriptively. Each prescribes a type of social justice for this world, but each from a different perspective. Every feature of this world may be looked at, accordingly, from a fourfold point of view; but the world and reality are not thereby split into four parts. The reality of racial justice in America remains one, but it may be understood and morally addressed from these four different aspects.

Passages from Kant's *Critique of Judgement* support and illustrate the importance of this proposition about different viewpoints on a single reality:

Our entire faculty of [reason] has two realms, that of natural concepts and that of the concept of freedom, for through both it prescribes laws *a priori*. . . . [T]he territory upon which its realm is established, and over which it *exercises* its legislative authority, is still always confined to the complex of all possible experience. . . .

Understanding [or reason in its theoretical or descriptive employment] and reason [or reason in its practical or prescriptive employment] . . . have two distinct jurisdictions over one and the same territory of experience. *But neither can interfere with the other.*[1]

In these passages Kant makes plain that it is the mind, or reason as a whole, employed in its different aspects, that creates radically different perspectives in a single world, or "territory." Except for the fact that each of the justifications for affirmative action combines descriptive and prescriptive elements, the schema of justifications from the respective modes of thought corresponds very closely to the Copernican point of view[2] that produces, in this example, the two distinct realms of thought found in the Kantian schema.[3] Indeed, it should be obvious by now that no one but an operationalist, like Kant, would create such a schema based on mutually exclusive and exhaustive modes of thought. It should also be clearer now why I say that operational is also the method of lawyers: Proceeding by the mind's powers of discrimination, this method enables the advocate to see all the points of view associated with an event or a set of facts, and to argue any or each of these points of view systematically and persuasively, directing those arguments to the powers of the minds of the audience. For the judge or juror who hears these arguments, operational reason requires him to be "a man of *enlarged mind*: [one who] detaches himself from the subjective personal conditions of his judgement, which cramp the minds of so many others, and [one who] reflects upon his own judgement from a *universal standpoint* (which he can only determine by shifting his ground to the standpoint of others)."[4] It is from the perspective of such an advocate and a judge that I conclude this inquiry.

LOGISTIC AND COMPENSATORY CAUSATION

Logistic and its rationale of compensatory causation plainly provide the prevailing judicial rationales.[5] Justice Powell's *Bakke* and *Wygant*, and O'Connor's *J. A. Croson* and *Adarand*, certainly represent the controlling law under the Fourteenth Amendment and may well become the prevailing view under Title VII.[6] The logistic frame of reference, upon which these cases rest, is also most congenial to the American mind, tutored in "Locke's modern concept of the soul as a[n] . . . introspected mental substance [giving] ego-centric form to the emphasis upon the individual conscience. [Such 'mental substances' or individuals have no regard for] the laws . . . of civil government [other than] as mere conventions . . . having their sole authority in the private, introspectively given opinions of the[se] independent atomic individuals and their joint majority consent."[7] Thus there is very little basis for "objective" norms, because there is no display, in a public space, of a common ground for such norms. The private completely dominates the public as a source of general mores.

Perhaps the strongest point for logistic and compensatory causation is that it reflects the American character. This may, however, also be its weakest point. Community and society are only an artificial construct, built up from the basic simples—individuals. "There is no *social entity* with a good that undergoes some sacrifice for its own good."[8] "What persons may and may not do limits what they may do through society."[9] There is, accordingly, no basis for a public interest that transcends individual interest. Indeed, the Court under logistic leadership has emphasized that great care must be taken to protect "innocent [white] victims" from the implementation of affirmative action. So there is little basis for a social conscience among the people in the majority, and little ground for experiencing any social guilt associated with our country's racial past and present. The "ego-centric . . . individual conscience" resists any stain of public guilt, having had no *personal* involvement (in most cases, perhaps) with doing a perceived harm to a person of a minority race or ethnic group. Moreover, because the community is merely an atomistic construction held together socially and legally by convention, there is no qualitative difference (or difference in kind) between the mores laid down for the social entity itself and the mores of the individuals comprising it. No new prescriptive relations obtain among the members of society, relations from which to make moral judgments about themselves *and* the community and from which to distinguish what *is* from what *ought to be* in a social context.[10]

Bound in this way to a very narrow basis for social conscience and to a narrow sense of social justice, compensatory causation and its proponents cannot readily generate the vision to address the wide panorama upon which race relations have been played out and continue to be played out on the American scene. Its vision is localized and limited to the most restricted time spans. The flaws in its normative perspective, just mentioned, and its conception of causation, limited in projection and frail in power to detect discrimination, will not allow the logistic mode to make more than piecemeal adjustments in racial justice. Yet there is a positive side to this limitation of affirmative action remedies, especially to an advocate of the logistic approach who embraces its view of the artificial and fragile nature of human society. "Classifications based on race carry a danger of stigmatic harm [that] may in fact promote notions of racial inferiority and lead to politics of racial hostility."[11] It may be better to limit sensitive changes in fundamental race relations to those that society can bear without risking serious social tensions. This logistic premise presupposes, of course, that avoidance of tensions in a postulated fragile polity outweighs in value the possible justice to be gained even at the price of some tension. In short, it reflects a rather Hobbesian emphasis on order.

As for the legal elements of this rationale, they are chiefly the concept of corrective justice and its major ingredient of causation, the latter largely taken from the common law of torts, where directness and the number and positioning of intermediaries have always been key. Nonetheless, the portrayal of this brand of causation in the affirmative action cases is quite indefinite and ambiguous. How direct must the causes be, and how many intermediaries between wrongdoer and victim (or beneficiary—the same?) are allowed? Justice Powell indicated that there may be some degree of attenuation in the causal chain and that the ultimate beneficiaries of a voluntary affirmative action plan need not have been actual victims of the plan's implementer/wrongdoer.[12] Justice O'Connor added to causation the conception of a "passive participant."[13] These views, however, present no clear conception of what a model, legally correct causal chain would be like, in large part because the cases in which these requisites for causation were presented (*Wygant* and *J. A. Croson*, respectively) were losing cases for the proponents of affirmative action, foundering on causation rather than exalting it. Thus there was no reason to develop fully the principles of causation in the context of a successful affirmative action plan. The standard of causation, though somewhat uncertain, is unquestionably daunting. It is no help, as already suggested, to advocates of affirmative action that there are no Supreme Court cases to serve as models on how to meet that standard (save perhaps *Fullilove*, though it is almost certainly overruled *sub silentio*); and the lower federal courts in cases like *Podberesky* and *Hopwood* have taken advantage of this weakness in the standard to fracture and squeeze the conception of causation in these cases far beyond the commonsense epistemology that most people (and the common law) apply.[14]

Corrective (or compensatory) justice is the other major element of this version of affirmative action. Both Kathleen Sullivan (through the allegory of sin)[15] and Cass Sunstein[16] have argued that it is a weakness. Corrective justice in the role of social justice is an outgrowth of the logistic belief in the ultimacy of the individual; it was designed to work on the level of individuals, to restore the *status quo ante* between them when a wrong by one deprived another of his individual entitlements. Its application to entire societies pushes the Lockean paradigm to an unbearable point. Justice Scalia's commentary on affirmative action involves nothing more than a shrinkage of corrective justice to its basic state, close to what Aristotle first set forth,[17] and resembles a modern-day individual disparate treatment case under Title VII because of Justice Scalia's apparent view that in most cases losing discriminators will be directly benefiting or compensating the actual victims of their discrimination. Richard Epstein, influential as an academic though not as a jurist, would take Justice Scalia's position even further and eliminate racial discrimination altogether as a subject for corrective justice, on the ground that such discrimination does not involve force, and thus by inference does not involve compensable injury.[18] Though his is an extreme position, it is supported by relying on the logistic idea of freedom understood as unimpeded motion—a freedom violated at its core whenever "persons can[not] sort themselves out in[to] environment[s] they like best, free of external restraint."[19] A paradox occurs here because a prohibition on discrimination would actually *restrict* freedom as so defined.

Finally, there are three more legal items, comprehended under the logistic mode of thought, that must be examined here: opposition to the idea of "benign" discrimination, opposition to the idea of societal discrimination, and promotion of strict scrutiny. All follow from the mechanistic individualism of logistic. Justice O'Connor, for example, has based her opposition to the idea of benign discrimination—a key concept in defending any setbacks that whites may encounter in affirmative action—on her firm conviction that it is "persons, not groups" who suffer from racial discrimination.[20] Those persons in the majority are protected by a "color-blind" constitutional standard, one whose prohibitions are uniformly triggered no matter what the race of the affected person. This is said to be the only standard that truly represents the protections of equal protection.[21] The projected values of the other two items follow from this reasoning. Strict scrutiny is needed to "smoke out" all racial classifications that do not follow this delicate equilibrium of color-blindness.[22] Societal discrimination, on the other hand, cannot support the deliberate use of race to upset the existing balance because its conception of causation is too indefinite and diffuse. It therefore provides "no logical stopping point," which can be adduced only with precise evidence of previous discrimination by and against definite individuals.[23] Strict scrutiny steps in to reveal a "stopping point" by, in large part, puncturing the arguably amorphous claims of societal discrimination.

All of these items of compensatory causation can be traced back to the Lockean idea that each person is bereft of any inherent social qualities.[24] If there is no way for a person to have a social or cultural heritage that is inherently distinct and *essentially* a part of him (and that could expose him to greater or lesser harm from discrimination), then, the reasoning goes, there truly is no way to distinguish between the nature of discrimination against members of one racially identified culture and members of another. All racial discrimination is the same and must be adjudged the same, because qualities like skin color and the associated history of persons *with* that skin color are irrelevant. Because Locke (and in a modified sense, Nozick) present society and its laws as mere convention, there is little wonder that discrimination, as part of this atomistic view of the world, is thought to proceed only from and to individuals.

PROBLEMATIC AND SOCIAL CAUSATION

Problematic and its corresponding justification social causation emphasize the proportionality of society and the unique history of social phenomena that prescriptively require the restructuring of that proportionality, in this instance to achieve racial justice. Individuals are not atoms but persons with essential social natures to be realized in the social whole. Causation is not a simple antecedent-consequent relation but a layering of social phenomena that accounts for and explains particular social institutions and their relations. This feature is accompanied by "a dramatic softening of causation"[25] that permits a holistic view of race relations not limited to events occurring in particular, precisely identifiable times and places.

In the leading problematic cases, decided under Title VII, *Weber* and *Johnson*, the Court sanctioned the affirmative action plans of employers who predicated those plans on the relation between the composition of their internal workforces and of the external labor pools—not on any present discriminatory effects traceable to these employers through a chain of causation to particular discriminatory acts at some precise place and time. The approval of these plans was in keeping with the Aristotelian view of *geometrical* proportionality in distributive justice,[26] not the *arithmetical* proportionality of corrective justice.[27]

Philosophically, problematic is neither atomistic nor reductionist (like logistic), nor is it assimilative or universalistic, reasoning to and from englobing wholes (like dialectic). It occupies a middle region where different subject matters, like law, on the one hand, and like, say, mathematics, on the other, have their own principles and methods of reasoning. Dewey thus finds the social and the political *sui generis*, noting that here knowledge emerges from observation of and reflection on the consequences of human action.[28] This knowledge, practical in nature, "inform[s] *desire* and thereby direct[s] action."[29] This approach concentrates on apprehending and in applying in its characteristic reasonings the particulars of action, not *a priori* concepts universal in scope.[30] And in a further important difference from logistic, Dewey as an adherent of problematic distinguishes the public from the private, identifying the former by its network of transactions beyond the immediate control of one person, a feature requiring that it be cared for through mores quite distinct from those of mere private individuals. Thus there is a basis for social conscience and for guilt beyond that concerned only about individuals' acts.

Cass Sunstein's primary contribution at this point is his "anticaste principle," which he identifies with opposition to the maintenance of groups, racially identified, who are virtually excluded from the "goods" of mainstream American life.[31] Only a scheme of distributive justice can effectively wipe away this strongly group-based discrimination supported by castelike social structures. Title VII's actions based on "societal discrimination" are particularly effective because they do not demand proof of intention but only proof of the *effects* of past discrimination. Interestingly enough, however, Sunstein opines that guilt and sin (even metaphorically) have no place in social causation because under this type of affirmative action there will no longer be identified wrongdoers or "harm to innocent victims."[32] Such a view shows that Sunstein is still beholden, in some respects, to logistic. President Abraham Lincoln did not trace the causes of slavery to specific individuals and their actions in order to find a national guilt about the existence of slavery, and to accept the Civil War as expiation for it, in his Second Inaugural Address.[33] "Yet, if God wills [the war] to continue until all the wealth piled by the bondsman's two hundred years of unrequited toil shall be sunk" is a statement from the deepest ground of faith revealing the entanglements of historical acts—not the product of an "incompletely theorized agreement" between the president and, say, General George McClellan and his Democratic sympathizers.

The major legal components of social causation are social or racial proportionality (often pejoratively referred to as "quotas"), rejection of the "colorblind" standard in favor of "benign discrimination," and the acceptance of disparate impact as a predicate for voluntary affirmative action. Justice Marshall's dissent in *J. A. Croson* illustrates the first component. There he urged a comparison between the minuscule proportion of blacks awarded contracts by the City of Richmond *and* the actual proportion of the black population (fifty percent) of the city. His argument contained references to castelike conditions among the blacks of Richmond and of others living in America, and by direct implication, he averred that there were many layers of causation related to race—not merely blacks' present one-dimensional "unqualified" state—that accounted for their virtual exclusion from the awarding of contracts in Richmond.[34] Justice Brennan argued in *Bakke* that the social and psychological effects of race discrimination are uneven when suffered by blacks and whites. With the former, the stain of stigma results in greater injury and the near certainty of invidiousness. With the latter, generally there is no invidiousness.[35] Intermediate scrutiny suffices to guard against invidious discrimination against whites, because the discrimination they receive is "benign."[36] With the reality of benign discrimination against whites understood, the social consequences of segregation, racial discrimination, and the erection of a caste system are more readily addressed through the acknowledgment of the asymmetry of the effects of racial classification than when the color-blind approach ignores the differential of stigmatization.

The Title VII cases did not require proof of the employer's intent to discriminate—only the existence of a "manifest . . . imbalance" in race.[37] Thus in both *Weber* and in *Johnson* the Court proceeded on the premise that the employer's previous activity violated the principle of disproportionality, though not necessarily amounting to actionable disparate impact. Even in *Bakke*, a constitutional case governed by precedent requiring proof of intent, Justice Brennan argued nonetheless that proof of "disparate racial impact [that is] the product of past discrimination" should have been sufficient to justify the medical school's plan.[38] Nothing could be a greater anathema to followers of logistic. Disparate impact is bottomed on the premise that there are group characteristics, which even when they unintentionally become the basis for discrimination, nonetheless affect each individual member of the group just as much as if he had been singly and intentionally harmed. Logistic jurists and figures cannot concede so much substance to the group. Problematic figures can and do, and thereby lies a major difference between the two.

But problematic, like logistic, is still driven by past events. The other two modes of thought and their corresponding rationales can escape the past—and transcend the present—as we strive to achieve freedom from the bondage of racial injustice.

DIALECTIC AND DIVERSITY

Dialectic is dialogue, the aperture to a world of reason and ideas behind the world of ordinary phenomena. Dialectic assimilates political and legal power to knowledge[39] and does not look to the emotions to initiate action from that knowledge, as does problematic.[40] Indeed, for dialectic, knowledge *is* action, and there is no need to distinguish the two as in problematic[41] or in operational.[42] Dialectic operating through diversity is not directly intended to be remedial, but it may lead to distributive justice incidentally,[43] and the revised power structure that multifaceted discourse can lead to may also bring a new degree of distributive justice.[44] Though dialectic, through reconciliation of the opposites, drives to integrate the many into the one, a monolithic whole does not result. Manifoldness is retained.[45]

The purpose of affirmative action through dialectic is to achieve or restore undominated equality—a status among persons requiring respect for their diversity.[46] Personal autonomy remains a *sine qua non* in the dialectical process. "*[A]utonomous will* . . . is freed from heteronomous features of contingent interests [*e.g.*, external features of race]. . . . The autonomous will is entirely imbued with practical reason."[47] "The conscious life conduct of the individual person finds its standards in the expressive will of self-realization [and in] the idea of freedom [founded on rights]."[48] Freedom is thus found in self-expression and realization through knowledge acquired from the broadest and most unrestricted of sources, not simply in the interstices of external forces (as in logistic), nor in the nature of one's political and social position in a particular polity (as in problematic).

The two most important characteristics of dialectic for justifying affirmative action through diversity are illustrated by my two figures' achievement of a rational unity from diversity by discursive or dialogic means. They also manifest an idea of historical progress—even a kind of secular providence—in which rational discourse achieves a society richer in possibilities of participation and more, simply in that society's formal organization of its legal and other norms.

As for the first point, both Habermas and Ackerman expressly eschew any reliance on so-called metaphysics or on religion to support their dialectical thought.[49] Indeed, Habermas is concerned with the tangible, actual deeds and words of human beings in association—not ostensibly with a transcendent, ontological ground of truth.[50] This focus on social phenomena as a source of knowledge has made him resemble John Dewey.[51] Yet Habermas informs us that discourse is "that form of communication that is *removed* from the contexts of experience and action [and through which] no force except that of the better argument is exercised."[52] The discursive unity produced by this dialectical process rests "on fundamental norms of rational speech that we must presuppose if we [are to] discourse at all—a *transcendental* character of ordinary language."[53] Ackerman, too, finds that a "deeper harmony" in the structure of society can be "glimps[ed]" through dialogue.[54] What Habermas and Ackerman indicate is that unity among diverse persons can be achieved when dialogue abstracts from coercive or nonrational elements in the language and thereby reaches a transcendent, rational ground that is capable of including everyone, no matter what his thoughts or ideas. This *is* the essence of dialectic.

History proceeds in epochs or periods of time usually associated with groups and their ideas and cultures, and both Habermas and Ackerman have adopted this pattern. Habermas, through his three paradigms of law, based successively on bourgeois, welfare state (bureaucratic), and discourse notions of law, shows movement or "shifts" over periods of time and an aim of legal history toward a participatory process of lawmaking that brings legitimization. Ackerman, if anything, tilts even more toward a dialectical version of history by his constitutional moments and their intervening epochs. Each constitutional moment represents the active participation of a vast number of the people in a dialogue about whether and how to transform the Constitution; it is clear that each such popular participation is the most fundamental source of support for and legitimacy of the Constitution. Between these moments of constitution making, the Court is forced to synthesize elements from different moments or epochs, because the people are not then engaged in participation. This historical development toward greater participation, wider inclusion of participants, and greater justice might be called a form of "secular providence." This kind of development is epochal, especially to the extent that it records, interprets, and synthesizes *all* the significant past events of our Constitution—including the enslavement and degraded treatment of several million black slaves and their descendants. It is characteristic of dialectical history to keep such events within its memory—which lasts more than one lifetime or even several lifetimes—and to interweave these elements with the present and the future. The element of destiny presages a resolution of conflicts and injustices perhaps never to be realized entirely—but which remains a powerful aim, nonetheless.

Justice Powell's opinion in *Bakke* remains the foremost legal authority for this rationale for affirmative action, though he wrote only for himself and would probably reject most of the express elements of dialectic, since most of his opinions rested predominantly on logistic premises. Five members of the Court reaffirmed *Bakkean* diversity in *Metro Broadcasting*.[55] Some lower courts, notably the Fifth Circuit in *Hopwood*, have attacked Powell's *Bakke* as lacking in vitality, but these attacks have dubious vitality themselves.[56] Justice Powell made diversity satisfy the compelling interest component of equal protection with a rationale highly compatible with dialectic—the marketplace of ideas of the First Amendment, understood as dialogue. The use of diversity satisfied all the three major purposes for the Free Speech Clause: self-government, self-expression, and the search for truth. Habermas's and Akerman's discursive thought is completely congruent with the decision.

Selection under *Bakke* of black and other minority students for admission to an academic institution was not, however, to be done on a proportional basis but, rather, on a more-or-less random basis according to the judgment of admissions officers. In recent years efforts have been made, largely unsuccessful so far, to extend the diversity rationale beyond academia to the workplace.[57] *Bakke* contains no express bar to such extension, and Habermas and Akerman present their supporting theories as general theories addressed to law formation throughout society. Finally, the Supreme Court has recognized that speech designated as "public," spoken or written by employees in public workplaces, has a high degree of protection.[58]

Dialectic enjoys several advantages over the modes of thought that have gone before in this conclusion. Because of dialectic's historical perspective, whether providential or a secular version thereof, and of its focus on pure rationality with a transcendent element, its creation of union within diversity is not controlled by past events seen as either narrow or broad causes—though the past is, paradoxically, ever at hand in the present. Dialectic can transcend the past and find new solutions to racial injustice, even beyond the stage at which diversity has initially been established. It can do so because "affirmative action will engender a ceaseless good faith debate,"[59] during which many new correctives for racial injustice and other injustices will surely be opened up through dialogue.

Expiation for the racial injustices of the past (and present) becomes a meaningful concept under dialectic. As noted before, its epochal view of history (Ackerman calls his approach a proposed synthesis of Christian and Greek traditions)[60] does not forget the past but synthesizes it into the present and the future. Expiation is not a phantom gesture in this vision; neither is it some form of civil religion. Expiation is rather a moral and a spiritual obligation of the dominant group to make amends for the wrongs of the past and the present, through which the groundwork for a new beginning can be laid. Finally, dialectic offers, through diversity, a symbol of unity that participates in society's composition as it exists but also serves prescriptively as an aspirational mark to inspire and to be achieved. The symbol of diversity, through participating in the life of the nation yet transcending it, offers a powerful means to achieve racial justice.

OPERATIONAL AND SOCIAL EQUALITY

Operational promotes social equality, not simply remedial justice linked to the past, through discourse and debate utilizing its method of discrimination. It presupposes a common human reason, to which all appeals are made, but also recognizes (and celebrates) the pluralism of comprehensive views and beliefs. Yet, from the point of view of dialectic, John Rawls (who is of the operational mode) has been accused "of establishing abstract equality behind the veil of ignorance, [and of having] reduced the social contract from a *dialogical* to a *monological* device . . . depriv[ing] his contractors [in the original position] of the means to perceive diversity."[61] Rawls, from the perspective of his development of an "overlapping consensus" to support justice as fairness as initially developed in the original position, responds: "[W]e also view the diversity of reasonable religious, philosophical, and moral doctrines found in democratic societies as a permanent feature of their public culture."[62] "[I]n the overlapping consensus consisting of [different reasonable] views . . . the acceptance of the political conception [of justice as fairness] is not a compromise between those holding different views, but rests on the totality of reasons specified within the comprehensive doctrine affirmed by each citizen."[63] Thus Rawls stakes a clear claim to diversity. To form such a consensus in order to support justice as fairness, "political groups must enter the public forum of political discussion and appeal to other groups who do not share their comprehensive doctrine."[64] So operational (cast as political liberalism), like dialectic, accepts diversity as desirable in society and offers (through Rawls) a means, "overlapping consensus," to build diversity into development of public norms while permitting to individuals the freedom to retain their moral and religious pluralism. All of this through discourse and debate among *real* interlocutors, who must come to terms both with other citizens' beliefs and with justice as fairness itself.[65]

The method behind the idea of "overlapping consensus" does involve the operational approach to achieving consensus or convergence. Richard McKeon has argued, for example "that the philosophic problem of UNESCO consists, not in the discovery of a single philosophy in which all men must agree, but rather in a common course of action and common solutions of problems on which men might agree for different reasons."[66] This is the same general[67] approach that Rawls has used in his idea of "overlapping consensus." Operational is one of two modes of thought readily capable of producing convergence or unity of thought, without force, among a diversity of views—by appeal to the mind through rational discourse.

Dialectic is the other such mode, although its method entails "resolut[ion] only by agreement on a single definition [or solution] and by abandonment of other meanings which are currently attached to the term [or solution]."[68] "Dialectic . . . employs terms which change their meanings in the course of the argument (or are 'analogical' or 'ambiguous'); contradictions are resolved by preseving what is essential to contradictories or contraries or opposites . . . ; and principles serve the function of providing an ontologically higher or historically later truth or status for that resolution."[69] So it is that dialectic, with its assimilative power to produce a *transformation* in interlocutors' diverse views, generates *unity* through reason as well. It might be argued that operational with its method of discrimination does not achieve such unity, but operational's power of persuasion upon the mental faculties of the interested public gives it the potentiality of producing widespread consensus, while operational symbols can similarly appeal to the public's minds.

Thinkers of operational bent are fiercely protective of individual rights while open to resolution of the racial and social problems associated with groups. Rawls's approach in justice as fairness is typified by his treatment of what he calls the "difference principle" and "the primary good of self-respect." The difference principle supports self-respect by assuring a sufficient distribution of wealth and income to "the least advantaged group" at a level below which self-respect could not be maintained.[70] As for self-respect, "nothing [w]ithout [it] may seem worth doing."[71] These two ideas, the difference principle and the primary good of self-respect, would steer an affirmative action plan both in the direction of distributive justice and toward benign discrimination to justify the use of racial classifications to attain equality.

Ronald Dworkin constructs an elegant theory of affirmative action by use of the distinctions between policy and principle (and its derivative, right),[72] and between equal treatment and treatment as a equal (*i.e.*, with equal concern and respect).[73] No one is always entitled to equal treatment by his government—

only to treatment with equal concern and respect. So whites do not suffer from illegal discrimination *ipso facto* when they lose some opportunities or benefits because of affirmative action and thus have no principled right with which to "trump" the policy of aiding minorities under the affirmative action plan. They, the dominant group with no history of stigmatization, suffer through affirmative action no invidious discrimination—no treatment lacking in equal concern and respect.[74] The concept of benign discrimination is also found in problematic, but there it is more an inference from empirical observation, and not the result of *a priori* reasoning, as it is under operational. Dworkin in fact exemplifies the rationalism and the rhetorical power of operational. He carries forward the characteristics of Rawls and of the operational mode—deep respect for the rights of individuals, attention to group dynamics, reliance on rational discourse, freedom from the causes of the past, and the lack of any bondage to theories of corrective justice. He carries his position one step further than does Rawls: He devises a logical, highly compelling, *and actual* plan for affirmative action—one ready to be taken off the shelf and implemented, without the obscurity found in so much of the work about this subject.

Justice John Paul Stevens has in his separate opinions shown his liberation from the past. In response to Justice Thomas's complaint in *Adarand* that "[s]o-called 'benign discrimination' . . . provokes resentment . . . and stamp[s] minorities with a badge of inferiority,"[75] Justice Stevens has replied, "I would not find Justice Thomas's extreme position—that there is a moral and constitutional equivalence between an attempt to subjugate and an attempt to redress the effects of a *caste* system—at all persuasive."[76] Justice Stevens has steadfastly supported the concept of benign discrimination, stating that the same disregard of the distinction between it and invidious discrimination "would disregard the difference between a 'No trespassing' sign and a welcome mat."[77] He has resisted resolution of cases through causal relation to the past, even when the theory was *social* causation in a Title VII case—*Johnson*. Thus in *Johnson* he counseled that "the employer may find it more helpful to focus on the future" than to examine its past conduct to devise an affirmative action plan.[78] In *Wygant* he showed his willingness to put the ideal of the public interest above the interest of white teachers who objected to the retention of black teachers under a "role model" justification: "I am persuaded that the decision to include more minority teachers served a valid public interest[,] that it transcends the harm to the [white teachers], and that it is a step toward the ultimate goal of eliminating entirely from governmental decisionmaking such factors as a human being's race."[79]

Though Justice Stevens has not always voted in favor of affirmative action plans before the Court,[80] the distinct thread of his judicial thought has favored it. Thus Justice Stevens has tacitly followed operational and its rationale, social equality, in ways entirely consistent with this approach. Principally his orientation is to the future, with the aim of ridding society of racism altogether; and he judges liberated *from* theories of remedial justice and *with* imagination and the power of mind that shapes events, rather than being shaped by them.

Operational and dialectic are the modes of thought that depend most on *a priori* rational discourse and are the ones whose rationales depend the least on causal links to the past. Logistic, while said to be workable by no less an authority than Justice O'Connor, makes too daunting demands on the employer or government agency or contractor about to launch an affirmative action plan. Problematic substantially supports affirmative action, but it too relies on a kind of causation, based on proportionality, that is frequently likened to "quotas"—anathema to the public. Moreover, though problematic relies on broader causes more flexibly proven up, such proof was decisively rejected in *J. A. Croson.* Though a constitutional case, *J. A. Croson* is headed ultimately for a showdown with the Title VII cases, *Weber* and *Johnson*, on their own statutory turf.

Operational and dialectic offer fresh approaches. They are, as pointed out above, alike in critical ways: They rely on rational discourse not only to work out and put the plan into effect initially but also to shape the outcome of the plans—either with dialectical discourse derived from diversity or through the smooth, informed rhetoric that can shape race relations, whether emanating from the classroom or the workplace. Both approaches have the power of eloquence to put affirmative action in a much better light with the public.

Dialectic and operational, especially the latter, are not bound to the past. They, of course, may look to the past, but it will be a past kept in proper perspective. The question here is whether operational can support a need for expiation or the need to make amends for the wrongs of racial injustice. This has been a theme of this inquiry.

[O]nly the supposition of a complete *change of heart* allows us to think of the absolution, at the bar of heavenly justice, of the man burdened with *guilt*; . . . therefore *no expiations*, be they penances or ceremonies, no invocations or expressions of praise . . . can supply the lack of this *change of heart*, if it is absent. . . .

When [the man with guilt] considers the verdict of his future judge (that is, of his own *awakening conscience* . . .) . . . it is from the action before him that he must infer his disposition.[81]

Interestingly, Kant disposes of the word "expiation" and its accoutrements "penances or ceremonies" because they imply the creation of a supernatural causal relation with God (the sense in which Kathleen Sullivan has used similar terms);[82] but such ideas have no place in a *rational* faith. Instead, he uses the term "change of heart" and later alludes to the "awakening conscience." Kant's terms here mesh with my own earlier use of the term *expiation* (which I distinguish from the sense of expiation that Kant here derides) to refer to the moral obligation of the dominant group to make amends for the wrongs of the past. Expiation means the end of a condition entangled with sin, an end—though painful—that makes possible a new beginning. Kant's words here convey the same message of the recognition of *social* injustice and a resulting reorientation of one's own moral self—a process that here might well be referred to as the awakening of the *social* conscience.

Kant also gives the answer whether operational can provide an inspiring symbol that represents and yet stands outside that which it represents:

Now I say, *the beautiful is the symbol of the morally good*, and only in this light (a point of view natural to every one, and one which every one exacts from others as a duty) does it give us pleasure with an attendant claim to the agreement of every one else, whereupon the mind becomes conscious of a certain ennoblement and elevation above mere sensibility to pleasure from impressions of sense. . . . In this faculty judgement does not find itself subjected to a heteronomy of laws of experience as it does in the empirical estimate of things—in respect of the objects of such a pure delight it gives to the law to itself [reason employed as judgment].[83]

This passage indicates that beauty, as a symbol, transcends the merely empirical and represents a universal claim to the power of reason—here employed as judgment. The reality that the symbol represents to judgment is in fact inaccessible to cognition, which deals only with mere sense data. Generally, then, because there is an analogy between the harmonies of beauty and the harmony said to be inherent in *just* racial relations, beauty can represent symbolically the justice of affirmative action. Charles Hartshorne affirms this relation *for all things* when he says that the more intensity invoked by beauty, the higher the value of the esthetic experience, and *diversity contributes to greater intensity in beauty.*[84]

The vivid conception of beauty as symbolic of morality would, indeed, be apt to stir the moral faculties of the mind. This symbolism points to a social reality with a vivacity that literalness alone could not convey. Who can dispute that Seurat's *Sunday Afternoon on the Isle de la Grande-Jalle* is symbolic of French bourgeois morals in the late nineteenth century, or that Edward Hopper's *Night Hawks* strikingly symbolizes the loneliness of the American spirit in the early twentieth?

Georgia O'Keefe's early abstractions, with their typically separate and parallel lines rising from a common base, can offer such symbolism for affirmative action. Despite their separateness, the lines *do* proceed from a common ground, and they reach out for each other in thickened strokes of charcoal or brush, with smaller, jutting lines in between that strive for connectedness. Thus both diversity in detail and unity of form are preserved in a single object of beauty. Proponents of affirmative action, especially in its dialectical configuration but in the operational mode as well, also strive toward just such unity in detailed diversity.

The faculty of judgment actively and freely produces the symbol, in the same manner that reason in its practical employment gives the moral law to itself. Reason as judgment is capable of presenting this same symbol-filled consciousness *in all men.* And the mind experiences "ennoblement" upon presentation of the symbol. These qualities—freedom from external restraints, a heightened awareness of morality, and the unity of humankind in the enjoyment of this awareness—all make beauty as the symbol of morality a striking example of the power of operational upon the soul. The virtues and qualities of operational—freedom, equality, the unity of mankind through universal participation in reason—emerge in this type of symbolism and have authentic value for promoting racial justice and harmony through affirmative action.

Operational, therefore, along with dialectic, has the capacity to summon genuine expiation and symbolism to the quest for racial justice. Of the four faces of affirmative action, I will risk the selection of two—*dialectic* and *operational*—that seem to me to offer the most intellectual power to address the problem of racial injustice in the United States, by providing the framework of ideas and methods to give new vitality to the efforts to achieve racial justice through affirmative action.

Finally, operational, which here receives the final word, regards history as the record of the men and women whose words and deeds, reflecting their spontaneity and autonomy from external causes, have spread the growth of freedom and of the moral law. The outstanding legacy in this country for national unity and for racial justice belongs to Abraham Lincoln. As I opened with his words of expiation, I now close with his words of destiny:

The dogmas of the quiet past are inadequate to the stormy present. The occasion is piled high with difficulty, and we must rise with the occasion. As our case is new, so we must think anew and act anew. We must disenthrall ourselves, and then we shall save our country.

Fellow citizens, we cannot escape history. . . . In giving freedom to the slave, we assure freedom to the free—honorable alike in what we give and we preserve. We shall nobly save or lose the last, best hope of earth. Other means could succeed; this could not fail. The way is plain, peaceful, generous, just—a way which if followed the world will forever applaud and God must forever bless.[85]

NOTES

[1] KANT, *KRITIK DER ÜRTEILSKRAFT* [CRITIQUE OF JUDGEMENT], supra Ch. 4, note 152, at 12, 13 (first two emphases in original; third, supplied) (A third power of reason, judgment, "has no peculiar realm of its own [but] renders possible the transition [between understanding and practical reason]." Id. at 14.).

[2] See notes and text at Ch. 4, notes 2 & 3, supra.

[3] Indeed, the schematism of the modes of thought themselves might make the better comparison, since they are *a priori*, or abstracted from normal experience, just as are the aspects of reason and their realms used here by Kant.

[4] KANT, *KRITIK DER ÜRTEILSKRAFT* [CRITIQUE OF JUDGEMENT], supra Ch. 4, note 152, § 40, at 153.

[5] Logistic and later problematic are taken up in this summation out of the order of their textual presentation for the rhetorical reason of allowing me to finish with the two modes that I most favor, dialectic and operational.

[6] See note and text at Ch. 3, note 131, supra, indicating that Justice O'Connor, when concurring in *Johnson*, asserted that the standard of proof on rebuttal under equal protection should replace the more lenient standard used under Title VII. The holding of the Court in *Johnson*, in favor of "manifest imbalance" (rather than "prima facie case," the standard later established under the Fourteenth Amendment by Justice O'Connor), was set down in 1987, and its major defenders, Justices Marshall and Brennan, are now off the Court.

[7] F.S.C. NORTHROP, THE MEETING OF EAST AND WEST: AN INQUIRY CONCERNING WORLD UNDERSTANDING 84, 87 (1947); see also generally LOUIS HARTZ, THE LIBERAL TRADITION IN AMERICA (1954) (Lockean thought pervades American political thought).

[8] See text at Ch. 2, note 10, supra.

[9] See text at Ch. 2, note 11, supra.

[10] See text at Ch. 2, note 12, and text at note 13, supra.

[11] See text at Ch. 2, note 198, supra.

[12] See text at Ch. 2, notes 131–34, supra.

[13] See notes and text at Ch. 2, notes 185, 189–90, supra.

[14] See notes and text at Ch. 2, notes 45, 168–69, supra.

[15] See note and text at Ch. 2, note 155, supra.

[16] See note and text at Ch. 3, note 41, supra.

[17] See note and text at Ch. 2, note 213, supra. See also note and text at Ch. 2, note 72, supra.

[18] See notes and text at Ch. 2, notes 40–49, supra.

[19] See note and text at Ch. 2, note 39, supra.

[20] See notes and text at Ch. 2, notes 195–97, 227–28, supra.

[21] See notes and text at Ch. 2, notes 97 & 98, supra.

[22] See notes and text at Ch. 2, notes 203–04, supra.

[23] See notes and text at Ch. 2, notes 121, 126, 147, 183, supra.

[24] See note and text at Ch. 1, note 131, supra.

[25] See note and text at Ch. 3, note 53, supra.

[26] See text of Ch. 1, note 101, supra; see also note and text at Ch. 2, note 70, supra.

[27] See text of note 100, Ch.1, supra; see also note and text at Ch. 2, note 71, supra.

[28] See notes and text at Ch. 3, notes 5–7, supra.

[29] See note and text at Ch. 3, note 8, supra.

[30] See Ch. 3, notes 2, 6, & 21–24.

[31] See note and text at Ch. 3, note 32, supra.

[32] See notes and text at Ch. 3, notes 50–52, supra.

[33] See note and text at Intro., notes 16 & 17, supra.

[34] See notes and text at Ch. 3, notes 69–75, supra.

[35] See notes and text at Ch. 3, notes 90–92.

[36] See note and text at Ch. 3, note 93, supra.

[37] See notes and text at Ch. 3, notes 113–17, supra.

[38] See notes and text at Ch. 3, notes 80–84, supra.

[39] See text following Ch. 1, note 87.

[40] See notes and text at Ch. 3, notes 5, 8, 14, supra.

[41] See note and text at Ch. 3, note 6, supra.

[42] See text at Ch. 3, note 94, supra.

[43] See text near end of Ch. 1, note 162, supra.

[44] See notes and text at Ch. 1, notes 96, 101, supra.

[45] See notes and text at Ch. 1, notes 13, 62, supra.

[46] See text above Ch. 1, note 88, supra; see also notes and text at Ch. 1, notes 189 & 190, supra.

[47] See note and text at Ch. 1, note 187, supra.

[48] See note and text at Ch. 1, note 188, supra.

[49] See notes and text at Ch. 1, notes 7 & 27, supra.

[50] See note and text at Ch. 1, note 8, supra.

[51] See Ch. 1, note 10, supra.

[52] See note and text at Ch. 1, note 15, supra (emphasis supplied).

[53] See note and text at Ch. 1, note 19, supra (emphasis supplied).

[54] See note and text at Ch. 1, note 84, supra.

[55] See notes and text at Ch. 1, notes 213, 214, 216, 217, supra. There have been attacks on diversity in *Metro Broadcasting* because of its intermediate standard of review. The standard, not the case and its reliance on diversity, was struck down in *Adarand*. See, *e.g.*, note and text at Ch. 3, note 265. I have rebutted these arguments. See text of note 1, Ch. 1; notes and text at Ch. 1, notes 268 & 269.

[56] See, *e.g.*, text of Ch. 1, note 162, supra, arguing that Powell's opinion on diversity was the holding of the case.

[57] See, *e.g.*, *Piscataway* (Title VII), 91 F.3d 1547; *Farmer*, 930 P.2d 730; *Lutheran Church-Mo. Synod*, supra notes and text at Ch. 1, notes 262–69, supra.

[58] See my "Public and Private Speech: Toward a Practice of Pluralistic Convergence in Free Speech Values," supra Ch. 1, note 257, 1 Tex. Wesleyan L. Rev. at 19–23.

[59] See note and text at Ch. 1, note 96, supra.

[60] See note and text at Ch. 1, note 113, supra.

[61] Rosenfeld, "Can Rights, Democracy, and Justice Be Received Through Discourse Theory? Reflections on Habermas's Procedural Paradigm of Law," supra Ch. 1, note 20, 17 Cardoza L. Rev. at 803 (emphasis supplied); reprinted in ROSENFELD AND ARATO (EDS.), HABERMAS ON LAW AND DEMOCRACY, CRITICAL EXCHANGES, supra Ch. 1, note 5, at 93.

[62] RAWLS, POLITICAL LIBERALISM, at 136.

[63] Id. at 170–71.

[64] Id. at 165.

[65] *Cf.* note and text at Ch. 1, note 5, supra.

[66] McKeon, "A Philosophy for UNESCO," supra Intro., note 42, 8 Phil. & Phenomenology at 573, 577.

[67] McKeon's version of convergence can occur when opposing views merely meet at a point of agreement on common action. This is the way in which I treated his method of achieving convergence in my "Public and Private Speech: Towards a Practice of Pluralist Convergence in Free-Speech Values," supra Concl., note 58, 1 Tex. Wesleyan L. Rev. 1. Rawls's device of "overlapping consensus" goes further by establishing more than mere agreement on action but a system of thought common to all divergent views. See notes and text at Concl., notes 62 & 63, supra.

[68] RICHARD MCKEON (ED.), DEMOCRACY IN A WORLD OF TENSIONS: A SYMPOSIUM PREPARED BY UNESCO 194 (1951) (untitled article by Richard McKeon on defining the term *democracy*).

[69] McKeon, "Dialectic and Political Thought and Action," supra Ch. 1, note 60, 65 *Ethics* at 6.

[70] See notes and text at Ch. 4, notes 26–32, supra.

[71] See text at Ch. 4, note 43, supra (quoting RAWLS, A THEORY OF JUSTICE, at 440).

[72] See notes and text at Ch. 4, notes 56–61, supra.

[73] See notes and text at Ch. 4, notes 81–83, supra.

[74] See notes and text at Ch. 4, notes 75–86, supra.

[75] See text of Ch. 4, note 95, supra.

[76] Id. (emphasis supplied).

[77] See text at Ch. 4, note 149, supra.

[78] Id.

[79] See text at Ch. 4, note 103, supra.

[80] See, *e.g., Bakke*, 438 U.S. 408–21 (Stevens, J., concurring in the judgment in part on nonconstitutional grounds and dissenting in part); *J. A. Croson*, 488 U.S. at 511–18) (Stevens, J., concurring in part and concurring in the judgment); *Fullilove*, 448 U.S. at 533–54 (Stevens, J., dissenting).

[81] KANT, *RELIGION INNERHALB DER GRENZEN DER BLÖSEN VERNÜNFT* [RELIGION WITHIN THE LIMITS OF REASON ALONE], supra Ch. 2, note 166, at 71 (emphasis supplied).

[82] Sullivan, "Sins of Discrimination," supra Ch. 2, note 154, at 484–92.

[83] KANT, CRITIQUE OF JUDGEMENT, supra Ch. 4, note 152, at 223–24 (emphasis supplied).

[84] HARTSHORNE, "The Esthetic Matrix of Value," in CREATIVE SYNTHESIS AND PHILOSOPHIC METHOD, supra Ch. 1, note 7, at 303; see also text at Ch. 1, note 61.

[85] Abraham Lincoln, Second Annual Message to Congress (Dec. 1, 1862), reprinted in BARTLETT'S FAMILIAR QUOTATIONS 522–23 (Emily Morison Beck ed. 1980).

Selected Bibliography

BOOKS

ACKERMAN, BRUCE, SOCIAL JUSTICE IN THE LIBERAL STATE (1980).
———, WE THE PEOPLE: FOUNDATIONS (1991).
CURRY, GEORGE E. (ed.), THE AFFIRMATIVE ACTION DEBATE (1996).
DEWEY, JOHN, DEMOCRACY AND EDUCATION: AN INTRODUCTION TO THE PHILOSOPHY
    OF EDUCATION (1916; 1944; Free Press ed. n.d.).
———, THE PUBLIC AND ITS PROBLEMS (1927).
DWORKIN, RONALD, FREEDOM'S LAW: THE MORAL READING OF THE AMERICAN CON-
    STITUTION (1996).
———, LAW'S EMPIRE (1986).
EPSTEIN, RICHARD A., FORBIDDEN GROUNDS: THE CASE AGAINST EMPLOYMENT DIS-
    CRIMINATION LAWS (1992).
HABERMAS, JÜRGEN, BETWEEN FACTS AND NORMS: CONTRIBUTIONS TO A DISCOURSE
    THEORY OF LAW AND DEMOCRACY (1992; Engl. trans. 1996).
———, LEGITIMATION CRISIS (1973; Engl. trans. 1975).
HACKER, ANDREW, TWO NATIONS: BLACK AND WHITE, SEPARATE, HOSTILE, UNEQUAL
    (1995).
HUME, DAVID, AN ENQUIRY CONCERNING HUMAN UNDERSTANDING (HACKETT ed.
    1977).
———, A TREATISE OF HUMAN NATURE (Selby-Bigge ed. 1968).
KAHLENBERG, RICHARD D., THE REMEDY: CLASS, RACE, AND AFFIRMATIVE ACTION
    (1996).
KANT, IMMANUEL, CRITIQUE OF JUDGEMENT (Creed Meredith trans. 1952; 1969).
———, CRITIQUE OF PRACTICAL REASON (Lewis White Beck trans. 1956).
———, CRITIQUE OF PURE REASON (Norman Kemp Smith trans. 1929).
———, FOUNDATIONS OF THE METAPHYSICS OF MORALS (Lewis White Beck trans.
    1959).

————, RELIGION WITHIN THE LIMITS OF REASON ALONE (Green & Hudson trans. 1960).

LOCKE, JOHN, AN ESSAY CONCERNING HUMAN UNDERSTANDING, in Great Books of the Western World, Vol. 35 (Robert Maynard Hutchins ed. 1952).

MCKEON, RICHARD (ed.), THE BASIC WORKS OF ARISTOTLE (1968).

———— (ed.), DEMOCRACY IN A WORLD OF TENSIONS: A SYMPOSIUM PREPARED BY UNESCO (1951).

————, FREEDOM AND HISTORY: THE SEMANTICS OF PHILOSOPHICAL CONTROVERSIES AND IDEOLOGICAL CONFLICTS (1952), reprinted in RICHARD MCKEON, FREEDOM AND HISTORY AND OTHER ESSAYS: AN INTRODUCTION TO THE THOUGHT OF RICHARD MCKEON 160–241 (Z. McKeon ed. 1990).

MYRDAL, GUNNAR, AN AMERICAN DILEMMA: THE NEGRO PROBLEM AND MODERN SOCIETY (1944).

NIEBUHR, REINHOLD, THE NATURE AND DESTINY OF MAN: HUMAN NATURE (1964).

NORTHROP, F.S.C., THE MEETING OF EAST AND WEST: AN INQUIRY CONCERNING WORLD UNDERSTANDING (1947).

NOZICK, ROBERT, ANARCHY, STATE, AND UTOPIA (1974).

RAWLS, JOHN, POLITICAL LIBERALISM (1993).

————, A THEORY OF JUSTICE (1971).

ROSENFELD, MICHEL, AFFIRMATIVE ACTION AND JUSTICE: A PHILOSOPHICAL AND CONSTITUTIONAL INQUIRY (1991).

———— AND ANDREW ARATO (EDS.), HABERMAS ON LAW AND DEMOCRACY: CRITICAL EXCHANGES (1998).

SKRENTNY, JOHN DAVID, THE IRONIES OF AFFIRMATIVE ACTION: POLITICS, CULTURE, AND JUSTICE IN AMERICA (1996).

SUNSTEIN, CASS R., LEGAL REASONING AND POLITICAL CONFLICT (1996).

————, THE PARTIAL CONSTITUTION (1993).

TILLICH, PAUL, 2 SYSTEMATIC THEOLOGY (1957).

————, 3 SYSTEMATIC THEOLOGY (1963).

WILLS, GARRY, LINCOLN AT GETTYSBURG: THE WORDS THAT REMADE AMERICA (1992).

ARTICLES

Amar, Akhil Reed and Neal Kumar Katyal, "*Bakke*'s Fate," 43 U.C.L.A. L. Rev. 1745 (1996).

Carrington, Paul D., "Diversity," 1992 Utah L. Rev. 1105.

Dworkin, Ronald, "Affirming Affirmative Action," *New York Review of Books* (Oct. 22, 1998).

————, "Bakke's Case: Are Quotas Unfair?" reprinted in RONALD DWORKIN, A MATTER OF PRINCIPLE 293–303 (1985).

————, "Hard Cases," reprinted in RONALD DWORKIN, TAKING RIGHTS SERIOUSLY 81–130 (1978).

————, "How to Read the Constitution," *New York Review of Books* (March 21, 1996).

————, "Is Affirmative Action Doomed?" *New York Review of Books* (Nov. 5, 1998).

————, "Justice and Rights," reprinted in RONALD DWORKIN, TAKING RIGHTS SERIOUSLY 150–83 (1978).

————, "Liberalism," reprinted in RONALD DWORKIN, A MATTER OF PRINCIPLE 181–204 (1985).

————, "The Model of Rules I," reprinted in RONALD DWORKIN, TAKING RIGHTS SERIOUSLY 14–45 (1978).

————, "Principle, Policy, Procedure," reprinted in RONALD DWORKIN, A MATTER OF PRINCIPLE (1985).

————, "Reverse Discrimination," reprinted in RONALD DWORKIN, TAKING RIGHTS SERIOUSLY 223–39 (1978).

Epstein, Richard A., "Causation and Corrective Justice," 8 J. Legal Stud. 477 (1979).

————, "Defenses and Subsequent Pleas in a System of Strict Liability," 3 J. Legal Stud. 165 (1974).

————, "Intentional Harms," 4 J. Legal Stud. 391 (1975).

————, "Nuisance Law: Corrective Justice and Its Utilitarian Constraints," 8 J. Legal Stud. 49 (1979).

————, "A Theory of Strict Liability," 2 J. Legal Stud. 151 (1973).

Habermas, Jürgen, "Morality and Ethical Life: Does Hegel's Critique of Kant Apply to Discourse Ethics?" 83 Nw. U. L. Rev. 38 (1988–89).

————, "Paradigms of Law," in HABERMAS ON LAW AND DEMOCRACY: CRITICAL EXCHANGES 13–25 (Michel Rosenfeld and Andrew Arato eds. 1998).

Hartshorne, Charles, "The Esthetic Matrix of Value," in CHARLES HARTSHORNE, CREATIVE SYNTHESIS AND PHILOSOPHIC METHOD (1983).

Howard, Roscoe C., Jr., "Getting It Wrong: *Hopwood v. Texas* and Its Implications for Racial Diversity in Legal Education and Practice," 31 New Eng. L. Rev. 831 (1997).

McCarthy, Thomas, "Legitimacy and Diversity: Dialectical Reflections on Analytical Distinctions," 17 Cardozo L. Rev. 1083 (1996), reprinted in MICHEL ROSENFELD AND ANDREW ARATO (eds.), HABERMAS ON LAW AND DEMOCRACY: CRITICAL EXCHANGES 115–56 (1998).

McKeon, Richard, "Dialectic and Political Thought and Action," 65 Ethics 1 (1954).

————, "Discourse, Demonstration, Verification, Justification," reprinted in RICHARD MCKEON, RHETORIC: ESSAYS IN INVENTION AND DISCOVERY 37–55 (Backman ed. 1987).

————, "Philosophic Semantics and Philosophic Inquiry," (unpublished contribution to the Illinois Philosophy Conference, held at Carbondale, Illinois, February 26, 1966, privately reproduced and distributed by the author; © 1987 by Zahava K. McKeon; copy in possession of the author of this book), reprinted in RICHARD MCKEON, FREEDOM AND HISTORY AND OTHER ESSAYS: AN INTRODUCTION TO THE THOUGHT OF RICHARD MCKEON 242–56 (Z. McKeon ed. 1990).

————, "A Philosophy for UNESCO," 8 Phil. & Phenomenology 573 (1948).

Meltzer, Bernard D., "The *Weber* Case: The Judicial Abrogation of the Antidiscrimination Standard in Employment," 47 U. Chi. L. Rev. 423 (1980).

Rosenfeld, Michel, "Can Rights, Democracy, and Justice Be Reconciled Through Discourse Theory? Reflections on Habermas's Proceduralist Paradigm of Law," 17 Cardozo L. Rev. 791 (1996), reprinted in MICHEL ROSENFELD AND ANDREW ARATO (eds.), HABERMAS ON LAW AND DEMOCRACY: CRITICAL EXCHANGES 82–114 (1998).

Sullivan, Kathleen M., "*City of Richmond v. J. A. Croson Co.*, the Backlash against Affirmative Action," 64 Tul. L. Rev. 1609 (1990).

————, "Sins of Discrimination: Last Term's Affirmative Action Cases," 100 Harv. L. Rev. 78 (1986).

Sunstein, Cass R., "The Anticaste Principle," 92 Mich. L. Rev. 2410 (1994).
———, "Public Deliberation, Affirmative Action, and the Supreme Court," 84 Calif. L. Rev. 1179 (1996).

CASE LAW

Supreme Court

Adarand Constructors, Inc. v. Pena, 515 U.S. 200 (1995).
City of Richmond v. J. A. Croson Co., 488 U.S. 469 (1989).
Firefighters Local Union No. 1784 v. Stotts, 467 U.S. 561 (1984).
Fullilove v. Klutznick, Secretary of Commerce, 448 U.S. 448 (1980).
Griggs v. Duke Power Co., 401 U.S. 424 (1971).
Hazelwood School District v. United States, 433 U.S. 299 (1977).
Johnson v. Transportation Agency of Santa Clara County, Calif., 480 U.S. 267 (1986).
Local No. 93, International Association of Firefighters v. City of Cleveland, 478 U.S. 501 (1986).
Local 28, Sheet Metal Workers International Association v. EEOC, 478 U.S. 421 (1986).
Metro Broadcasting, Inc., v. FCC, 497 U.S. 547 (1990).
Regents of the University of California v. Bakke, 438 U.S. 265 (1978).
St. Mary's Honor Center v. Hicks, 509 U.S. 502 (1993).
United Steelworkers of America v. Weber, 443 U.S. 193 (1979).
Wygant v. Jackson Board of Education, 476 U.S. 267 (1986).

Lower Courts

Coalition for Economic Equality v. Wilson, 122 F.3d 692 (9th Cir.), *cert. denied*, 522 U.S. 963 (1997).
Hopwood v. Texas, 78 F.3d 932 (5th Cir.), *cert. denied*, 518 U.S. 1033 (1996).
Lutheran Church-Missouri Synod v. FCC, 141 F.3d 344 (D.C. Cir. 1998).
Podberesky v. Kirwan, 956 F.2d 52 (4th Cir. 1992) (*Podberesky I*).
Podberesky v. Kirwan, 38 F.3d 147 (4th Cir. 1994), *cert. denied*, 514 U.S. 1128 (1995) (*Podberesky II*).
Taxman v. Board of Education of the Township of Piscataway, New Jersey, 91 F.3d 1547 (3d Cir. 1996) (en banc), *cert. dism'd*, 522 U.S. 1010 (1997).
Wessmann v. Gittens, 160 F.3d 790 (1st Cir. 1998).

Index

About the Author

W. ROBERT GRAY is Professor of Law at Texas Wesleyan University School of Law. Prior to academia, he practiced law in Washington, D.C. and for the Attorney General of Texas.